IMAGES
of America

Cape St. George Lighthouse and Apalachicola Bay

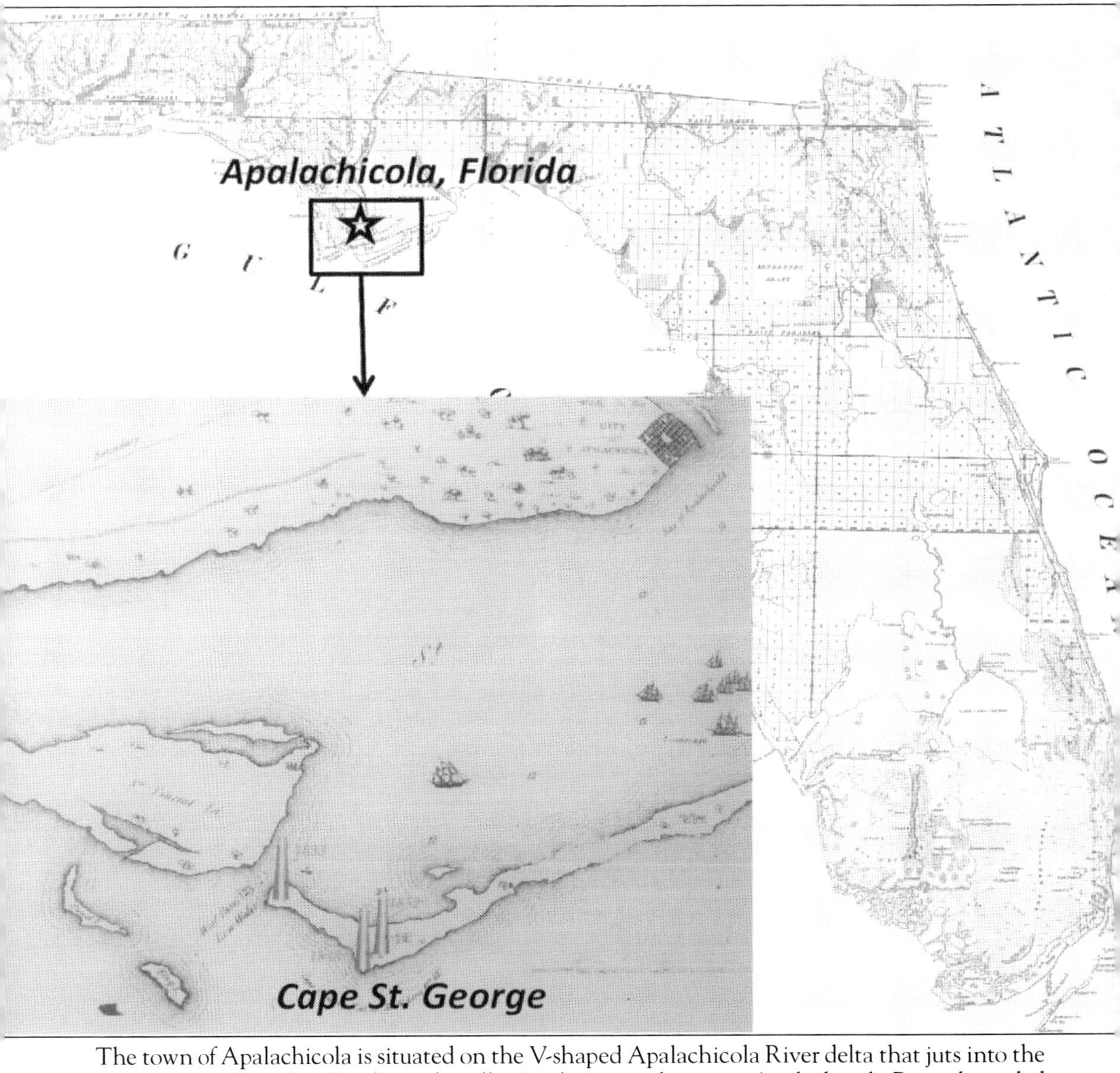

The town of Apalachicola is situated on the V-shaped Apalachicola River delta that juts into the Gulf of Mexico in the Florida Panhandle. As shown in the inset, Apalachicola Bay is bounded by a string of barrier islands that includes St. George Island. In 1833, a lighthouse was built on St. George Island at West Pass, but ship captains complained that the light failed to guide them past the shoals. In 1848, the lighthouse was moved to Cape St. George, the southernmost curve of St. George Island. After the keeper's dwelling and tower were destroyed by a violent hurricane in 1851, the lighthouse was rebuilt on pilings driven into a high sand ridge 400 yards inland. In 2005, the tower was undercut by storm surges and collapsed into the Gulf of Mexico. It was salvaged by the St. George Lighthouse Association and rebuilt in Lighthouse Park on St. George Island. (SGLA.)

On the Cover: A member of the US Coast Guard beach patrol stands at attention in front of the Cape St. George Lighthouse during World War II. The Bureau of Lighthouses was transferred from the Department of Commerce to the Coast Guard in 1939, and its principal functions during the war were to guard shipping from U-boat attacks and intercept German saboteurs.

IMAGES
of America

Cape St. George Lighthouse and Apalachicola Bay

James L. Hargrove and Carol A. Talley

ARCADIA PUBLISHING

ISBN 978-1-4671-2497-3

Published by Arcadia Publishing
Charleston, South Carolina

Printed in the United States of America

Library of Congress Control Number: 2017930450

For all general information, please contact Arcadia Publishing:
Telephone 843-853-2070
Fax 843-853-0044
E-mail sales@arcadiapublishing.com
For customer service and orders:
Toll-Free 1-888-313-2665

Visit us on the Internet at www.arcadiapublishing.com

This book is dedicated to the visitors, volunteers, and staff at the Cape St. George Lighthouse who have shared family stories about the 1852 lighthouse.

Contents

ACKNOWLEDGMENTS

We thank the officers, members, and volunteers of the St. George Lighthouse Association (SGLA), without whom Lighthouse Park and the Cape St. George Lighthouse would not exist. Without the work they did in salvaging and rebuilding the tower and keeper's home, the lighthouse would now be a reef in the Gulf of Mexico.

We thank Terry Kemp for sharing the digital archives of the SGLA with us. This body of material from local sources and the National Archives was used to build the museum display and to determine the keepers and assistant keepers from 1833 on. One objective of this book is to retell the many personal stories that comprise the 153-year history of the 1852 lighthouse on Cape St. George and its predecessors.

A special thanks to Lois Swoboda for sharing her research on Old Neb, the lighthouse horse, and island developer William Popham; to Mark Curenton and the Apalachicola Historical Society; and to Bill Roberts, son of keeper Walter A. Roberts Jr. Thanks also to historians William Warren Rogers and Harry Owens, plus lighthouse historians Neil Hurley, Thomas Taylor, and David Cipra.

Our deepest gratitude goes to Leonard Montgomery and Aulray White Bozeman, who explained what it was like to grow up on Cape St. George with our last lighthouse keepers, John W. Montgomery and Sullivan R. White. White's grandchildren Theresa Crosby and Michael Millender kindly provided photographs of their grandfather, who was present during World War II when German U-boats patrolled the Gulf of Mexico.

Thank you to all of the above for giving us a glimpse of life at the Cape St. George Lighthouse and a special view of shipping and commerce from the port of Apalachicola, along the great river, and through Apalachicola Bay.

Below is a key to the abbreviations included in the courtesy lines:

LOC	Library of Congress
NYPL	New York Public Library Digital Collection
SGLA	St. George Lighthouse Association
SAF	State Archives of Florida, Florida Memory
TC/MM	Theresa Crosby and Michael Millender
USCG	US Coast Guard
USLHS	US Lighthouse Society

Introduction

The Cape St. George Lighthouse, standing in Lighthouse Park on St. George Island today, is a result of commitment, hard work, a respect for history—especially lighthouses—and the generations of keepers who maintained them. However, the most important ingredient was the can-do attitude demonstrated by the members of the St. George Lighthouse Association.

This book introduces many of the keepers and their families, who were the only permanent residents of St. George Island for almost 100 years.

The original 1833 lighthouse at West Pass was not well situated and was dismantled and rebuilt on the Cape in 1847–1848. A 12-foot storm surge from the great hurricane of August 1851 destroyed that structure as well as the lighthouse on Cape San Blas to the west and Dog Island to the east. That storm destroyed much of Apalachicola and caused loss of life, including the Dog Island Lighthouse keeper's wife and infant. A third lighthouse was built in 1852. Although it was sometimes known as "the leaning tower of Florida," it stood for 153 years.

Certainly, the lives of lighthouse keepers satisfy our romantic yearning for a simpler time when loyalty, discipline, and a desire to help and rescue others were expected virtues. However, it should not be forgotten that the Cape St. George Lighthouse served a purpose in commerce—that is, as commerce developed, lighthouses played an important role in protecting the flow of goods. From 1820 to 1917, the United States had no income tax, and revenue from duties and tariffs on imported goods supported the entire US government. Because of this, lighthouse keepers were members of the Department of the Treasury up to 1910, when the Lighthouse Bureau was transferred to the new Department of Commerce.

Because lighthouse keepers were part of the Treasury, they were hired by the local customs collectors under a spoilage system in which newly elected politicians could replace governmental employees with new hires from their own party. The spoilage system lasted until the Lighthouse Board took over in 1852. The customs collectors in Apalachicola served dual roles as superintendents of lighthouses up to roughly 1870, when the lighthouse board gradually split lighthouse administration into districts, and Apalachicola was assigned to the lighthouse district inspector in Key West and later transferred to New Orleans. Prior to that time, the customs collectors reported to the fifth auditor of the Treasury, Stephen Pleasonton, who was the commissioner of lighthouses for the entire United States from 1820 to 1852.

Apalachicola Bay has been a center of conflict and change for the entire history of the United States. The port of Apalachicola came into being because the great river for which it is named can be navigated from the river mouth to the falls of the Chattahoochee River at Columbus, Georgia. For 100 years, steamboats plied those waters, bringing supplies upriver and carrying cotton, naval stores, and iron goods downriver. This book will review that history, as much as possible from the viewpoint of lighthouse keepers, ship captains, and merchants involved with commerce from Apalachicola, along the river and into the Gulf of Mexico with ports of call from New Orleans to New York and Liverpool, England.

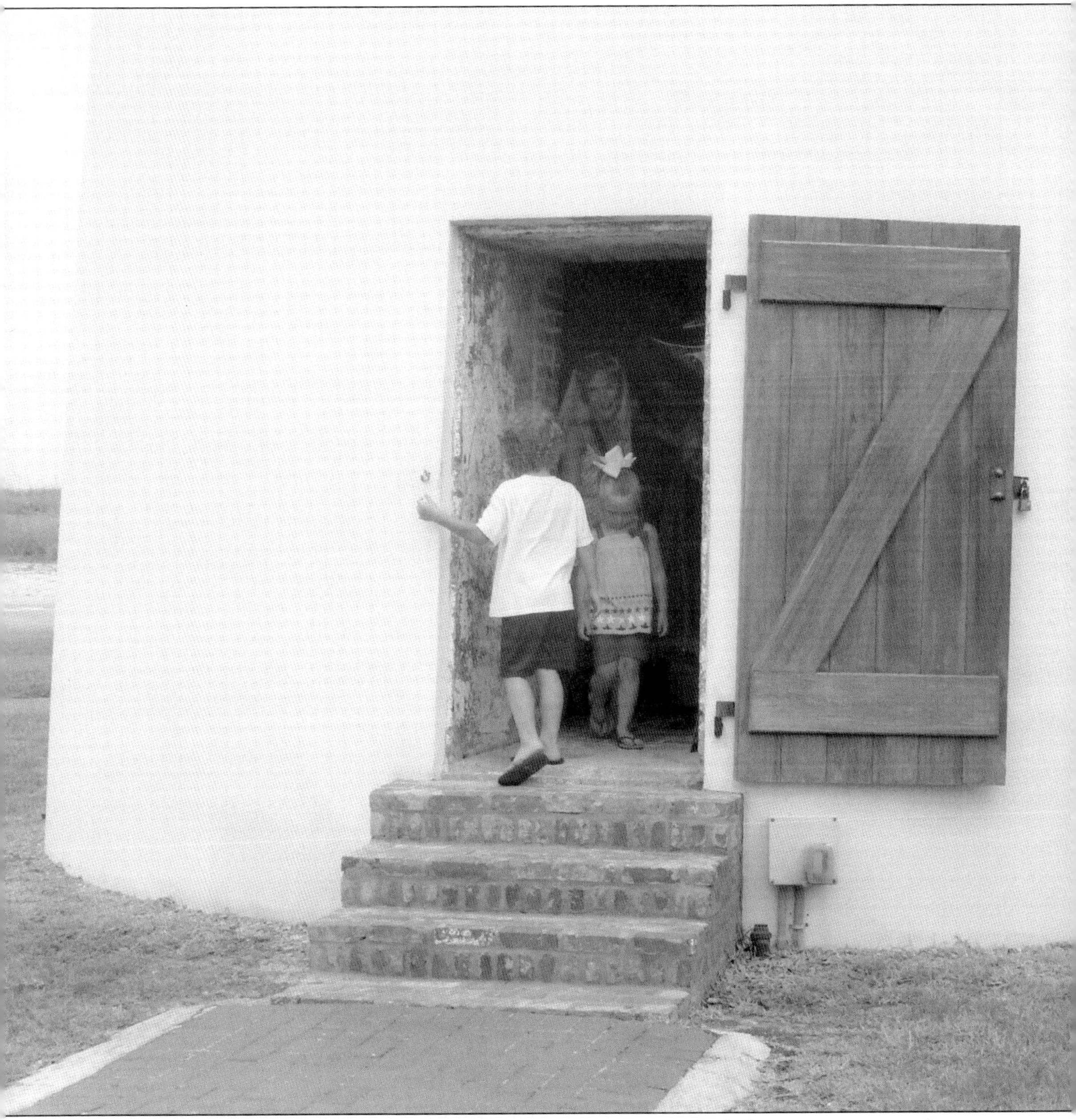

Visitors walking through the doorway of the Cape St. George Lighthouse step across the same granite threshold that lighthouse keepers and visitors have stepped across since 1852. Step inside and look up; every brick passed while climbing the stairway stood as part of the old lighthouse tower for 153 years. The threshold, window sills, and over 22,440 bricks were recovered and cleaned by dedicated volunteers after the old lighthouse collapsed during the hurricane season of 2005. (Photograph by JLH.)

One

Lighthouse Keepers and Families at Cape St. George

This chapter introduces some of the lighthouse keepers and families who cared for the lighthouse on Little St. George Island and Cape St. George, Florida. Sadly, there is no record in photographs or portraiture of any lighthouse keeper at Cape St. George from before the Civil War. Their names and annual salaries (usually less than $450) are listed in a keeper's register that was maintained in the US Department of Treasury. A few fragmentary notes exist in which the keepers or inspectors wrote to the local collector of customs. Unfortunately, most correspondence comes from the collectors, not the keepers.

The first keeper for whom a photograph exists is James Albert Williams, who was hired as assistant keeper in 1857 when his father, Braddock Williams, was head keeper. It seems that an assistant was needed after the lighthouse board installed a new Fresnel lens to replace the old chandelier of Lewis lamps. James Albert became head keeper in 1875, the second of four generations of Williams men who kept lighthouses and lighthouse tenders. James Albert and his wife, Lucretia, are included in a photograph from 1906 that portrays three generations of lighthouse keepers.

The photographic record for the Cape St. George lighthouse keepers improved greatly after 1893 when Edward G. Porter and his wife, Josephine, transferred from Cape San Blas to Cape St. George. Better still, their daughter Pearl Porter Marshall wrote a memoir describing what it was like to grow up at the isolated light station, which was about 12 miles from Apalachicola over a difficult sand road and 10 miles of open water.

The family of Walter A. Roberts Jr. and his wife, Bessie Pryor Roberts, also left a photographic and written legacy. Their son William Roberts also described growing up and working with his parents and siblings in a book called *Lighthouses and Living Along the Florida Gulf Coast.*

Please turn these pages and meet some of the lighthouse keepers' families who were the caretakers at Cape St. George for 153 years. Having no sick leave or annual vacation, each keeper taught his wife, daughters, and sons how to operate the lighthouse equipment. Their love, loyalty, and discipline were always a family affair, and they are owed a debt of respect and gratitude.

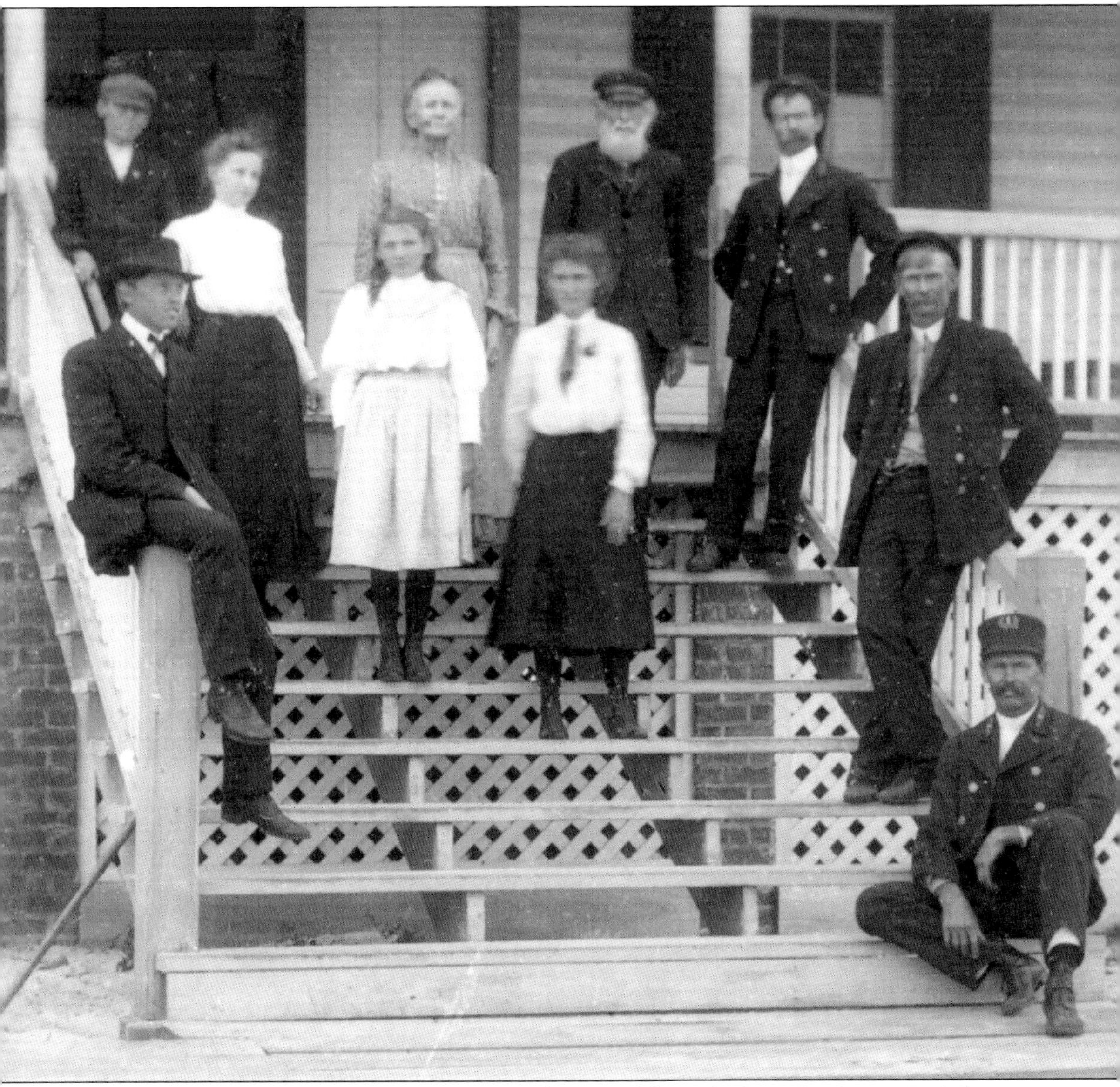

James Albert Williams became first assistant keeper of the 1852 Cape St. George Lighthouse in 1857 when his father, Braddock Williams, was keeper. An assistant keeper was needed when a new third-order Fresnel lens was installed to replace the old, inadequate lighting apparatus comprised of a chandelier of 13 Lewis lamps, each one fueled by whale oil, with silvered parabolic reflectors. James A. Williams was promoted to keeper in 1875 after his brother Arad fell to his death while white-washing the lighthouse tower. In this photograph from 1906, the white-bearded James Albert stands next to his wife, Lucretia Foster Williams, at the top of the steps of the Crooked River Lighthouse in Carrabelle at the east end of Apalachicola Bay. From left to right are Buford Williams, James Tabor Williams (on railing), Delia Cornelia Vause Williams, unidentified, Lucretia Foster Williams, unidentified, James Albert Williams, Albert Arad Williams, James Chester Williams, and Charles Henry Williams (seated). Four generations of the Williams family served as lighthouse keepers and upheld a reputation for hard work, reliability, and devotion to the US Lighthouse Establishment. (SAF.)

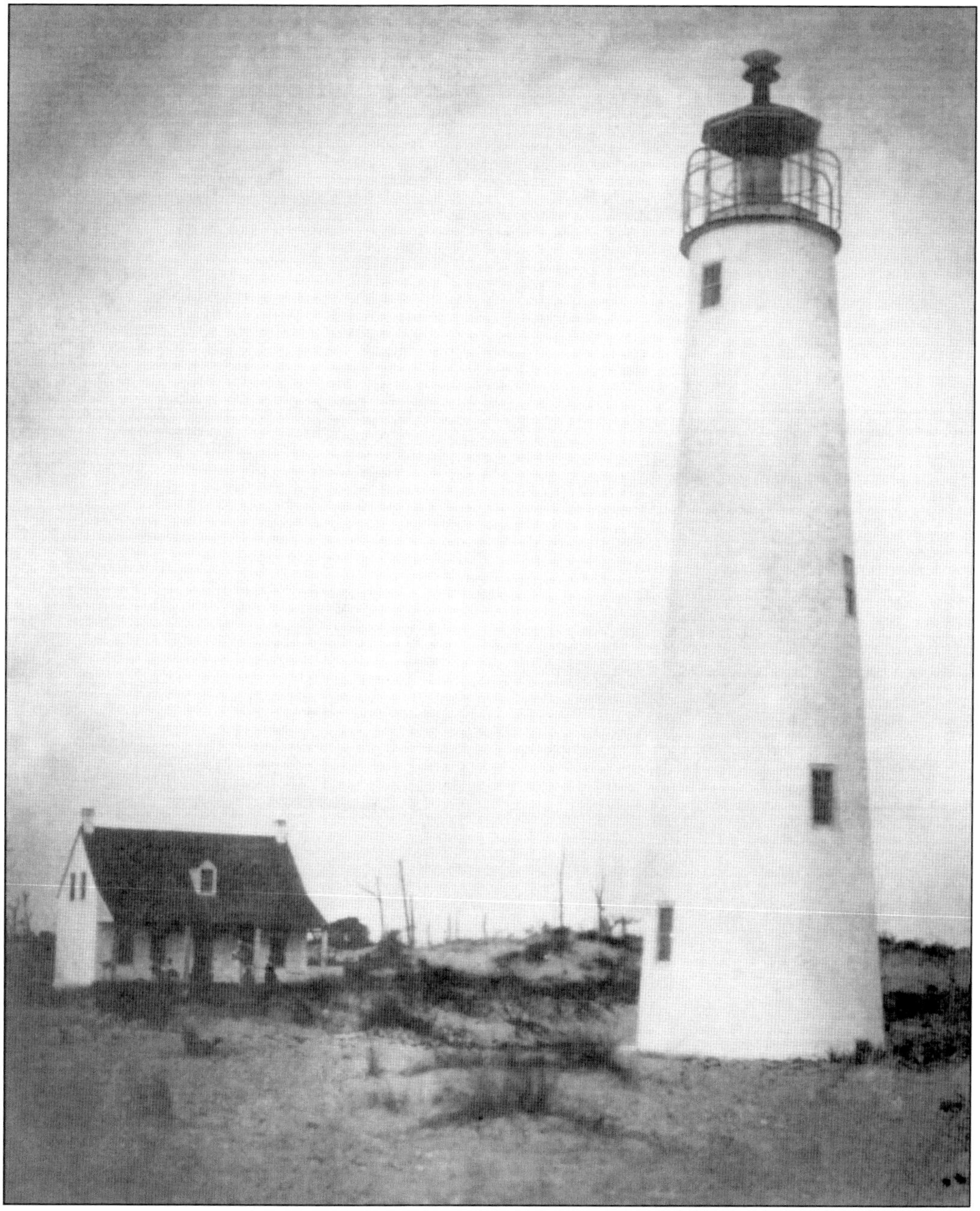

Denuded trees and sand dunes in the earliest photograph of the 1852 lighthouse reservation demonstrate the power of the 1851 hurricane that toppled the first lighthouse built on Cape St. George in 1847. A man is sitting on the porch in front of the dwelling. William Austin served as keeper here from 1850 to 1854 and was succeeded by Braddock Williams, who served from 1854 to 1861 when the lighthouse governance was transferred to the Confederate Lighthouse Service. The contract for the 1852 lighthouse stipulated that ventilation would be provided by an Emerson Patent Ventilator, which protrudes from the top of the lantern room along with a lightning rod. The original ventilator was later replaced with a round vent ball that is shown in every other photograph of the Cape St. George Lighthouse. (SGLA.)

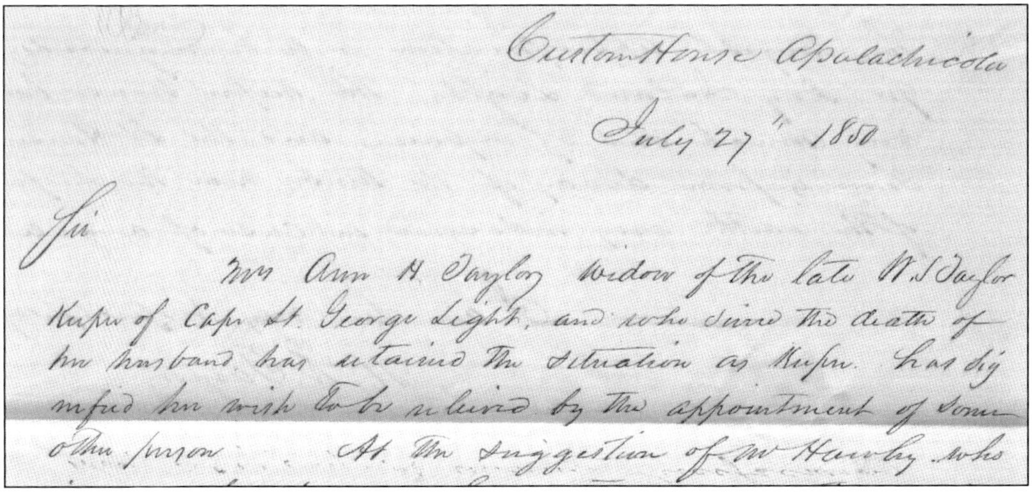

Custom House Apalachicola

July 27th 1850

Sir

Mrs Ann H. Taylor widow of the late W. J. Taylor Keeper of Cape St. George Light, and who since the death of her husband has retained the situation as Keeper, has signified her wish to be relieved by the appointment of some other person. At the suggestion of Mr Hawley who

Only one woman, Ann H. Taylor, ever served as temporary lighthouse keeper on St. George Island. She kept the light from April until August 1850 after her husband, William Taylor, died. Because the lighthouse had to be "manned" every day of the year, keepers frequently taught their wives and children how to operate the lamps. This letter from the deputy superintendent of lights indicates that she had requested a replacement. Her timing was excellent, for a hurricane struck the island just after she left and washed away the lighthouse boat, leaving no way to get to Apalachicola. Her replacement, William Austin, endured the great hurricane of 1851, which destroyed the dwelling and tower. (SGLA.)

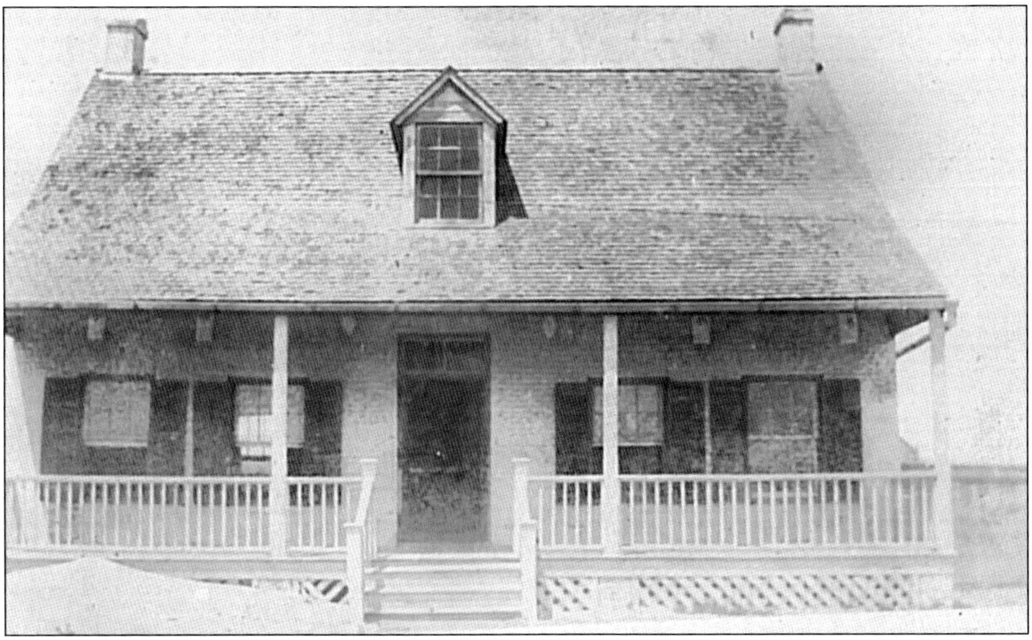

From 1852 to 1878, lighthouse keepers and assistant keepers shared this small, two-story dwelling that was built with separate hearths at each end of the building and a loft that was reached through a central staircase. A separate cookhouse extended behind the cottage, and water was supplied from a cistern that collected rainwater from the gutters. With no refrigeration or electricity, keepers' families relied on fresh seafood to supplement their rations of rice and beans that were delivered quarterly by US Lighthouse Establishment tenders. (Silva family archives, SGLA.)

James Chester Williams, son of James Albert Williams, served as assistant keeper at Cape St. George from 1886 to 1893 while his father was the head keeper. Both families moved to the Crooked River Lighthouse at the east end of Apalachicola Bay when it was completed and lit in 1895. James C. Williams is pictured here with his wife, Delia Cornelia Vause Williams. (SAF.)

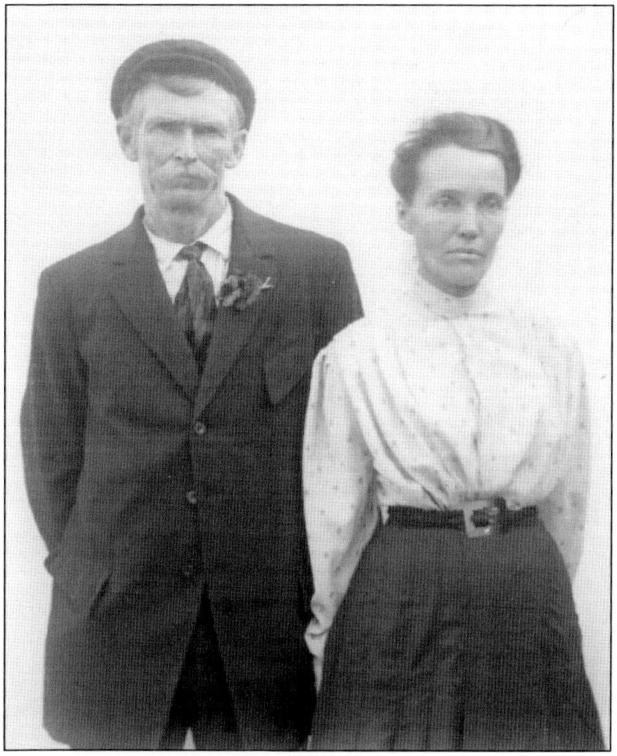

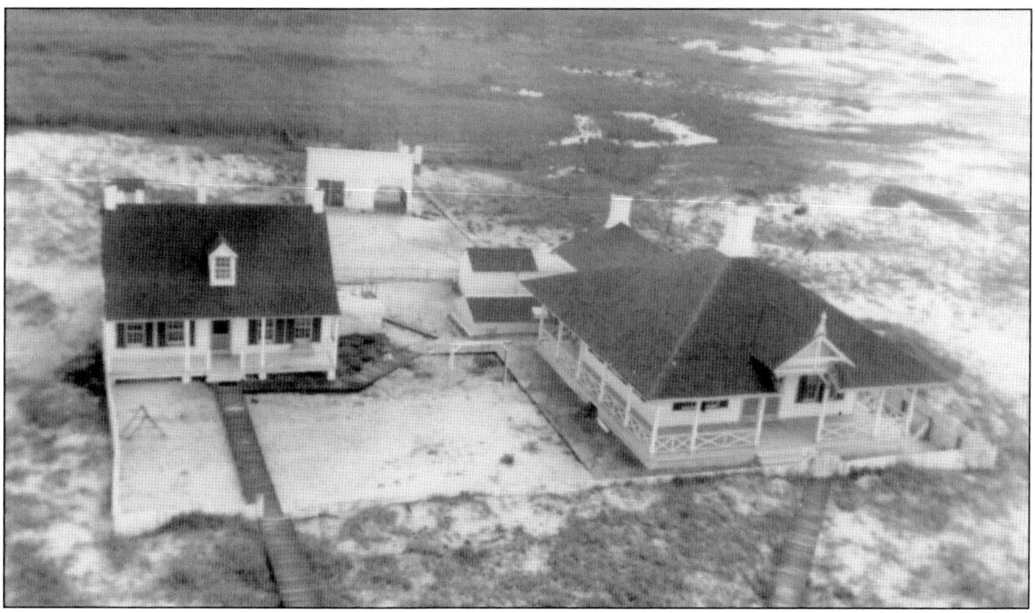

This c. 1950 aerial photograph shows the assistant keeper's dwelling at left next to the larger, single-story keeper's home. The keeper's dwelling was built in 1878 so the light station could house the two large families who usually lived at Cape St. George. The walkways in front of the two dwellings lead to the lighthouse tower. Other buildings included a washhouse, a stable, and a privy behind the stable. A brick oil house was built to store drums of kerosene, which was more flammable than the whale oil and oil rendered from lard that had been used earlier. (SGLA.)

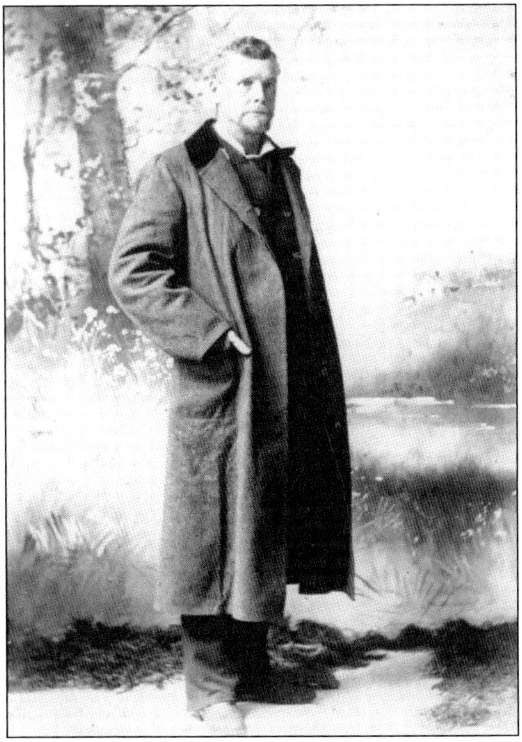

When James A. Williams transferred from the Cape St. George Lighthouse to Crooked River, the US Lighthouse Establishment asked Edward Porter to relocate from the Cape San Blas Lighthouse in 1893 and assume duties as keeper at Cape St. George. Porter and his wife, the former Josephine C. Wakefield, moved into the keeper's dwelling. During the next 23 years, they raised six children on what is now Little St. George Island. (SGLA.)

Edward and Josephine Porter loved living at the lighthouse so much that they purchased 1,515 acres on Little St. George Island and raised their family there. In this photograph from about 1902, Josephine poses with five of her children on the porch of the keeper's dwelling. From left to right, her children include Ethel, Josephine, baby Pearl, Eleanor, and Bernard. Their housekeeper, possibly Pearl Byrd, stands behind them in the doorway. (SAF.)

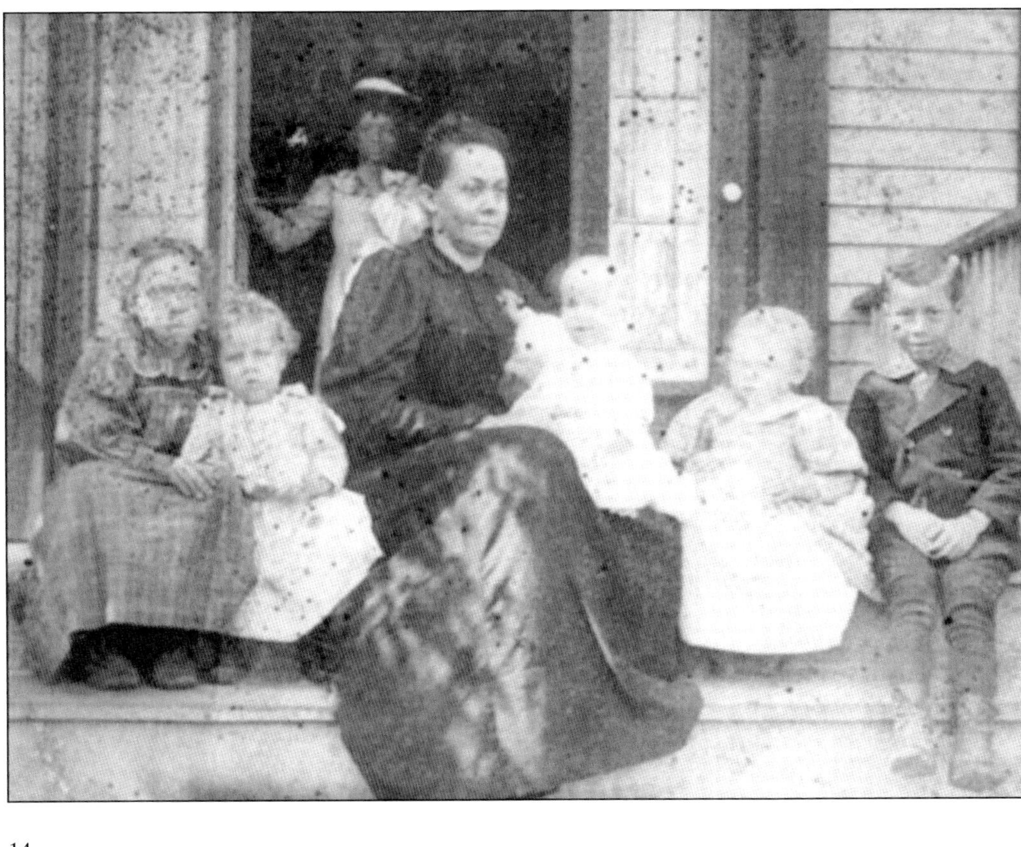

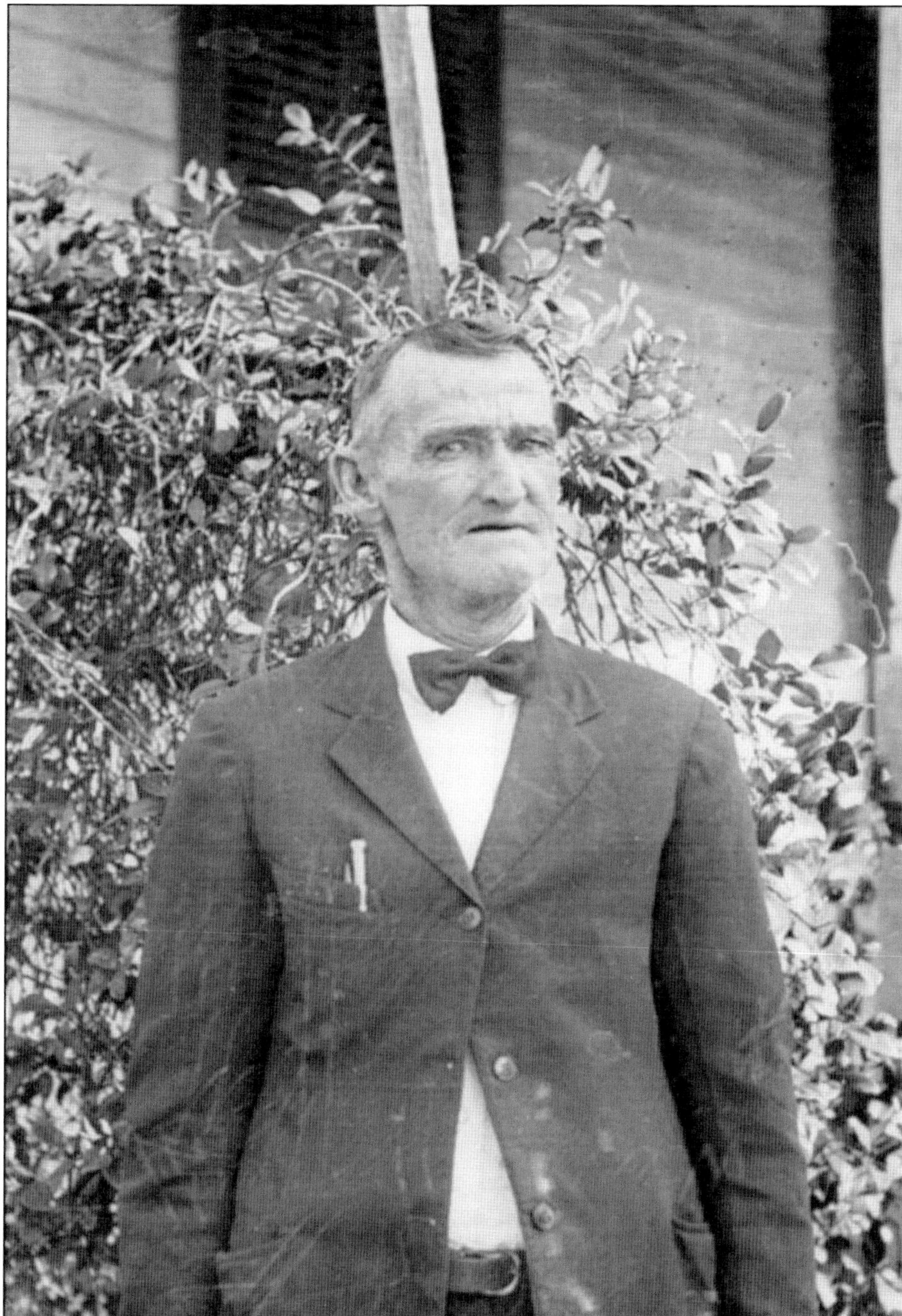

Walter Andrew Roberts Sr. served as assistant keeper at Cape St. George from 1894 to 1902 and from 1909 to 1912, when Edward Porter was the head keeper. His son Walter A. Roberts Jr. grew up at the light station and returned as assistant keeper in 1920. Walter Andrew Roberts III, the grandson of the senior Walter Roberts, joined the US Coast Guard in 1941 and was assigned to the Crooked River Lighthouse near Carrabelle, the third generation of lighthouse keepers in the Roberts family. (SGLA.)

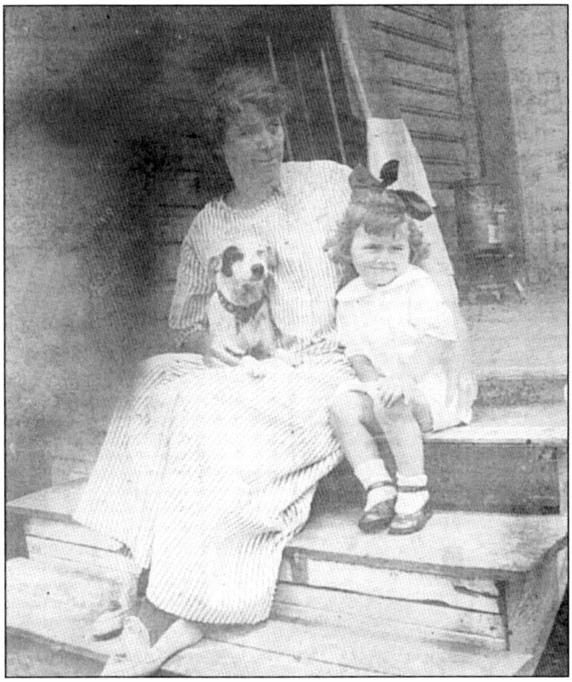

David Silva's daughter, Marjorie Silva Hilton, and his granddaughter, Helen Hilton, sit with their dog on the deck of the keeper's cottage (Silva family collection, SGLA.)

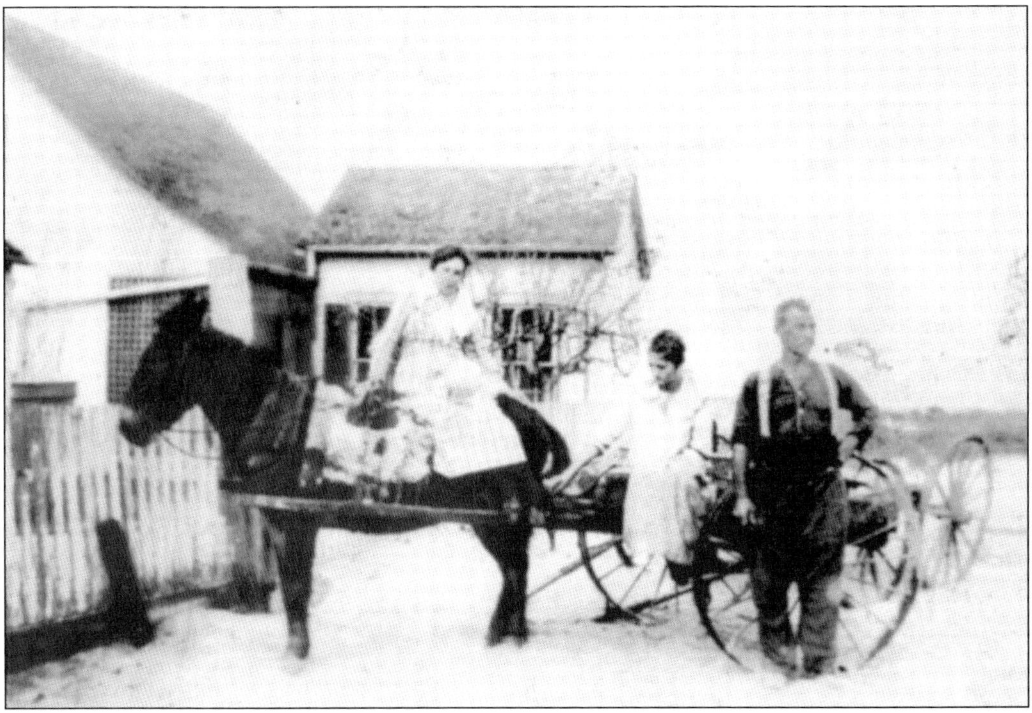

Keeper David Silva has hitched the lighthouse horse, Old Neb, to a wagon for the two-mile journey over sand roads to reach the boat dock on the bay. Bessie Roberts is on the horse, and Silva's daughter-in-law Malveena is getting into the wagon. At the dock, the horse would be unhitched, and the keeper or assistant keeper would load the lighthouse launch for the 10-mile boat trip across the bay to Apalachicola. (SGLA.)

There was never a bridge to St. George Island when the lighthouse operated. During the entire 19th century, the only option for the trip from Cape St. George to Apalachicola was to take a boat, or launch, as the US Lighthouse Establishment called the watercraft. In 1905, funds were approved to build a single-masted catboat similar to the one shown in this image. (Library of Congress.)

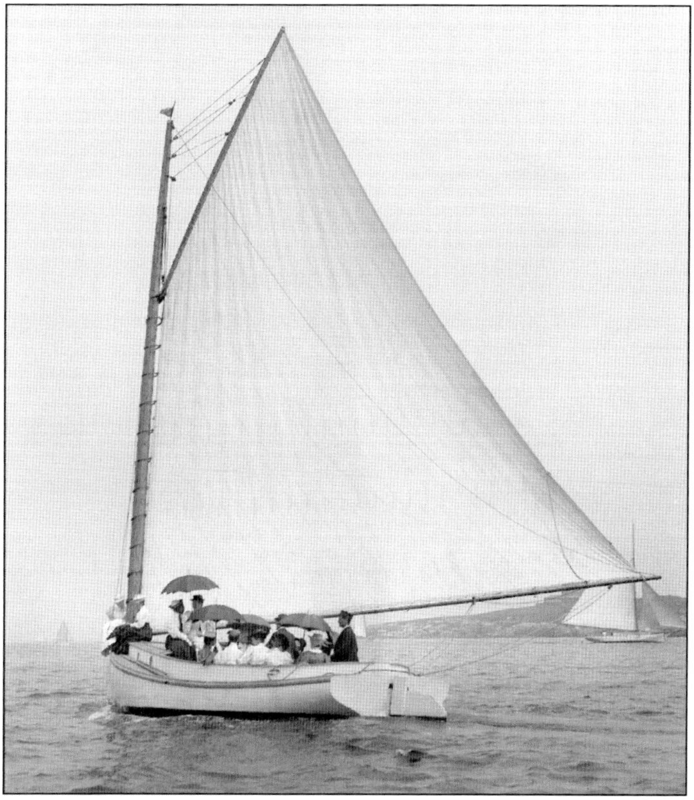

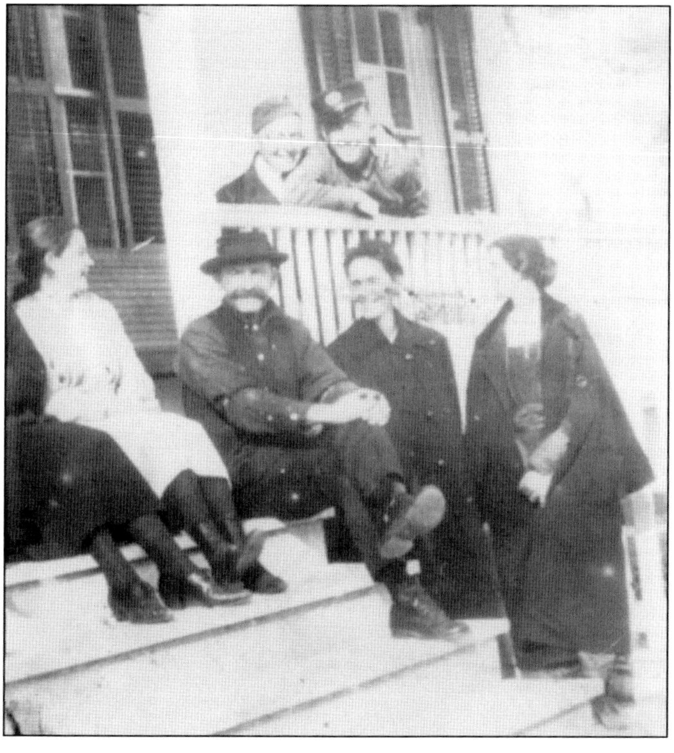

Emma Brooks (far left) shares a joke with her father, Clairmon (or Clement) Brooks, who is sitting next to his wife, Emma Pryor Brooks. "Clem" Brooks served as keeper at Cape St. George from 1921 to 1925 and kept the Apalachicola Front Range Lights at the river's mouth. He was noted for his generosity and bravery. He received a citation for saving the life of a drowning boy. Two other lighthouse keepers, Shafter Johnson and Walter A. Roberts Jr. (in lighthouse keeper's cap), smile from the porch above Brooks. (SGLA.)

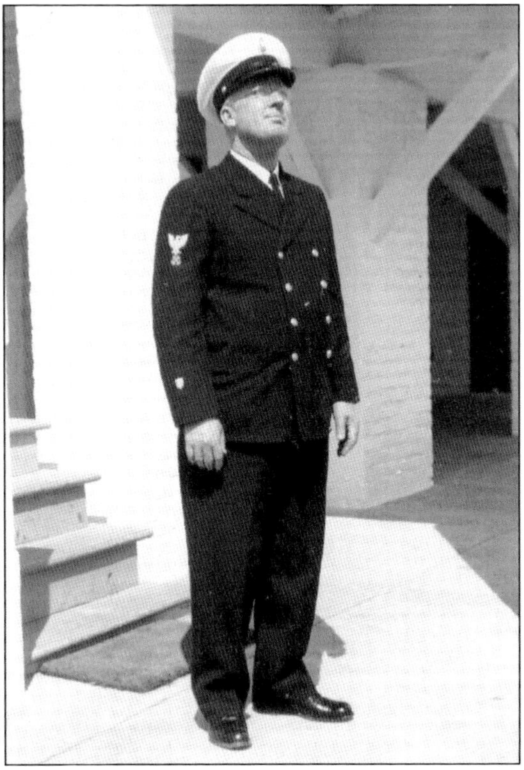

Walter Andrew Roberts Jr. joined the US Lighthouse Establishment after serving as an Army medic during World War I. First assigned to the Pensacola lighthouse, he was transferred to Cape St. George as first assistant keeper in 1925. Usually called "Pete," he was promoted to keeper in 1932 and served until 1938, when he was transferred to the St. Joseph Bay Rear Range Lighthouse. When the Lighthouse Service was merged with the US Coast Guard in 1939, Roberts enlisted and continued serving as a chief petty officer until 1952. (SAF.)

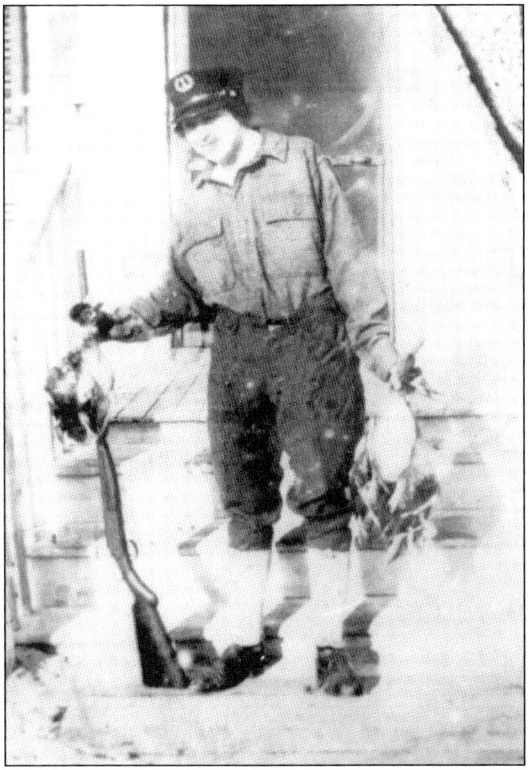

Bessie Pryor married Walter Roberts Jr. in Pensacola in 1920 and raised their family of four children on Cape St. George. Here, she is depicted wearing a jaunty keeper's cap after returning from a successful duck hunt. With no refrigeration until after 1920, most of the lighthouse keeper's families at Cape St. George supplemented their diets with fresh seafood, ducks, and garden vegetables whenever possible. (SAF.)

Louis Buras, assistant keeper from 1923 to 1924, poses in his US Lighthouse Service uniform next to his sister Mollie. Written permission from the district superintendent in New Orleans was required for any visitor who stayed at the lighthouse dwellings overnight.

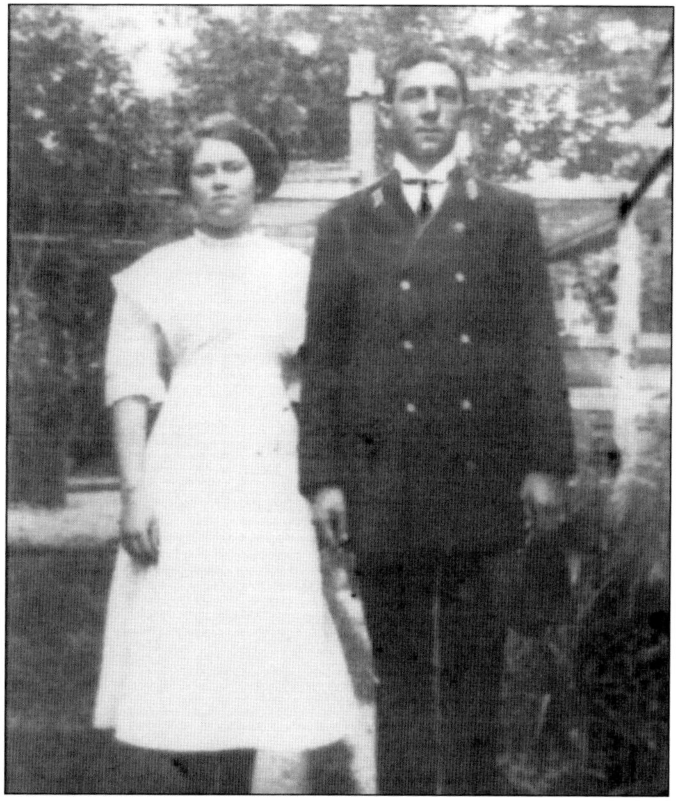

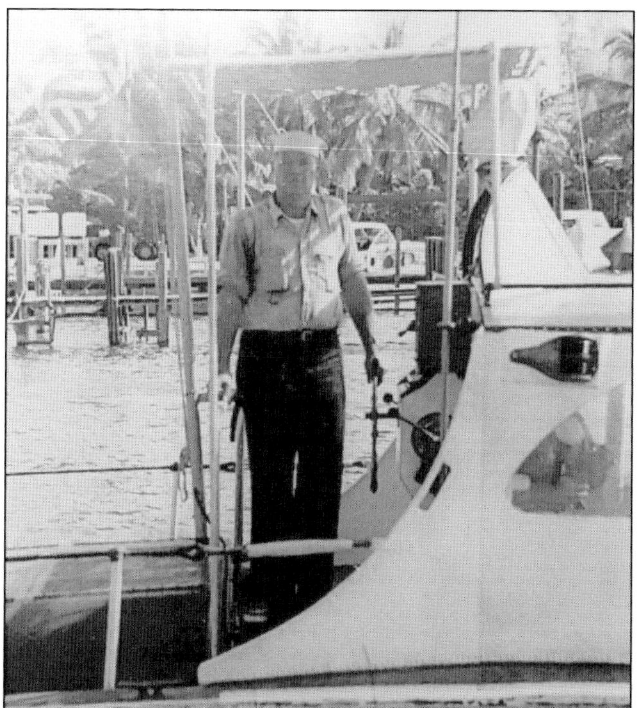

John W. Montgomery entered the US Lighthouse Service as assistant keeper at Cape San Blas, and transferred to Cape St. George in 1938. When the US Coast Guard assumed command of all lighthouses and lighthouse tenders, Montgomery enlisted and served as a boatswain's mate first class. When keeper Sullivan White retired in 1946, Montgomery became the last trained lighthouse keeper at Cape St. George. In this photograph, he is manning a Coast Guard launch en route from Dinner Key to the lighthouse at Carysfort Reef south of Miami. (Leonard Montgomery.)

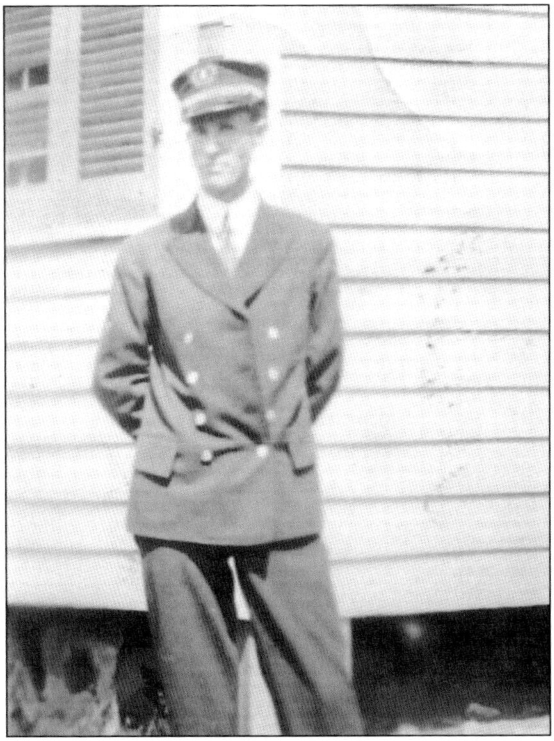

Sullivan R. White was the last official head keeper at Cape St. George, arriving from prior stations in Louisiana and Cape San Blas just before the US Coast Guard took command of the lighthouses in 1939. He enlisted in the Coast Guard and served as a boatswain's mate first class until the end of World War II. Below, Sullivan White wears his Coast Guard fatigues outside his home in Apalachicola. Like many of the keepers, White and his wife, Bertha, purchased a home in town where their children could reside during the school year. There was no way for family members to travel to town on a daily basis, whether for school or church. All of these keepers and their families were bound to the Cape St. George Lighthouse and St. George Island by a sense of love and dedication to the work they did and the joys of living independently on a remote island with the emerald-tinted Gulf to the south and the abundant marine life in Apalachicola Bay to the north. (Both, TC/MM.)

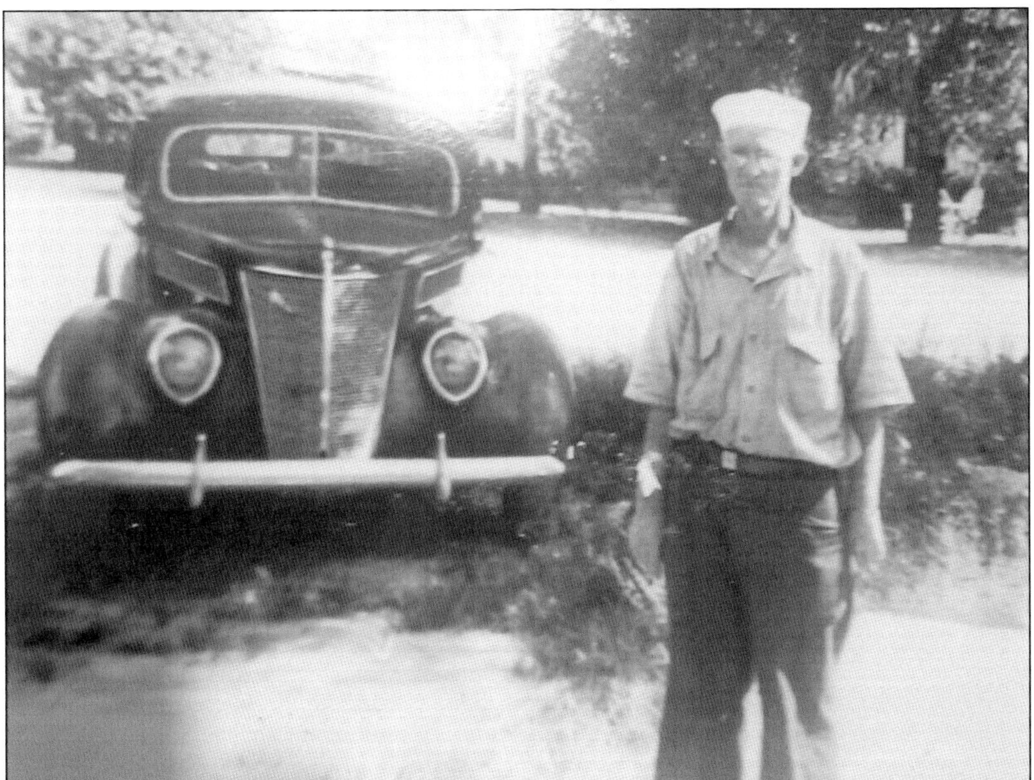

Two

The Need for a Lighthouse on Apalachicola Bay

From 1789 onward, all US lighthouse keepers were employees of the federal government. Specifically, the Treasury Department operated the US Lighthouse Establishment until 1910, and then the Department of Commerce and Labor managed the Bureau of Lighthouses from 1910 to 1939 when lighthouse operations were transferred to the US Coast Guard.

Lighthouses were placed at strategic locations along the entire United States coastline where they aided the safe navigation of ships past dangerous shoals into harbors where custom collectors could collect duties and tariffs on imports and exports. There was no permanent income tax in the United States until 1917, and the revenue for running the government and its military branches primarily came from duties, tariffs, whiskey taxes, and land sales. However romantic the modern view of lighthouse keepers may be, they all reported to the local collector of customs, who was also the superintendent of lights, and the collector reported to a Treasury auditor who only cared that expenses were less than revenues.

The story of Apalachicola and its lighthouses began when Pres. James Monroe set up a territorial customs district that ran from Cape Florida to the Apalachicola River, which is navigable for 350 river miles to the falls of the Chattahoochee River at Columbus, Georgia. It is the only river system in Florida whose headwaters lie in the Appalachian Mountains, and the prospects for commerce were great. Accordingly, the first collector of customs built a dwelling at the river mouth, and a town of merchants and squatters sprang up. Citizens in the Territory of Florida (1821–1845) soon petitioned Congress for lighthouses to guide ships past the reefs and barrier islands, through the passes and into port.

It might have been simple to build lighthouses on Apalachicola Bay, if only someone could have provided a valid deed for St. George Island or, for that matter, the rest of Franklin County. No one could until after a Supreme Court decision in 1835 and the Seminole Wars that lasted past statehood, but few settlers let such trivial concerns get in their way. They knew they were land squatters, but if possession was truly nine-tenths of the law, the land was free for the taking until the rightful owner sued you.

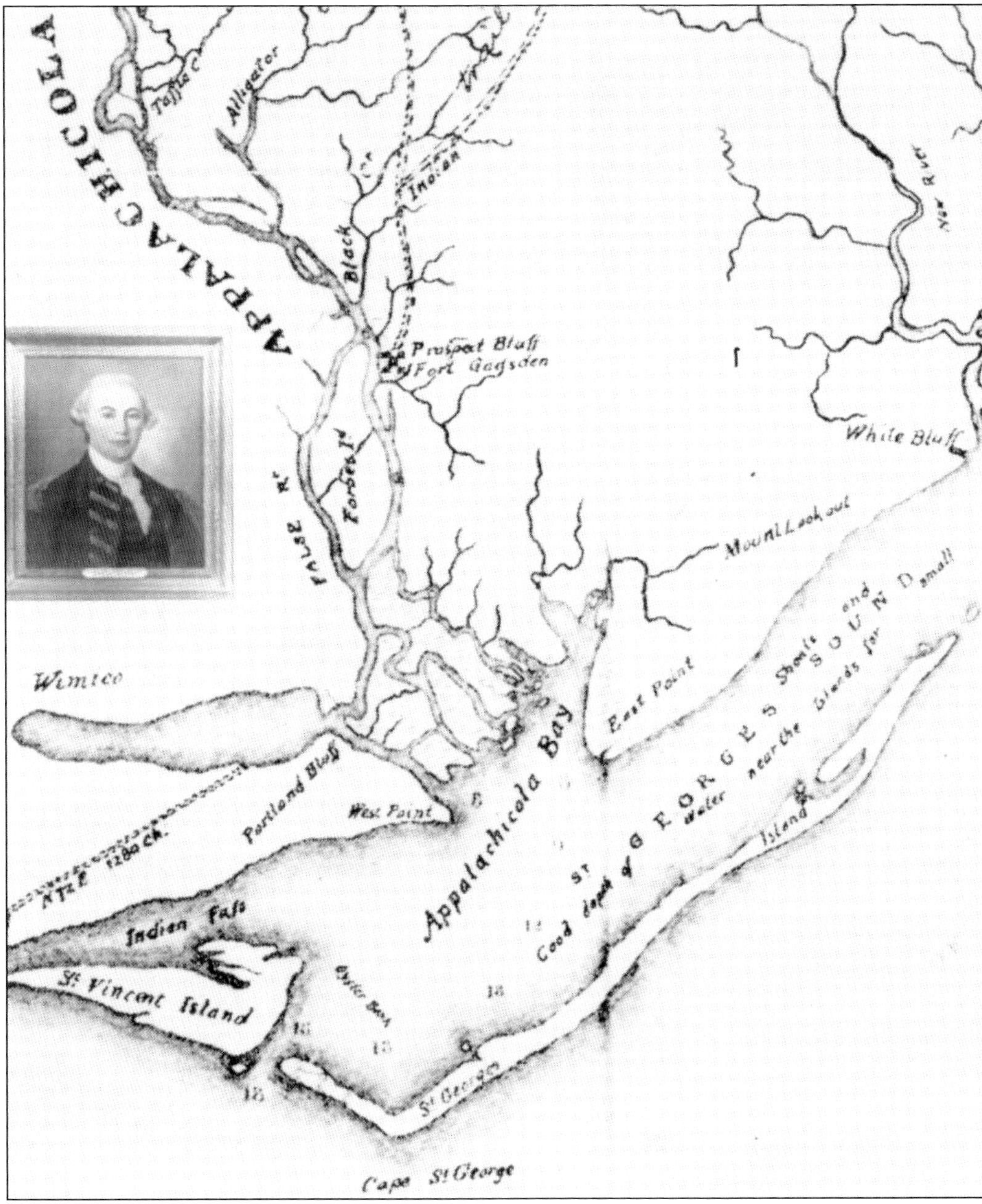

The first obstacle to the plan to build lighthouses or establish a city at the mouth of the Apalachicola River after Florida became a US territory in 1821 was that no one, including the federal government or the Territory of Florida, could obtain a valid land claim. Under the Spanish government, the land was regarded as property of the Muscogee Creek Indians. However, Spain allowed the Creeks to settle disputes with John Forbes's trading company by ceding large parcels of land. Forbes and Company claimed over 1.2 million acres extending from St. George Island far up the Apalachicola River and east to the Wakulla River. Forbes (inset in map) sold the land claim to John Innerarity and others, who formed the Apalachicola Land Company. Not until the US Supreme Court validated their claim in 1835 did it become possible to survey the land and offer it for sale. (SAF.)

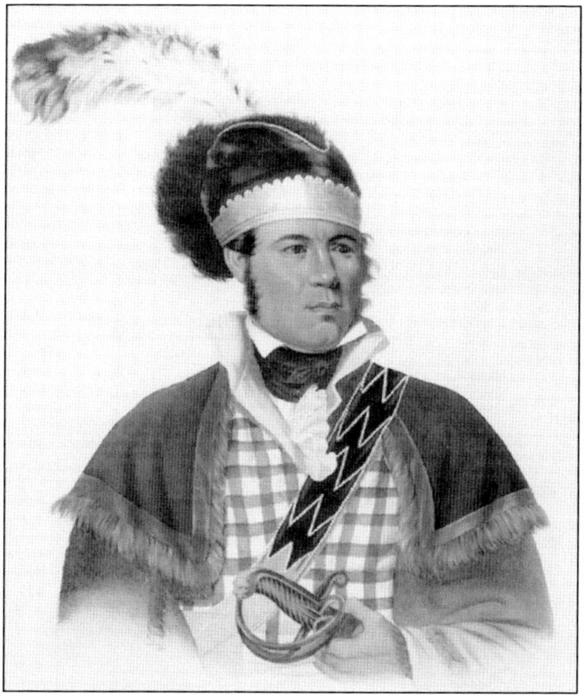

Like the Cherokee, the Muscogee or Creek Indians had been trading with and marrying British, Scots, and American traders for many years before Florida became a US territory. This influence is exemplified by the garb and name of Creek chief William McIntosh. Most of the villages along the Apalachicola were regarded as peaceful, and the name Apalachicola can be translated as "the land of friendly people." Despite this goodwill, the Indian Removal Act of 1830 sparked intense conflict as it became US policy to relocate all native peoples west of the Mississippi River. (LOC.)

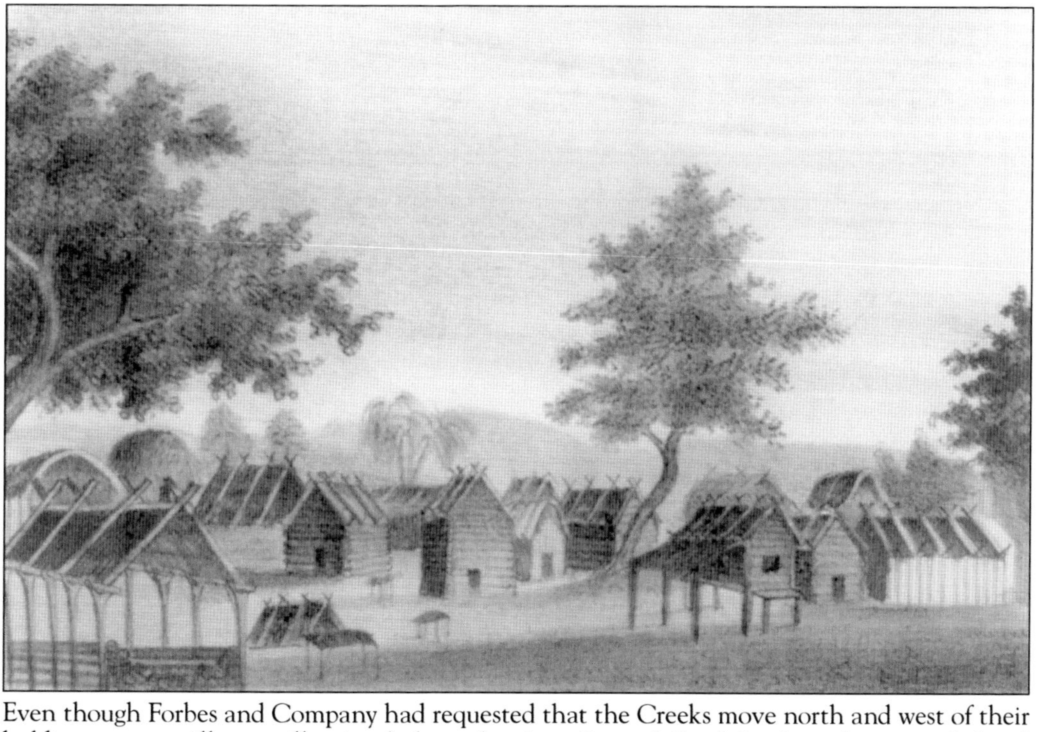

Even though Forbes and Company had requested that the Creeks move north and west of their holdings, many villages still existed along the river. Several Creek leaders whose people lived along the Apalachicola River agreed to let the federal government buy their lands or swap them for land west of the Mississippi. Many others resisted, and US troops were sent to forcibly remove them. (LOC.)

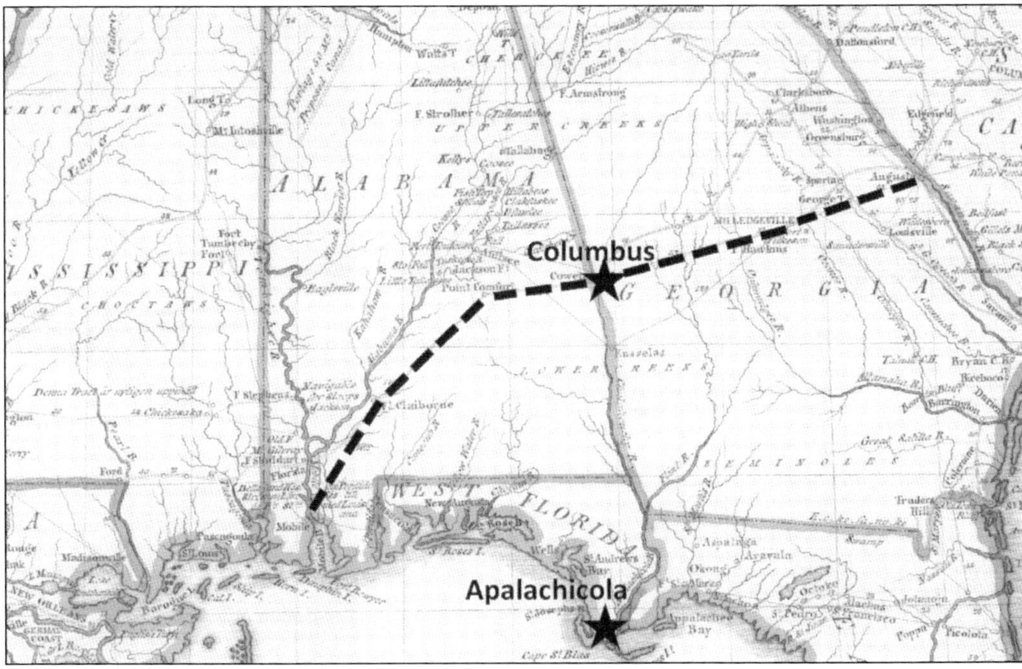

In 1828, a steamboat named *Fanny* reached the falls of the Chattahoochee River at Columbus and loaded passengers and freight including cotton, lumber, and hogsheads of sugar. With commerce beginning to grow, Apalachicola was destined to become the third largest port on the Gulf of Mexico, and a lighthouse was needed on St. George Island to guide ship traffic. Columbus was located on the old Federal Road, one of the major routes for east-west movement of settlers headed for Florida, Alabama, and lands along the Mississippi River that opened after the Louisiana Purchase of 1804. (JLH.)

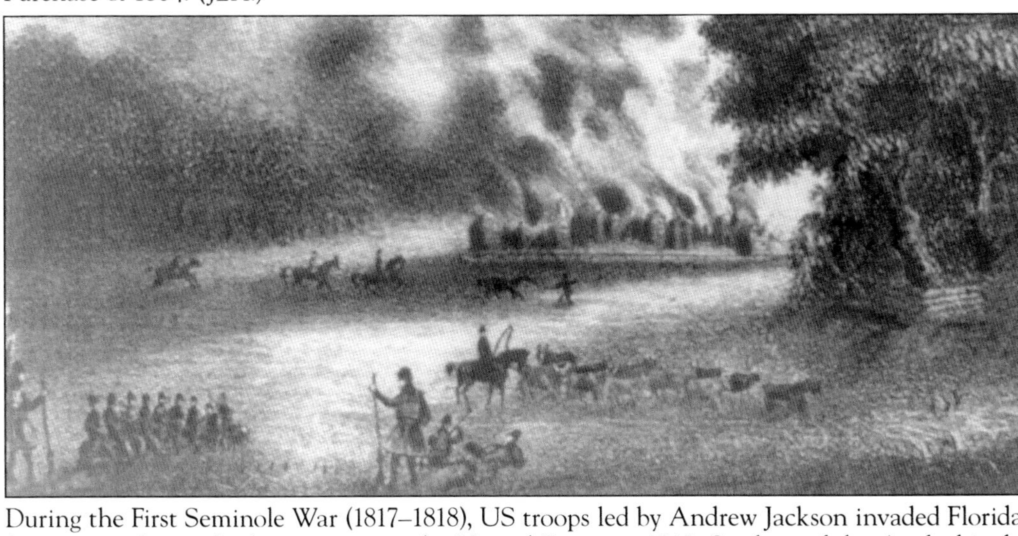

During the First Seminole War (1817–1818), US troops led by Andrew Jackson invaded Florida. Spain agreed to cede the territory to the United States in 1819. Settling of the Apalachicola, Chattahoochee, and Flint River valleys contributed to the Second Seminole War, which was fought from 1835 to 1842. This lithograph from 1837 depicts the burning of the Creek village Pilaklikaha by troops under Gen. Abraham Eustis. Despite the conflict, farmers moved into the river valleys and established cotton plantations based on slave labor. (LOC.)

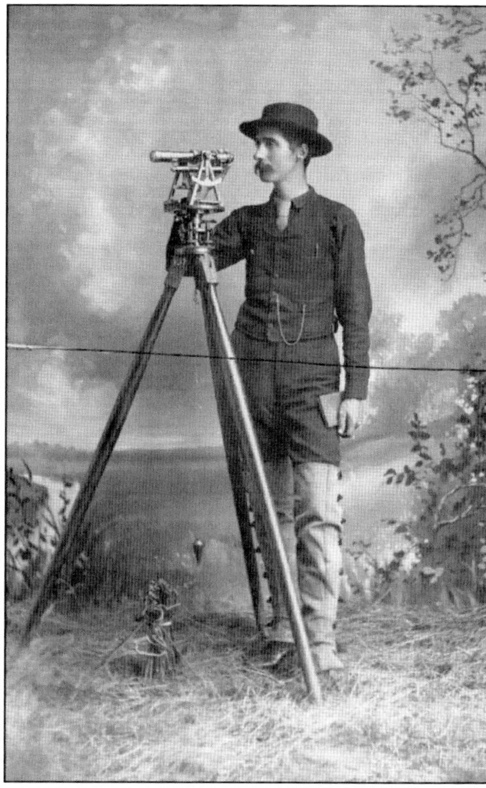

A surveyor from 19th-century Florida is portrayed engaged in his work, enabling future land sales and the great land boom of the early 20th century. (SAF.)

All land deeds in Florida are linked to a basis line and prime meridian located in Cascade Park in Tallahassee. This plat map from 1845 shows where the basis line intersects the prime meridian (arrow). Because there were only a few surveying crews and much of the area in the Forbes Purchase was swampy, there were no detailed surveys of St. George Island or Apalachicola yet. (USGS.)

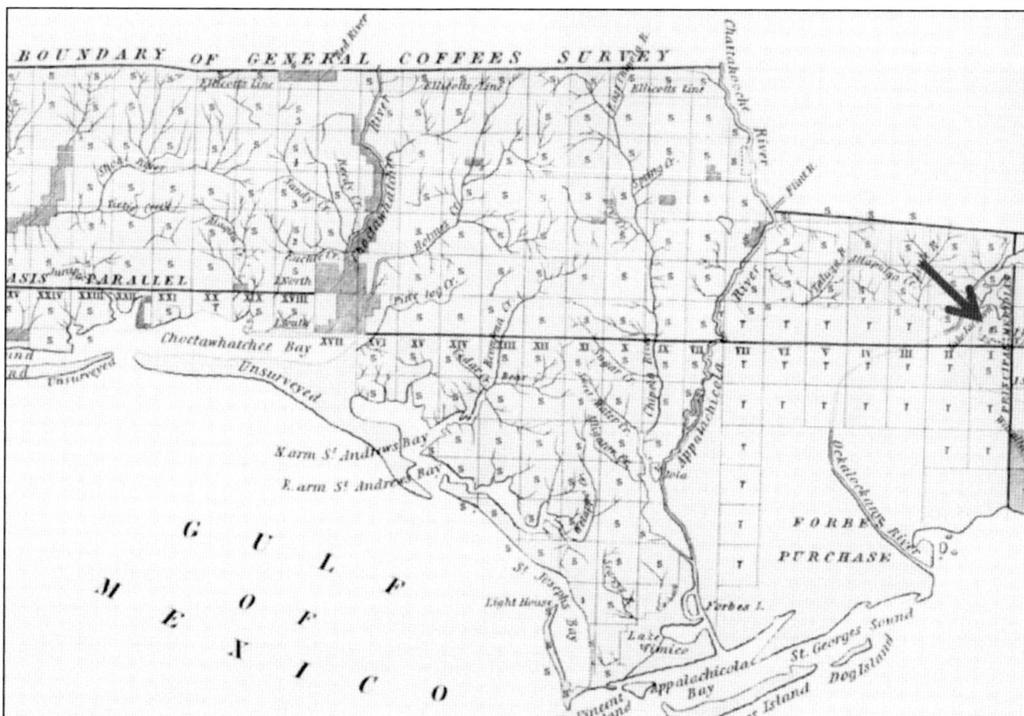

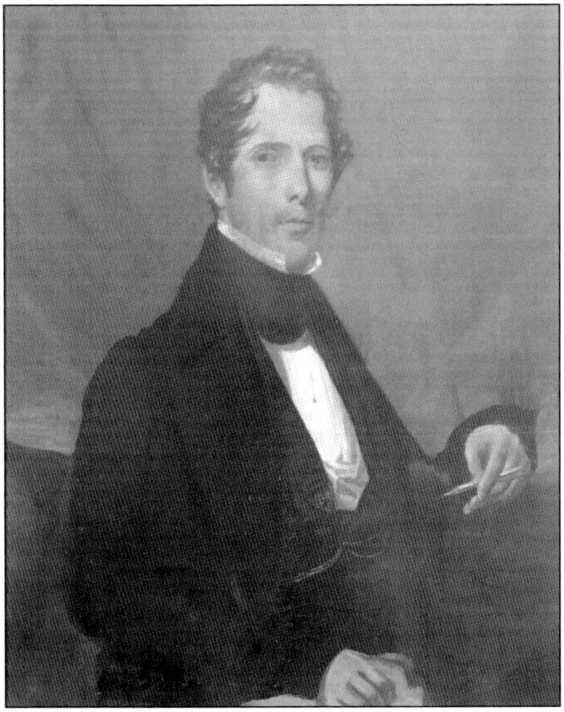

In 1831, Congress appropriated $11,400 for building a lighthouse on the west end of St. George Island and added $400 for buoys to guide ships through West Pass and up to the city of Apalachicola at the river's mouth. The collector of customs added the title of superintendent of lights to his responsibilities. Hiram Nourse, shown here, is the first superintendent of lights at Apalachicola for whom a portrait exists. Until 1852, each superintendent reported to a man named Stephen Pleasonton, the fifth auditor of the US Treasury. (Courtesy of the estate of Francis Nourse O'Bryan Jr.)

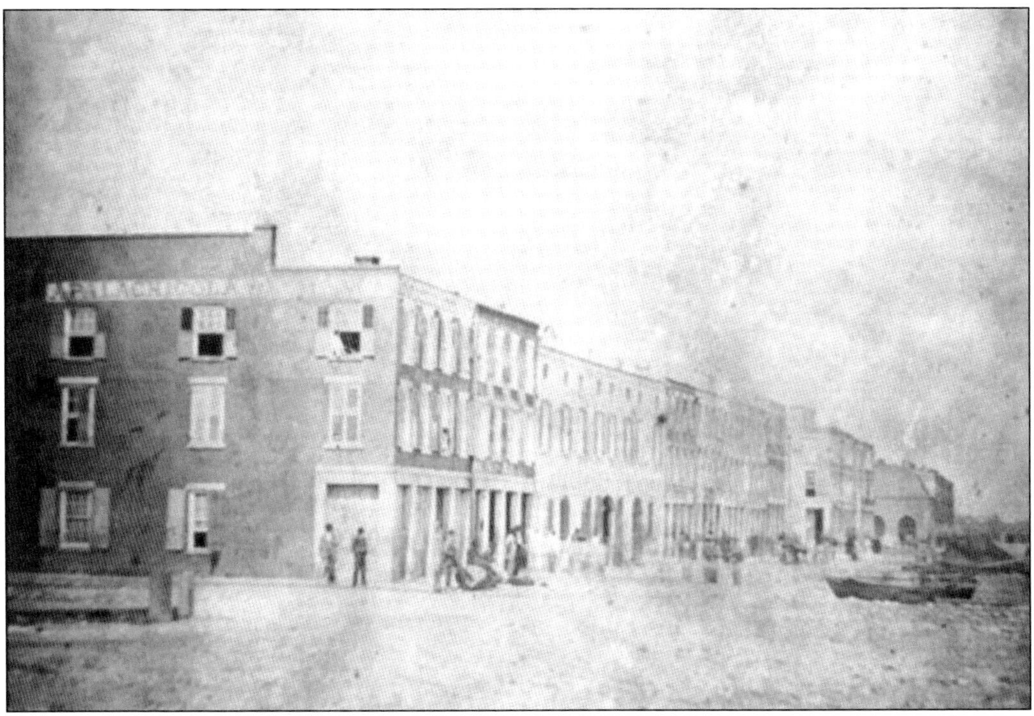

The customs house in Apalachicola was located on the riverfront and often also served as the post office. This view of Water Street from the 1870s shows the area where lighthouse keepers would report each week to pick up mail, their pay, and supplies. Sadly, the earliest customs houses burned or were destroyed by hurricanes, and nearly all their records were lost. (SAF.)

This is a portrait of Stephen Pleasonton, fifth auditor of the US Treasury, who was responsible for issuing lighthouse contracts in territorial Florida and corresponding with local superintendents of lights. The dour Pleasonton adhered scrupulously to his goal of minimizing expenses that had to be borne by the United States. Although that was laudable, Pleasonton also turned down requests to improve US lighthouse quality by installing newly invented Fresnel lenses. (LOC.)

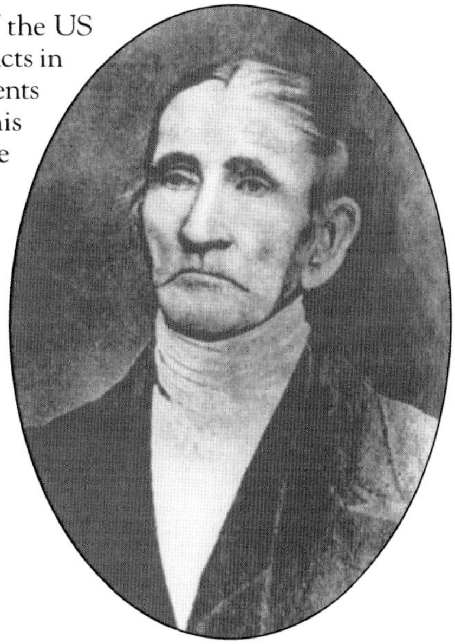

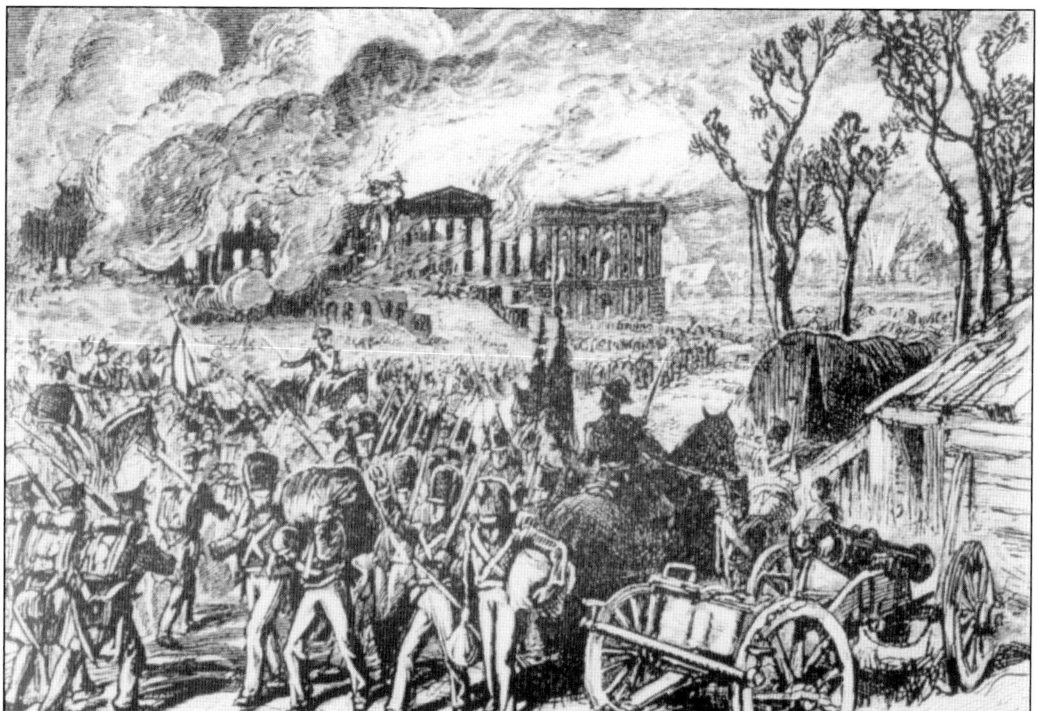

When British forces were marching on Washington in August 1814, Stephen Pleasonton was clerking in the State Department. Secretary of State James Monroe sent an urgent warning that ended, "You had better remove the records." Along with two other clerks, Pleasonton loaded several wagons with documents, including the Declaration of Independence, and drove them to safety in Leesburg, Virginia. Perhaps because of his reputation for quick, responsible action, he was promoted to the fifth auditor of the Treasury and oversaw the expansion of the US Lighthouse Establishment from 1820 to 1852. (LOC.)

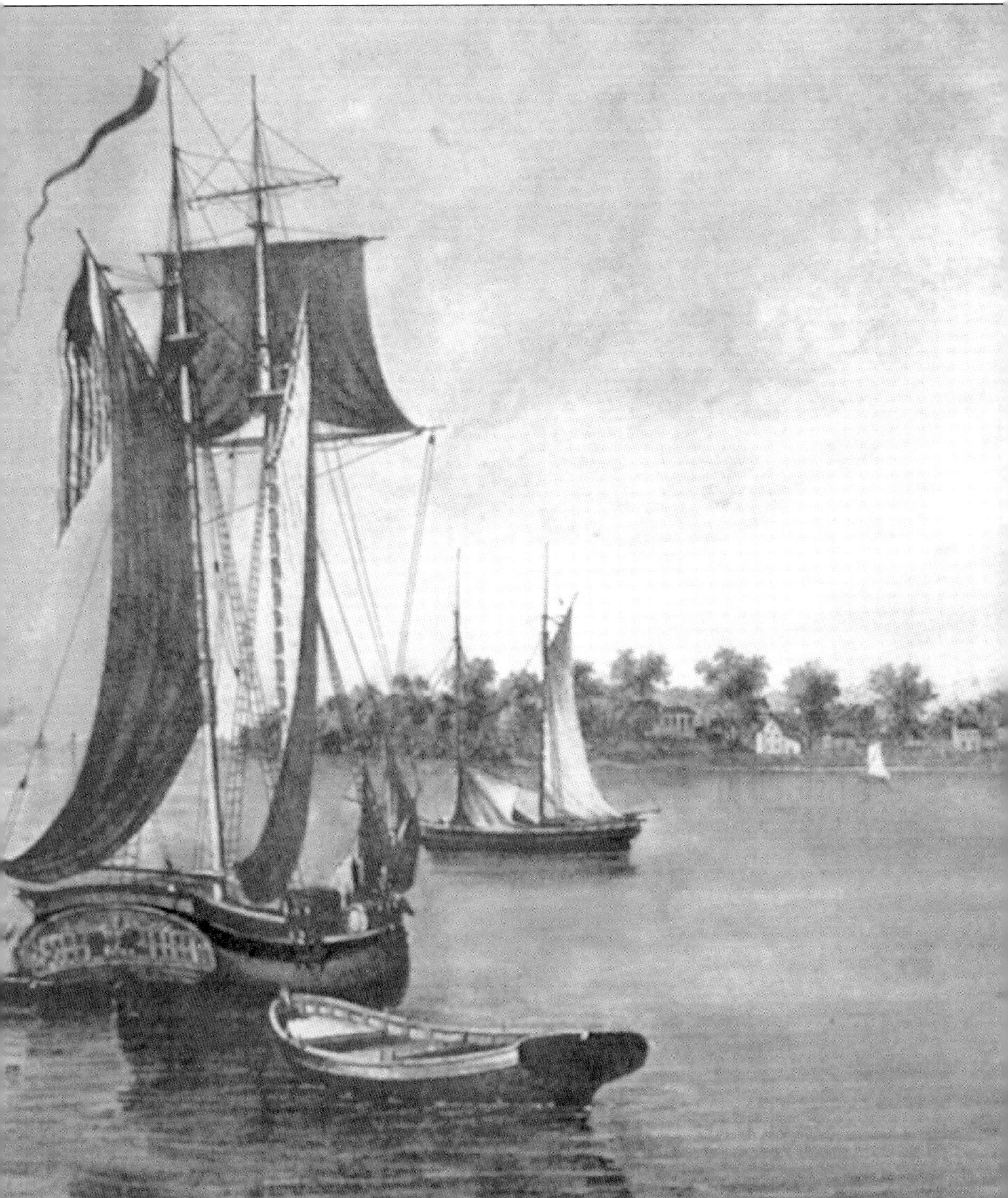

By 1837, Apalachicola was a thriving harbor engaged in shipping cotton and lumber downriver from the falls of the Chattahoochee River at Columbus. The lighthouses of Apalachicola Bay were important in guiding deep-draft, ocean-going ships past the shoals and oyster bars to an

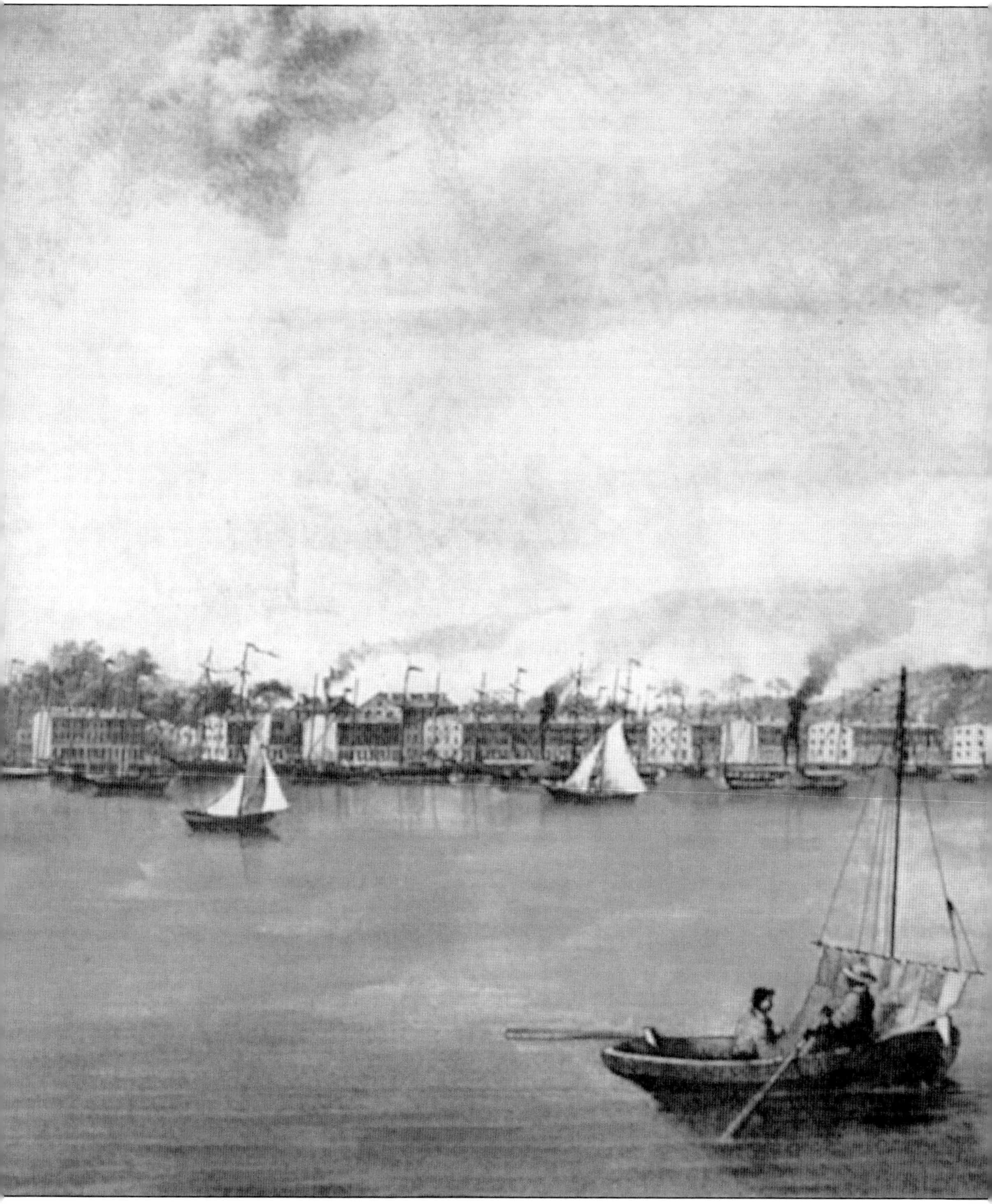

anchorage about three miles from the city wharves. Small sailing vessels called lighters ferried goods from the docks to the larger ships so the wares could be transported to New York and Liverpool, centers for the burgeoning textile trade. (SAF.)

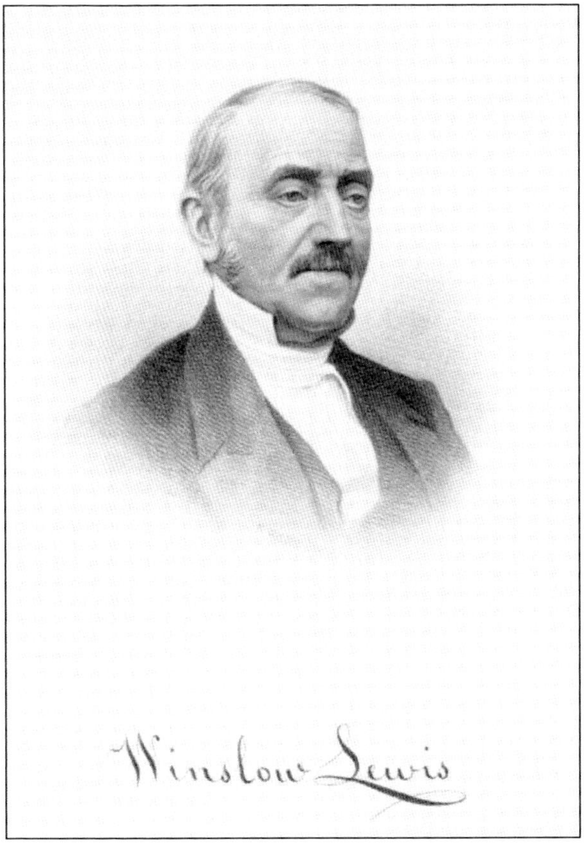

Captain Winslow Lewis of Boston, Massachusetts, built the first lighthouses on St. George Island, at Dog Island on the East Pass into Apalachicola Bay, and St. Marks, Florida. He had obtained a US patent for a chandelier of lamps, each with a silvered reflector, and a magnifying lens he called a bull's-eye. Lewis loaded building materials and work crews onto ships and sailed to sites selected for new construction. (LOC.)

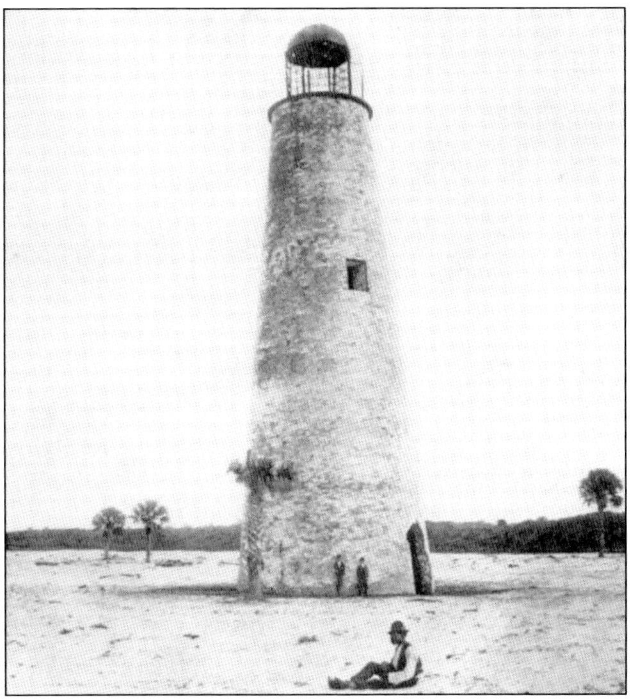

Although no photograph exists of the 1833 lighthouse at West Pass, this image shows the similar lighthouse Captain Lewis built on the St. Johns River in 1830. At the time, the contracts did not stipulate that the lighthouses should be erected on a foundation of pilings. This tower is already leaning three years after it was built. The men in the photograph were part of a crew that dismantled the faulty structure so the bricks could be reused. (SAF.)

A contract for building a lighthouse on St. George Island was issued to Winslow Lewis in 1833 by auditor Stephen Pleasonton. (SGLA.)

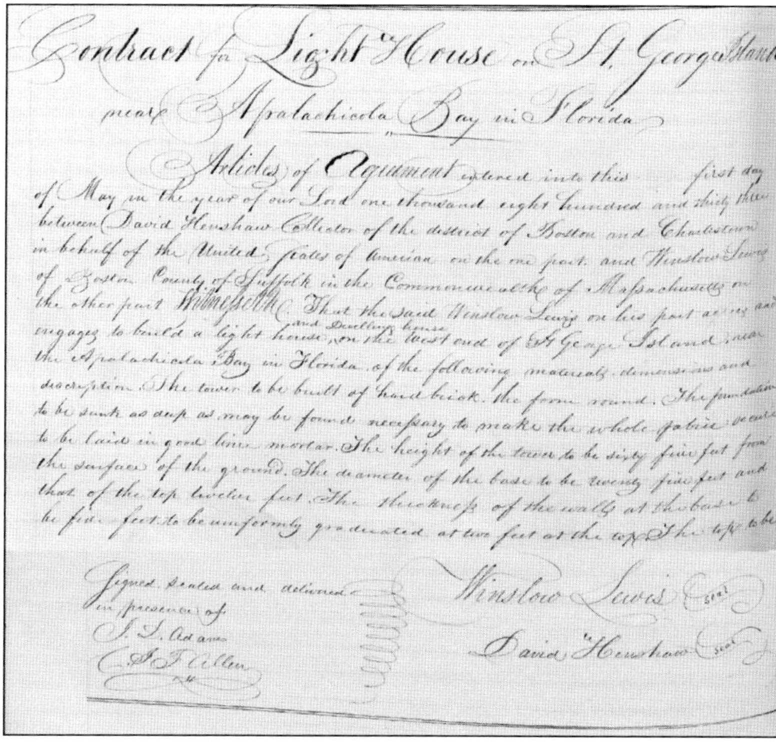
Contract for Light House on St. George Island
near Apalachicola Bay in Florida

Articles of Agreement entered into this first day of May in the year of our Lord one thousand eight hundred and thirty three between David Henshaw Collector of the district of Boston and Charlestown in behalf of the United States of America on the one part and Winslow Lewis of Boston County of Suffolk in the Commonwealth of Massachusetts on the other part Witnesseth That the said Winslow Lewis on his part agrees and engages to build a light house, and Dwelling house on the west end of St George Island near the Apalachicola Bay in Florida of the following materials dimensions and description. The tower to be built of hard brick. the form round. The foundation to be sunk as deep as may be found necessary to make the whole fabric secure to be laid in good lime mortar. The height of the tower to be sixty five feet from the surface of the ground. The diameter of the base to be twenty five feet and that of the top twelve feet. The thickness of the walls at the base to be five feet to be uniformly graduated at two feet at the top. The top to be

Signed sealed and delivered in presence of
J. L. Adams
A. F. Allen

Winslow Lewis (seal)
David Henshaw (seal)

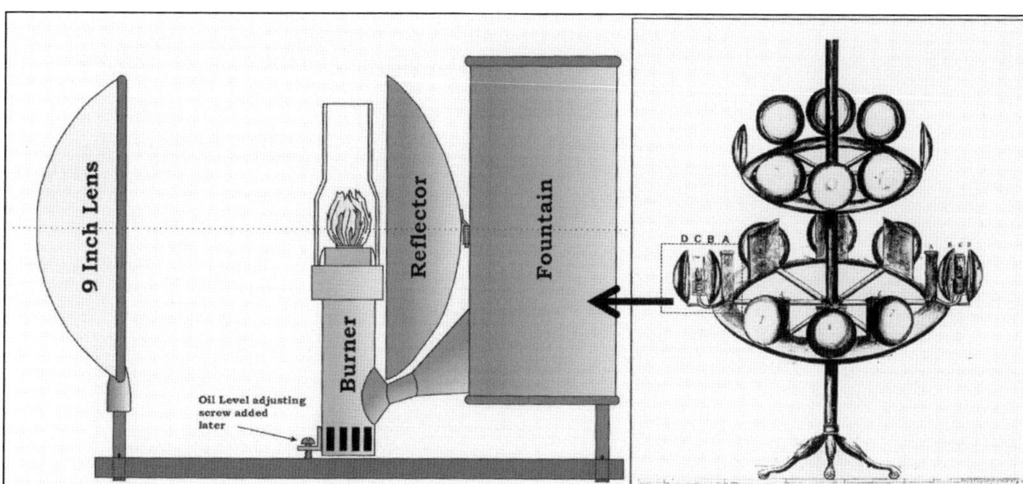

The Lewis lighting apparatus was a chandelier of 13 lamps with silvered, parabolic reflectors that each included a bull's-eye lens. The drawing at right depicts the chandelier envisioned by Winslow Lewis in his original US patent application. At left, an individual fuel reservoir, reflector, burner and magnifying lens are shown. Lighthouse keepers had to refill the fuel reservoirs frequently and spent their nights trimming wicks and polishing the reflective surfaces, which unfortunately rubbed away. (USLHS.)

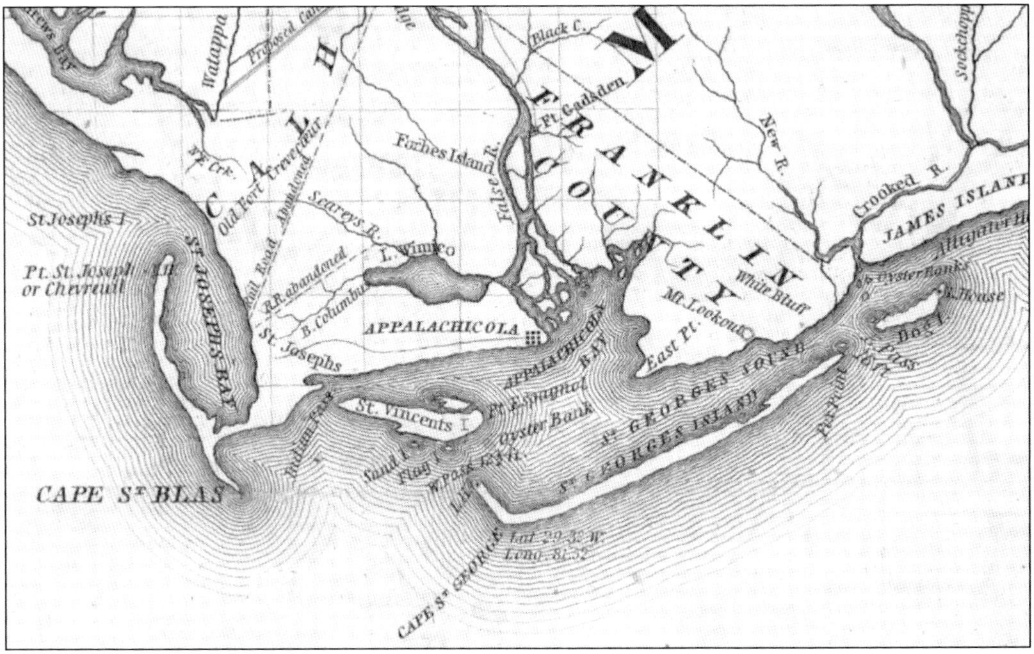

This nautical chart from 1846 shows the location of the lighthouse at West Pass on St. George Island. It also marks some of the shoals and oyster bars that made the lighthouse important for aiding navigation. In addition, a tidal surge from the hurricane of 1837 opened two channels across St. George Island and separated Little St. George Island from its eastern neighbor until it was filled in by storms after 1907. (USGS.)

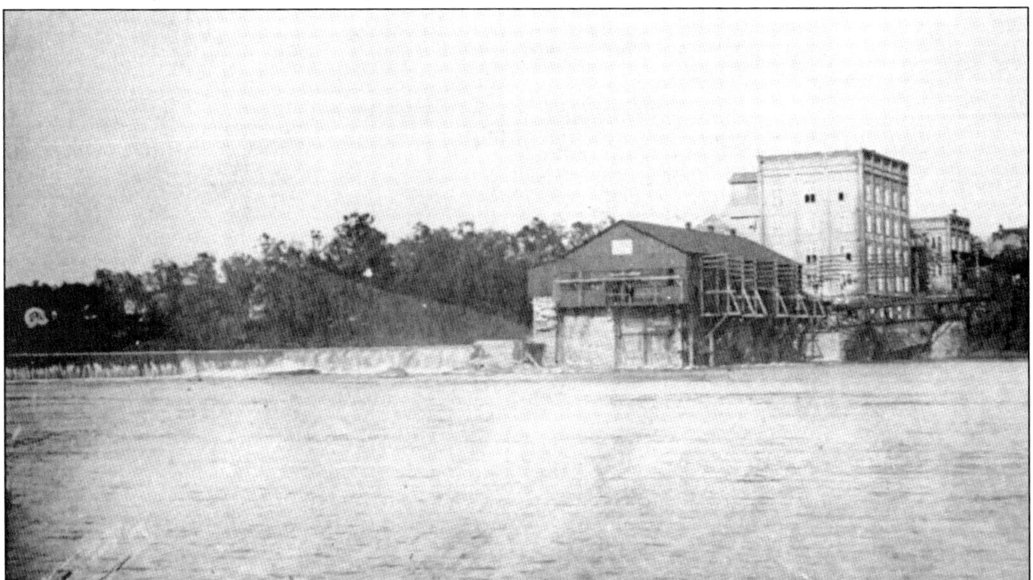

Columbus, Georgia, flourished as Apalachicola's sister city upriver. Located along the waterfalls of the Chattahoochee, its grist mills and textile mills used power generated by water turbines. Sources of iron ore and coal in the Appalachian foothills enabled the largest iron foundry in the South to be set up at the Columbus Iron Works. Most of these goods were either shipped downriver to Apalachicola for export or sold to settlers along the river valley.

Before the Civil War, the port of Apalachicola engaged in packing and shipping cotton from agricultural lands along the river in Georgia and Alabama. The plantation system was established, primarily relying on the work of black slaves (upper panel). Shallow-draft steamboats brought the cotton to the docks during the fall and winter. Much of the work of ginning and packing cotton into compressed bales for international shipment also relied on steam engines, as shown in the lower panel. (SAF.)

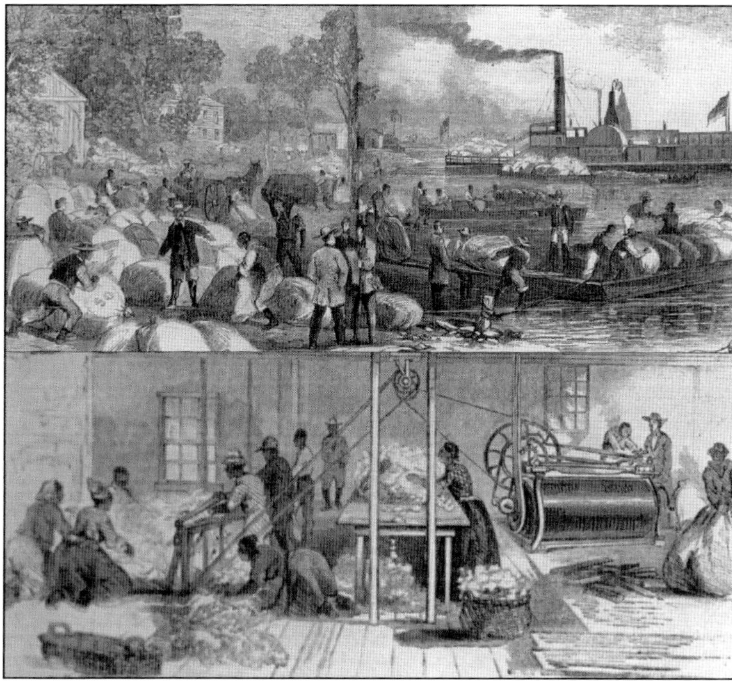

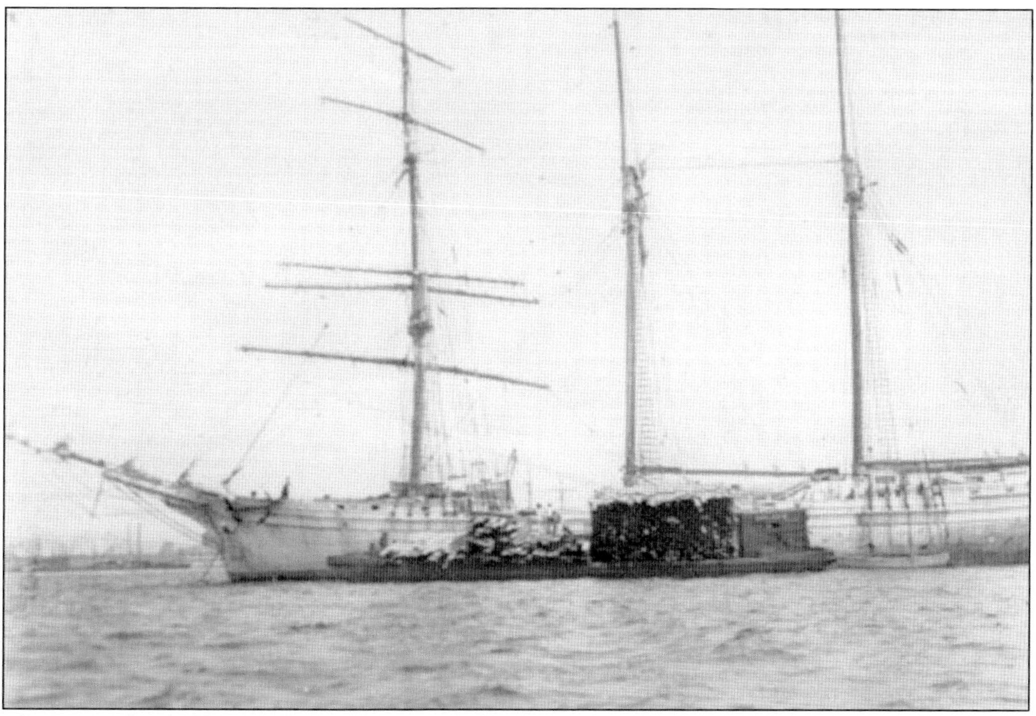

The crew of a shallow-draft boat called a lighter is shown transferring lumber cargo to a three-masted sailing ship in Apalachicola Bay. Until the advent of railroads, lightering fees were charged to all shipments that required deep-draft, ocean-going vessels. (SGLA.)

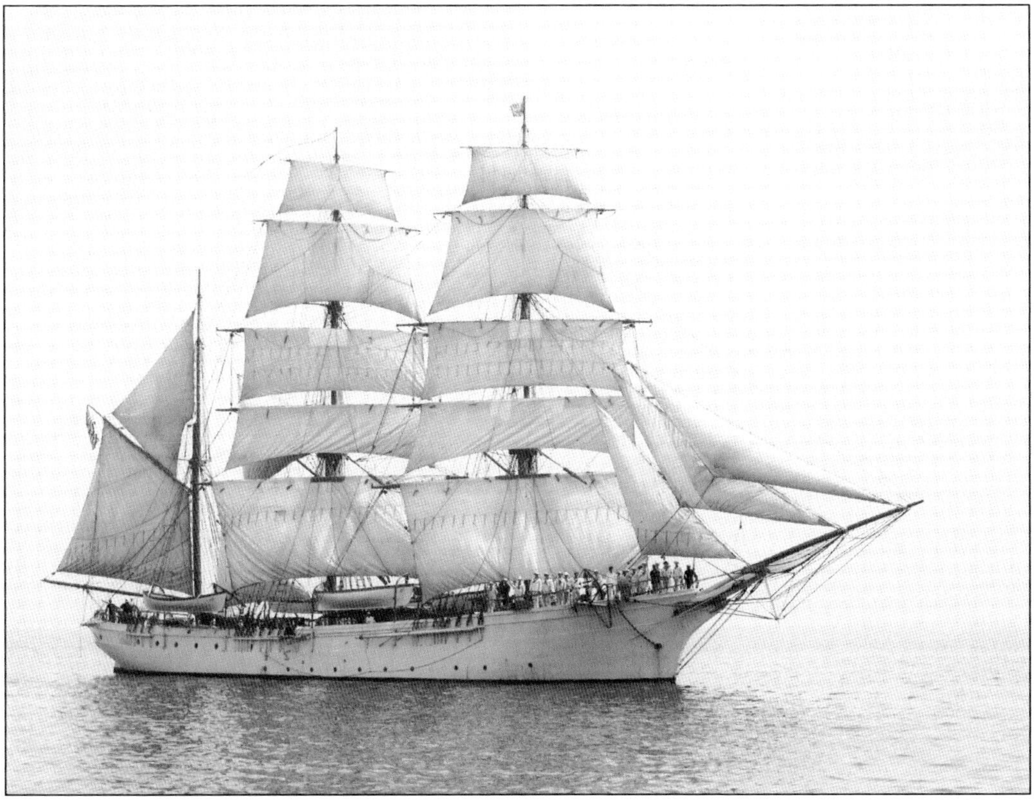

This barque is similar to the wood-hulled, ocean-going ships that carried goods from Apalachicola through West Pass and on to New York and other ports. By 1850, some vessels were hybrids powered by sails and steam engines. By the end of the Civil War, many steamships had iron hulls, and paddlewheels were being replaced by screw propellers. (LOC.)

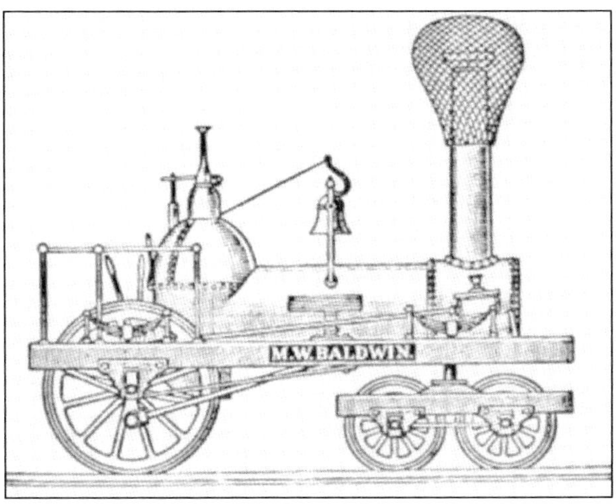

After 1835, the rival town of St. Joseph attempted to compete with Apalachicola by transporting goods by rail from the Apalachicola River to its deepwater port along St. Joseph Bay 25 miles west of Apalachicola. By 1839, a Baldwin locomotive engine operated on one of the first railroads chartered in the territory of Florida. An epidemic of yellow fever ended St. Joseph's prospects in 1841 and it was soon deserted, but the short-lived railroad foreshadowed how much transportation would change a few decades later. (LOC.)

Three

THE 1852 LIGHTHOUSE, A LOVE STORY

The hurricane of August 1851 destroyed the 1848 lighthouse on Cape St. George and washed away the keeper's dwelling. William Austin, who was the keeper at the time, survived the storm. Benjamin Hawley, the superintendent of lights in Apalachicola, also supervised the lighthouses on Cape San Blas and Dog Island. He and his deputy wrote to Stephen Pleasonton to explain that all three towers had been destroyed and would need to be rebuilt. Keepers were expected to be on duty at all times, especially during storms. With no way to forecast hurricanes, families were in great jeopardy during hurricanes.

It had been a mistake to build a lighthouse within 150 yards of the Gulf of Mexico, and the deputy superintendent noted that a sand hill about 400 yards inland would provide a favorable site. Commerce in Apalachicola was still burgeoning, and a request for bids to rebuild the lighthouses was issued promptly. The superintendent noted that the illuminating apparatus (the Lewis lamp chandelier) could be salvaged and reused and recommended that bricks from the old tower should also be salvaged to reduce costs. The contract was issued to two contractors from Boston, Emerson and Adams, in December 1851, and construction began promptly. One of Stephen Pleasonton's last tasks before he retired from the Treasury Department was to request funds to rebuild the lighthouses of Apalachicola Bay.

By 1852, the task of managing the lighthouses and buoys that mark navigation channels had grown far beyond the capabilities of the fifth auditor of the Treasury. Congress established a new lighthouse board made up of military men, engineers, and surveyors. The board remained a part of the Treasury Department, but hiring practices would gradually shift from the patronage system used by collectors of customs to the superintendents of lighthouse districts. Each district set up supply depots with ships called tenders that would deliver supplies, bring inspectors, and maintain buoys in the navigation channels. Perhaps to distinguish the tenders from navy vessels, tenders were named after flowering plants, such as the *Arbutus*, the *Camellia*, and the *Magnolia*.

In 1857, the US Lighthouse Board replaced the old Lewis lamps with a beautiful, third-order Fresnel lens and requested that an assistant keeper be hired. However, just as the new lighthouse began to function at peak efficiency, the Civil War broke out. The Union blockade of Apalachicola Bay eliminated commerce on the bay and river. The population of Apalachicola plummeted, and decades would be needed to rebuild the economy.

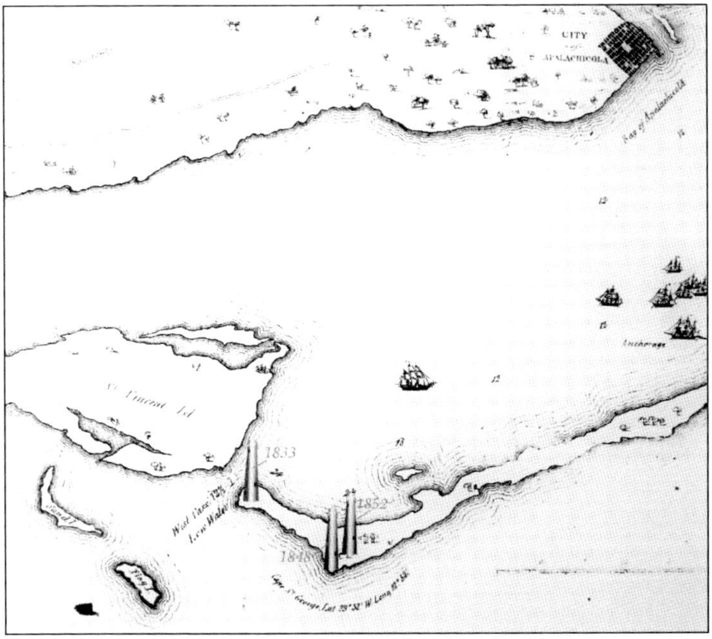

The 1833 lighthouse had been built at West Pass, as seen on this map. It was dismantled and rebuilt as the 1848 tower on Cape St. George, where sea captains could see it sooner when arriving from the east. Major hurricanes in 1850 and 1851 damaged and then toppled the lighthouse, and it was rebuilt in 1852 on a small hill about 400 yards from the Gulf of Mexico. The new foundation was built on sturdy pilings, and the tower stood for 153 years until beach erosion and storm surges toppled it in 2005. (SGLA.)

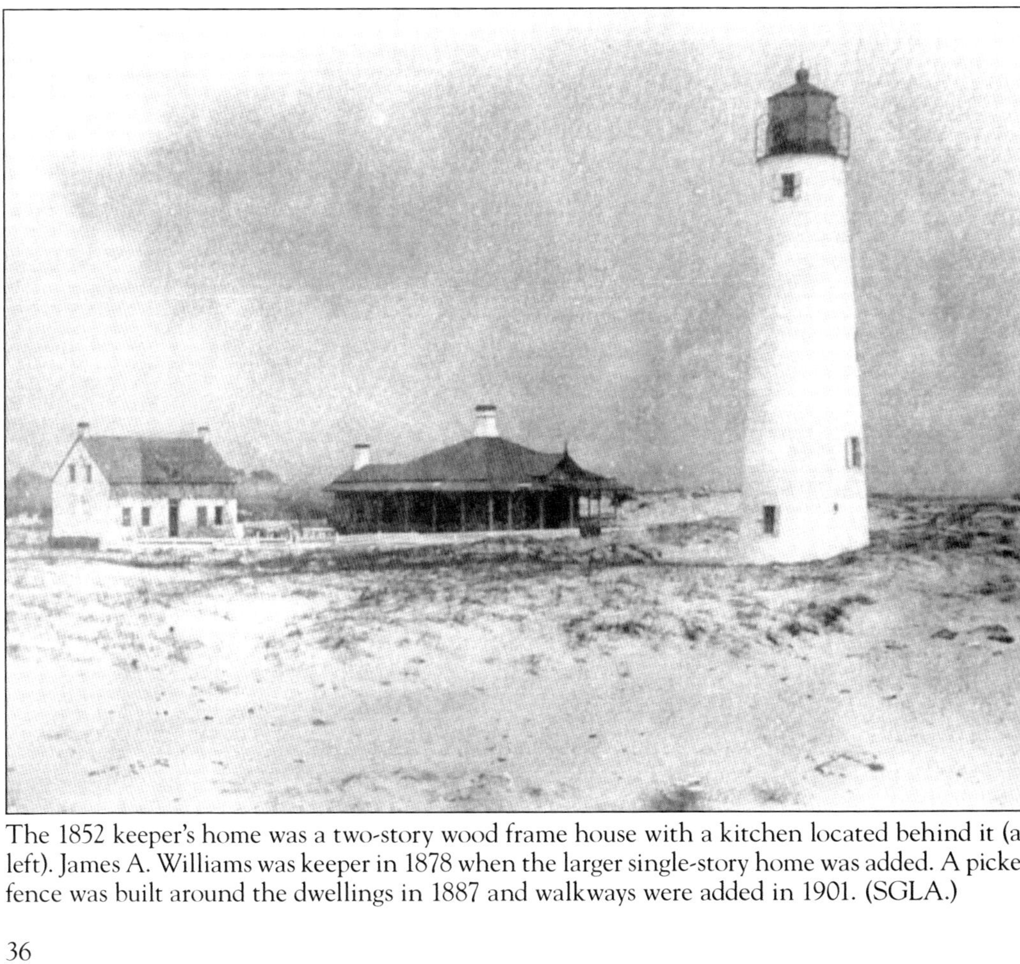

The 1852 keeper's home was a two-story wood frame house with a kitchen located behind it (at left). James A. Williams was keeper in 1878 when the larger single-story home was added. A picket fence was built around the dwellings in 1887 and walkways were added in 1901. (SGLA.)

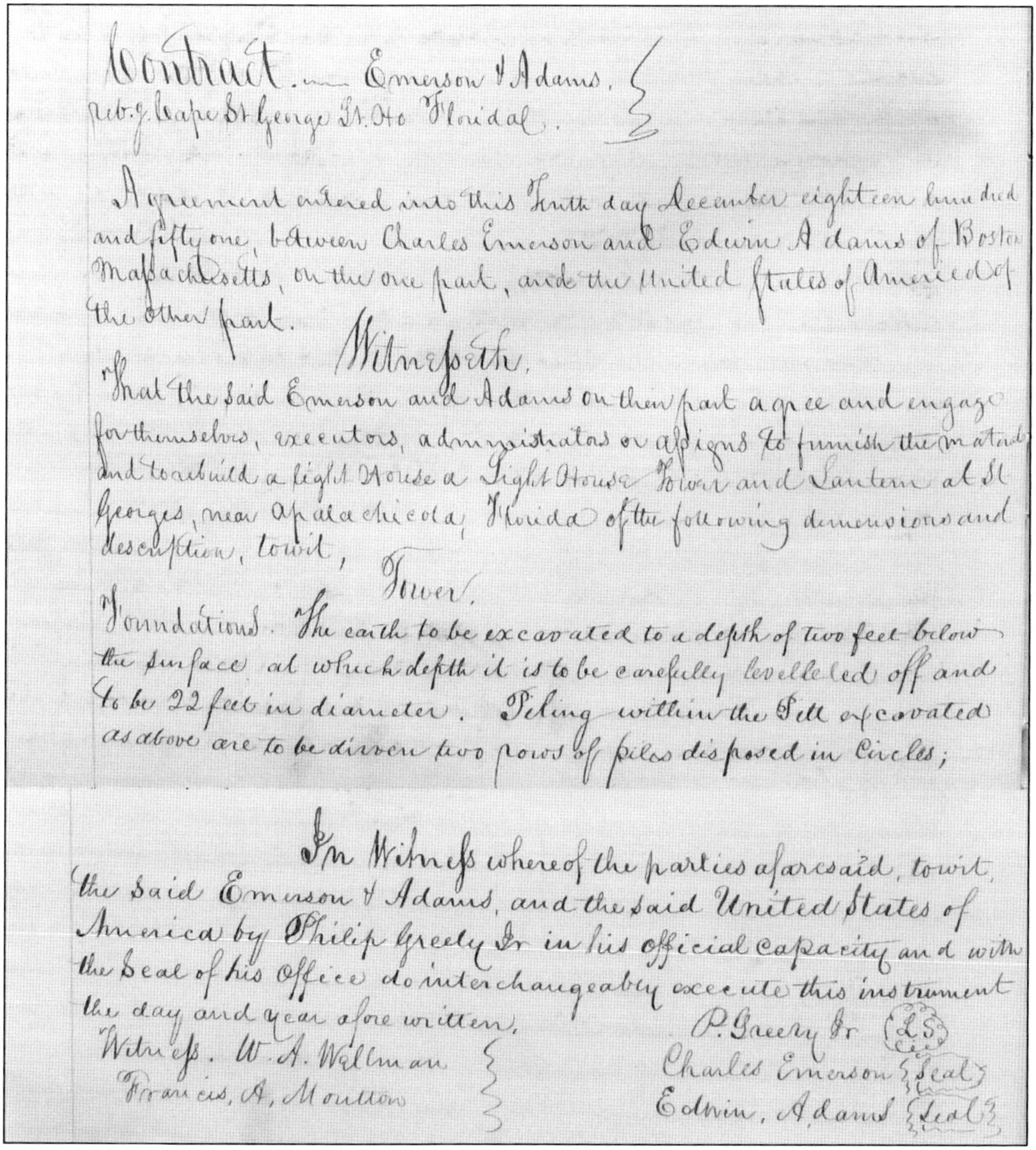

Contract. — Emerson & Adams.
reb.g Cape St George Lt. Ho Florida.

Agreement entered into this Tenth day December eighteen hundred and fifty one, between Charles Emerson and Edwin Adams of Boston Massachusetts, on the one part, and the United States of America of the other part.

Witnesseth,

That the said Emerson and Adams on their part agree and engage for themselves, executors, administrators or assigns to furnish the material and to rebuild a Light House a Light House Tower and Lantern at St Georges, near Apalachicola, Florida of the following dimensions and description, to wit,

Tower.

Foundations. The earth to be excavated to a depth of two feet below the surface at which depth it is to be carefully levelled off and to be 22 feet in diameter. Piling within the cell excavated as above are to be driven two rows of piles disposed in Circles;

In Witness whereof the parties aforesaid, to wit, the said Emerson & Adams, and the said United States of America by Philip Greely Jr in his official capacity and with the Seal of his Office do interchangeably execute this instrument the day and year afore written.

Witness. W. A. Wellman
Francis, A, Moulton

P. Greely Jr (L.S.)
Charles Emerson {Seal}
Edwin, Adams {Seal}

After the hurricane of 1851, Philip Greely, the superintendent of lights in Boston, issued a contract for rebuilding the lighthouse tower and keeper's home on Cape St. George. The contract was issued to Charles Emerson and Edwin Adams on December 10, 1851, for the price of $6,390. Benjamin Hawley, superintendent of lights in Apalachicola, was responsible for overseeing the construction. After 32 years of service, Stephen Pleasonton resigned, and Congress created a new lighthouse board to manage all operations of US lighthouses. (National Archives, SGLA.)

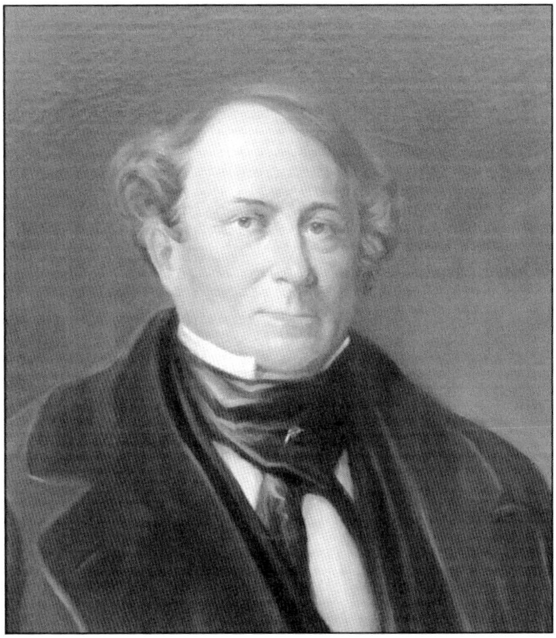

George S. Hawkins was appointed collector of customs and superintendent of lights in 1855. Hawkins was a lawyer and judge who moved to Apalachicola from New York. He served in the territorial legislature and was an associate justice on the Florida Supreme Court. For several years after the US Lighthouse Board was founded in 1852, local customs collectors still influenced hiring and firing of lighthouse keepers and relied on aids to navigation that allowed ships to enter Apalachicola Bay and pay tariffs and duties. (SAF.)

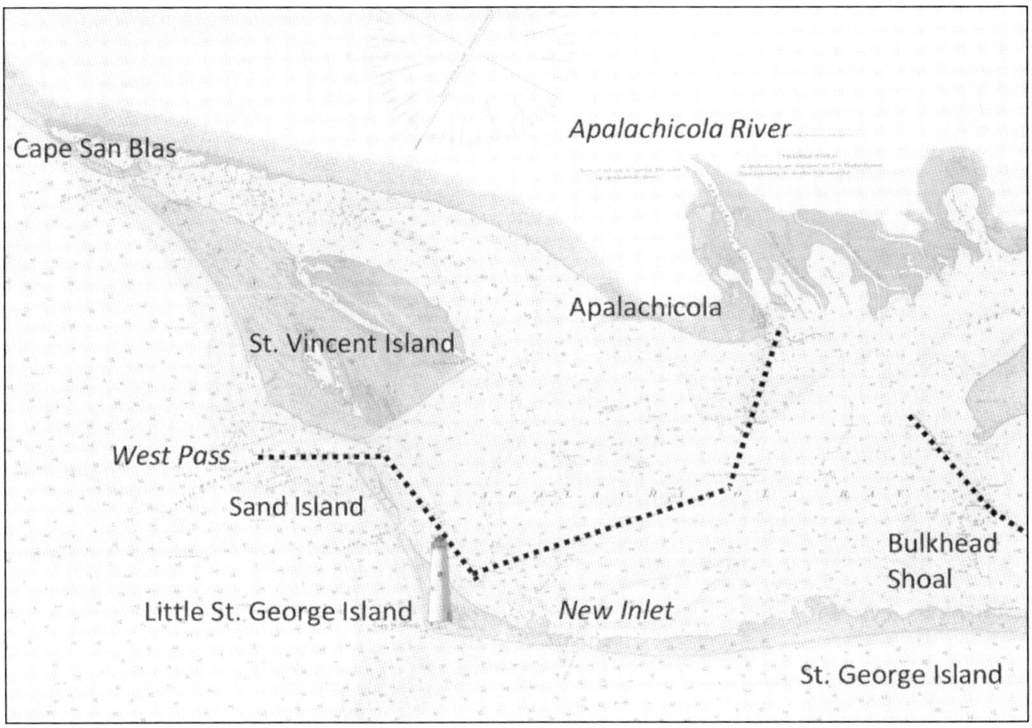

This map of the west end of Apalachicola Bay shows the position of the lighthouse on Cape St. George and the inlets cut by hurricanes that formed Sand Island and separated Little St. George Island from the rest of St. George Island at the time. Sailing ships entered West Pass and navigated along the marked channel (dotted line) to Lower Anchorage near the island or Upper Anchorage in the middle of the bay. Apalachicola is situated at the river's mouth toward the top. (US Geological Survey, JLH.)

In 1852, the US Congress created a nine-member lighthouse board to manage the 331 lighthouses then in operation. US Navy commodore William B. Shubrick (pictured) was appointed the first head. Comprised of military men, surveyors, and engineers, the committee created the well-trained service that would become known for its neat blue uniforms and its professionalism. By 1910, the board was managing 1,200 lighthouses, 54 lightships, and thousands of lesser aids to navigation. (LOC.)

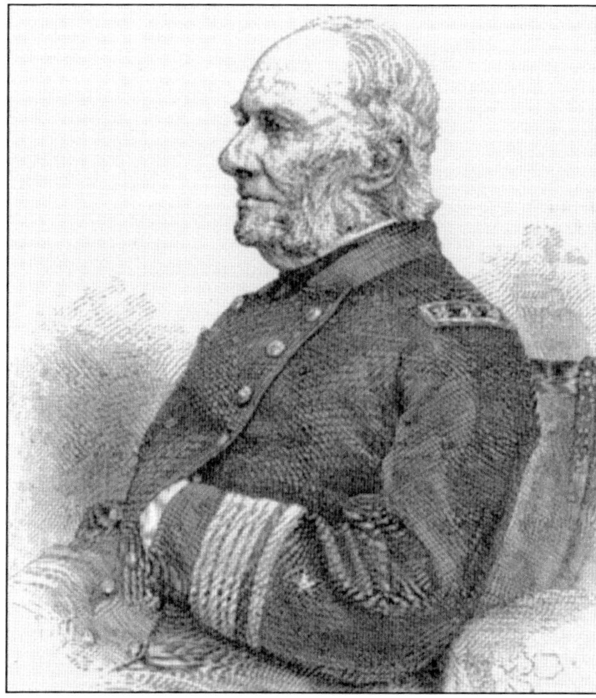

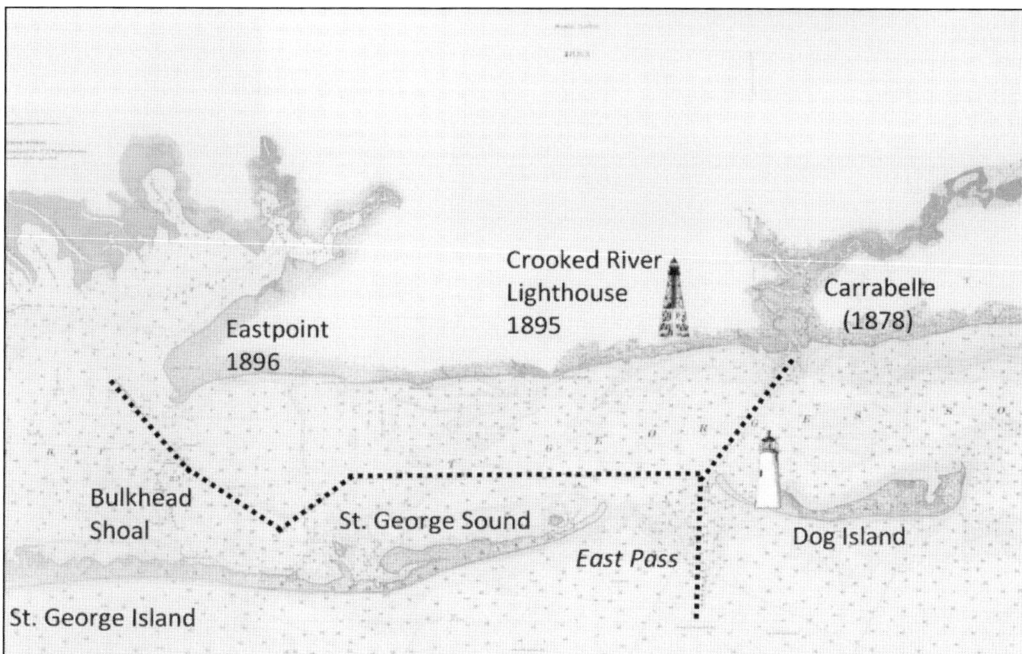

This map of the east end of Apalachicola Bay and St. George Sound (east of Bulkhead Shoal, an oyster bar) shows East Pass, Carrabelle, Crooked River Lighthouse, and Eastpoint. Replaced after the hurricane of 1851, the Dog Island lighthouse was finally destroyed by a hurricane in 1873. A steel frame tower was built in 1895 at a point called Crooked River north of East Pass. Until a channel was dredged through Bulkhead Shoal, East Pass was primarily used for ships carrying lumber from Carrabelle. (US Geological Survey, JLH.)

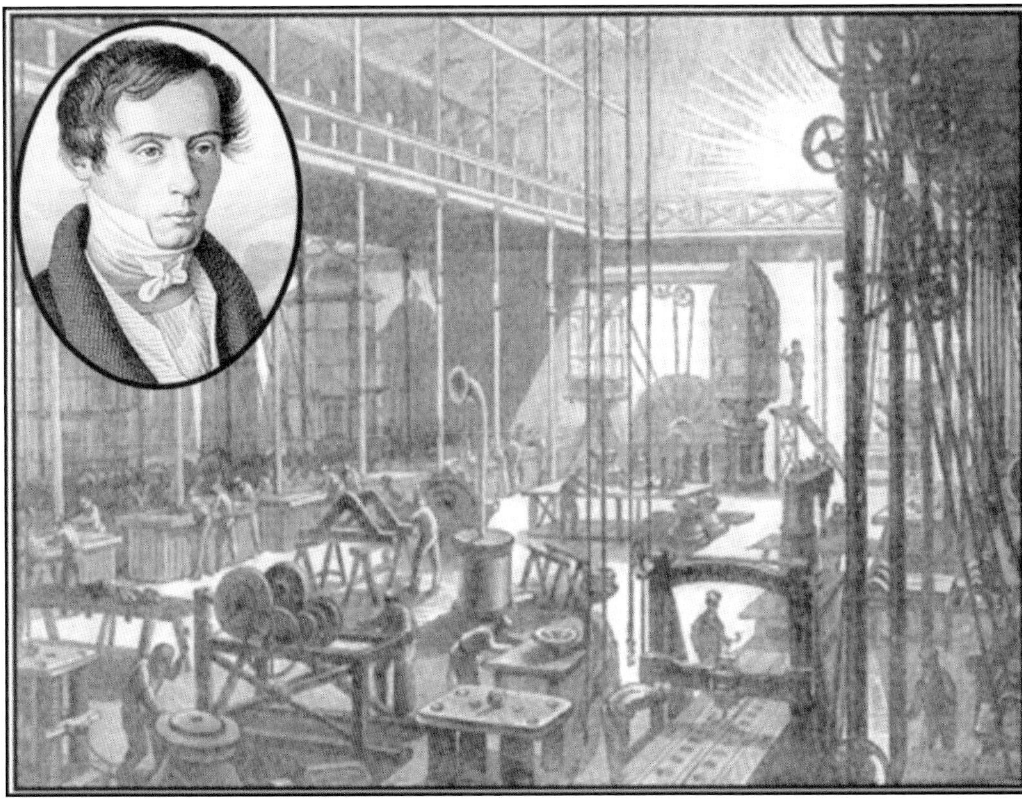

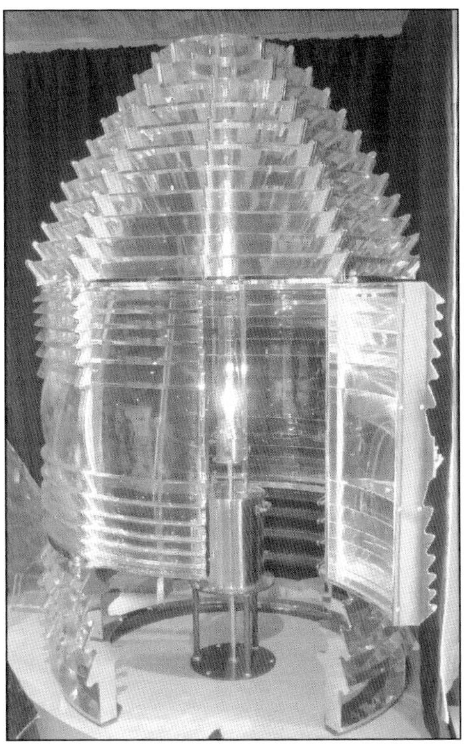

The US Lighthouse Board immediately began replacing the inefficient Lewis reflector chandeliers with a very efficient lens system invented by Augustin Fresnel (inset). Pictured is the Parisian lens factory of Sautter, Lemonnier and Sons that ground and assembled Fresnel lenses. Even though Fresnel lenses cost more to install, only one lamp was required per lighthouse, resulting in a significant savings in fuel. Whale oil was still used until the Civil War. (USLHS.)

This replica of the third-order Fresnel lens that was first installed at Cape St. George in 1857 shows the access panel open, revealing a replica lamp. Fresnel's innovation was a central focusing lens surrounded by prisms that captured nearly all the light emitted by the lantern and focused it into a single beam. Unlike older lenses, no mirrors were required. The beacon from the lantern could be seen from 13 miles offshore. The characteristic, or night mark, at Cape St. George was a fixed beacon until 1949 when the Coast Guard adopted a flash at six second intervals. (JLH, SGLA.)

The Fresnel lens was probably shipped from Paris to the lighthouse depot on Staten Island and then to a depot in Mobile, Alabama. US Navy commander Raphael Semmes (foreground) signed the receipt at Mobile when the lens was shipped to Cape St. George. Semmes would later serve as the first superintendent of lights in the Confederate States of America, but resigned to take command of the famous confederate raider *Alabama*. The image shows Semmes and Lt. John Macintosh Kell on board the CSS *Alabama*. (US Naval Historical Archives, SGLA.)

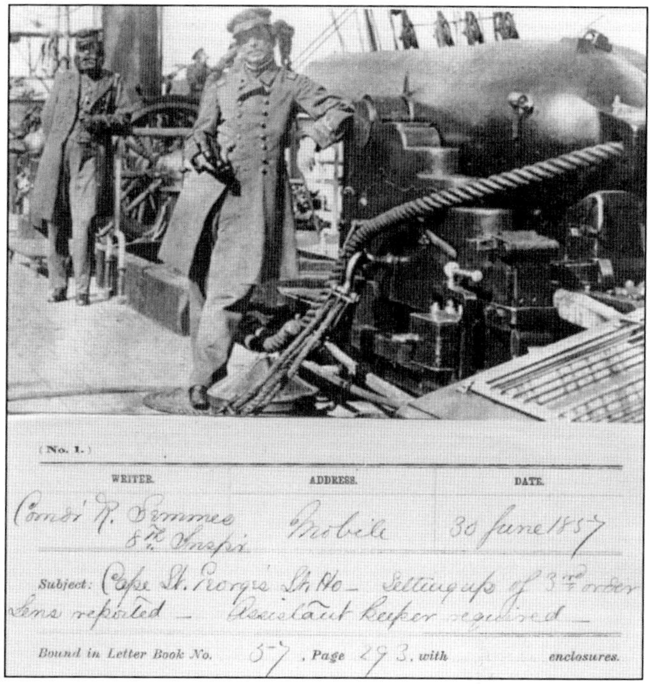

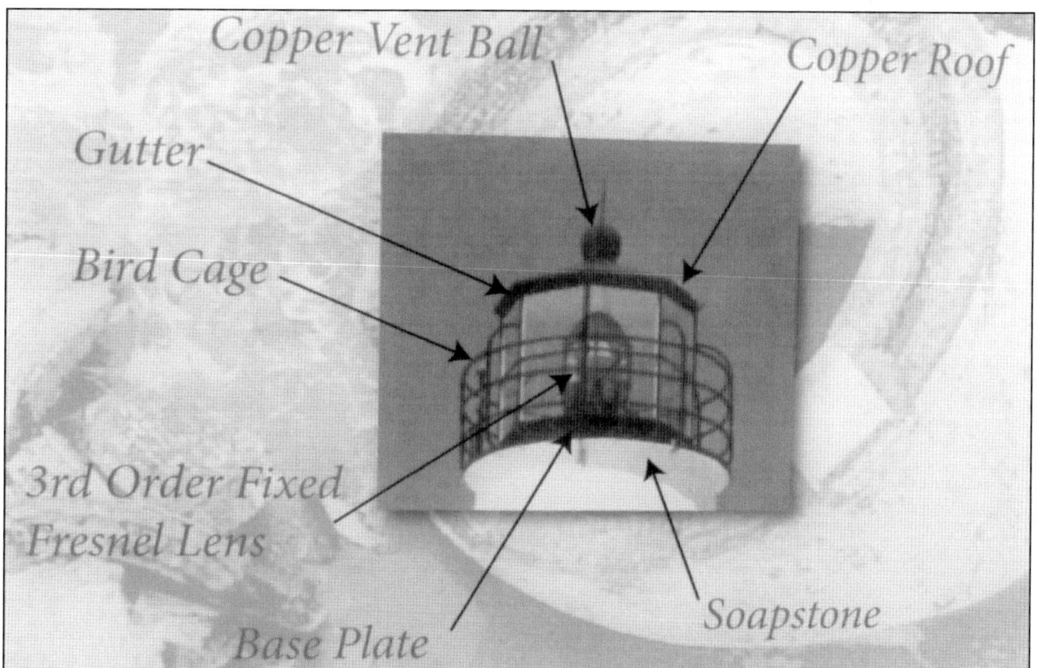

To lighthouse keepers, the "lantern" referred to the entire lighting apparatus, including the oil lamp, the lens system, and the plate-glass windows on the top of the tower. This diagram from the Cape St. George Lighthouse Museum names the other parts of the tower. The spike on top of the vent ball is a lightning rod that is attached to a thick copper wire that runs to the ground. Lightning strikes are common on the coast of Florida, and keepers had to be present during the storms, no matter how severe. (SGLA.)

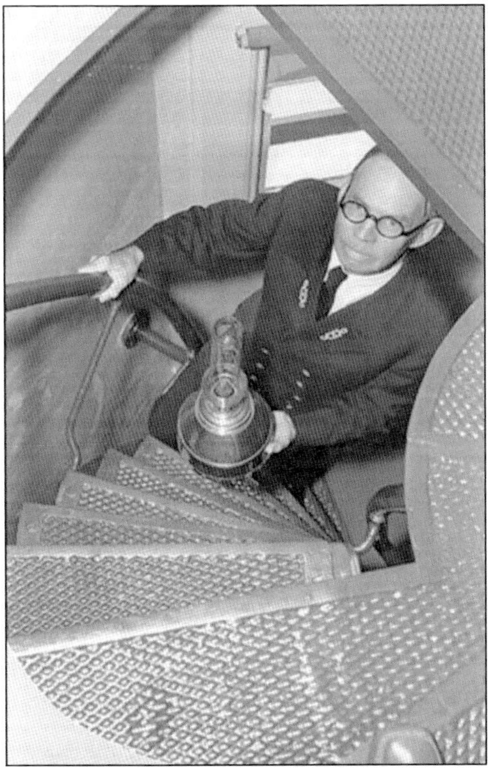

A lighthouse keeper climbs the stairs on his way to the watch room to begin preparing to light the lamp at sunset. Imagine climbing the 92 steps at least four times a day, usually carrying five gallons of fuel oil or cleaning supplies, in summer and winter, fair weather and foul. Keepers used handheld service lamps or Aladdin lamps, but often simply ascended the familiar stairs using only starlight or moonlight to guide their steps. (USLHS.)

The watch room display at the Cape St. George Lighthouse Museum includes a wooden chair and desk, a keeper's log, a barometer for forecasting weather changes, and tools used to maintain the station. Here, the keeper could pause before climbing a ladder through a rectangular "scuttle" to gain entry into the lantern room with the oil lamp and Fresnel lens. When an assistant keeper was present, one of the two was expected to keep watch at all times. (SGLA.)

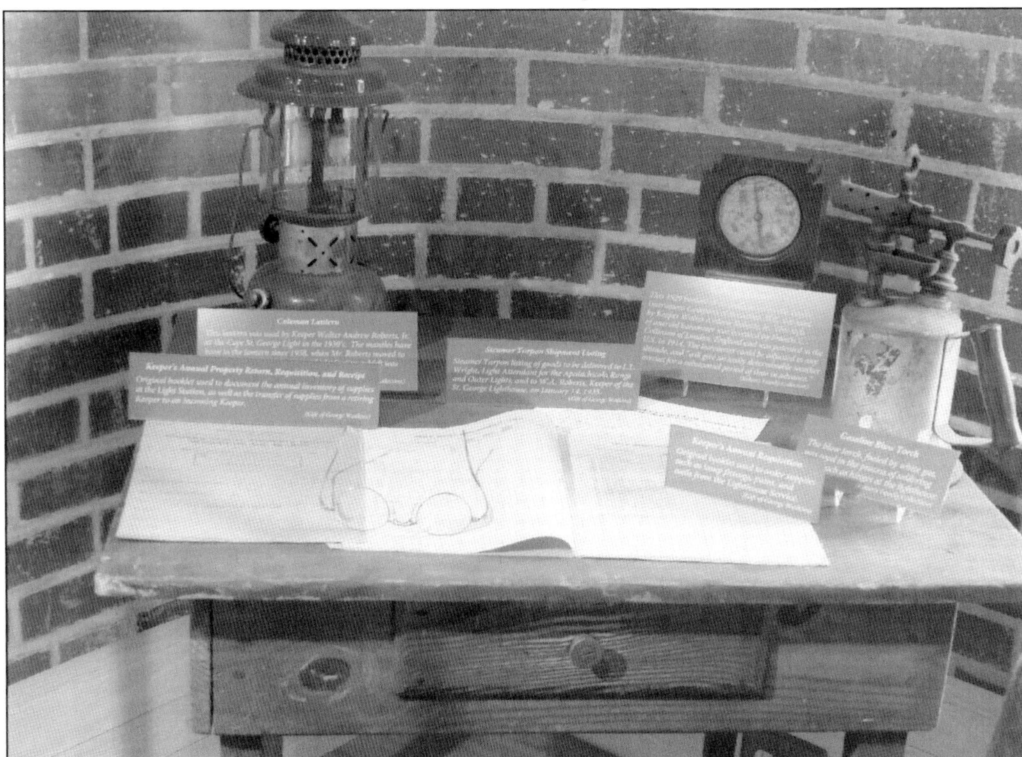

The first light source for the new Fresnel lens was probably a piston-driven moderator lamp. A keeper's first duty before sundown was to fill the oil reservoir and turn a key to raise the piston so it would push oil through the wick. Moderator lamps needed to be rewound every four hours during the night, and it became important for each lighthouse to hire an assistant keeper to help with the night watches. (USLHS.)

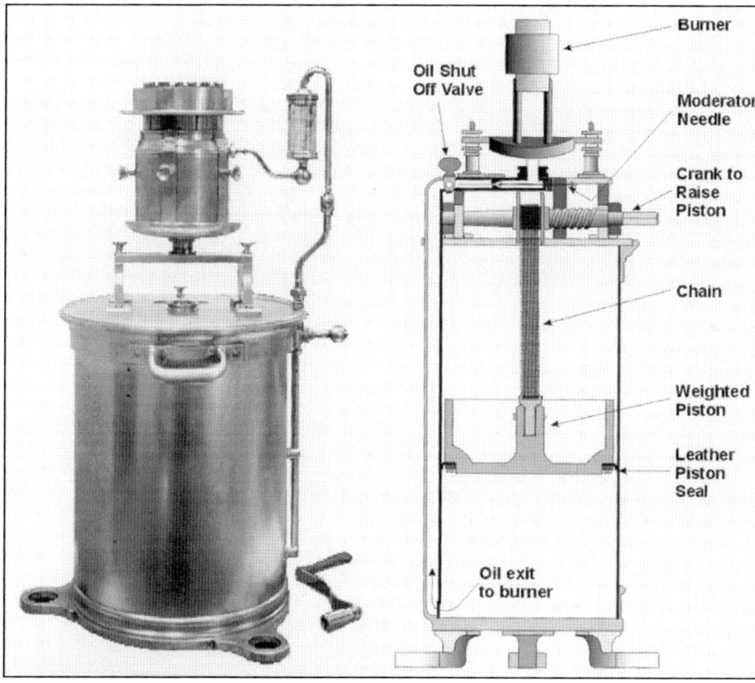

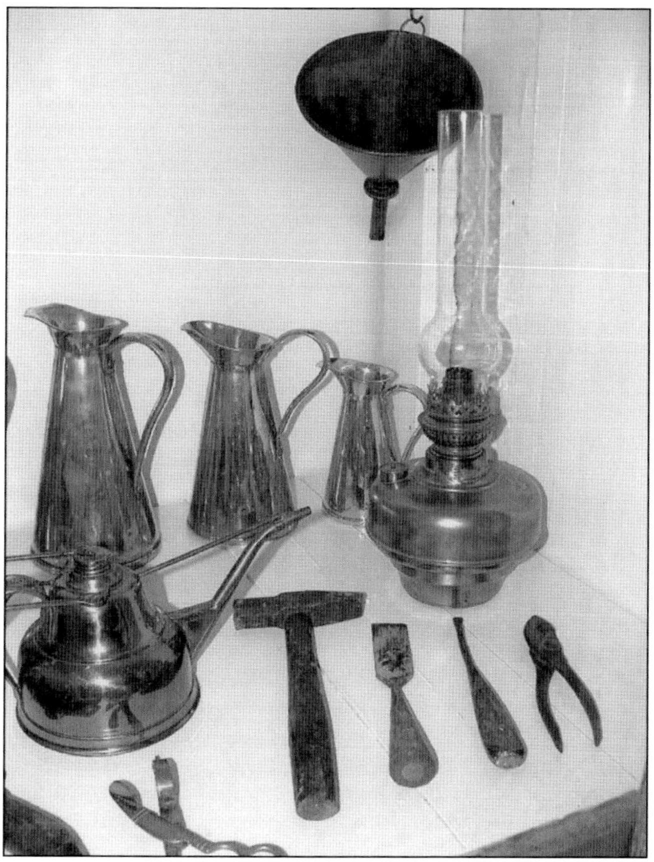

Lighthouses had many brass fixtures that needed daily polishing. Here is an assortment of oil transfer pitchers along with tools needed for trimming wicks and making general repairs. Keeper Fred Morong wrote a poem, one stanza of which laments, "The lamp in the tower, reflector and shade / The tools and accessories pass in the parade / As a matter of fact the whole outfit is made Of BRASSWORK." (USLHS.)

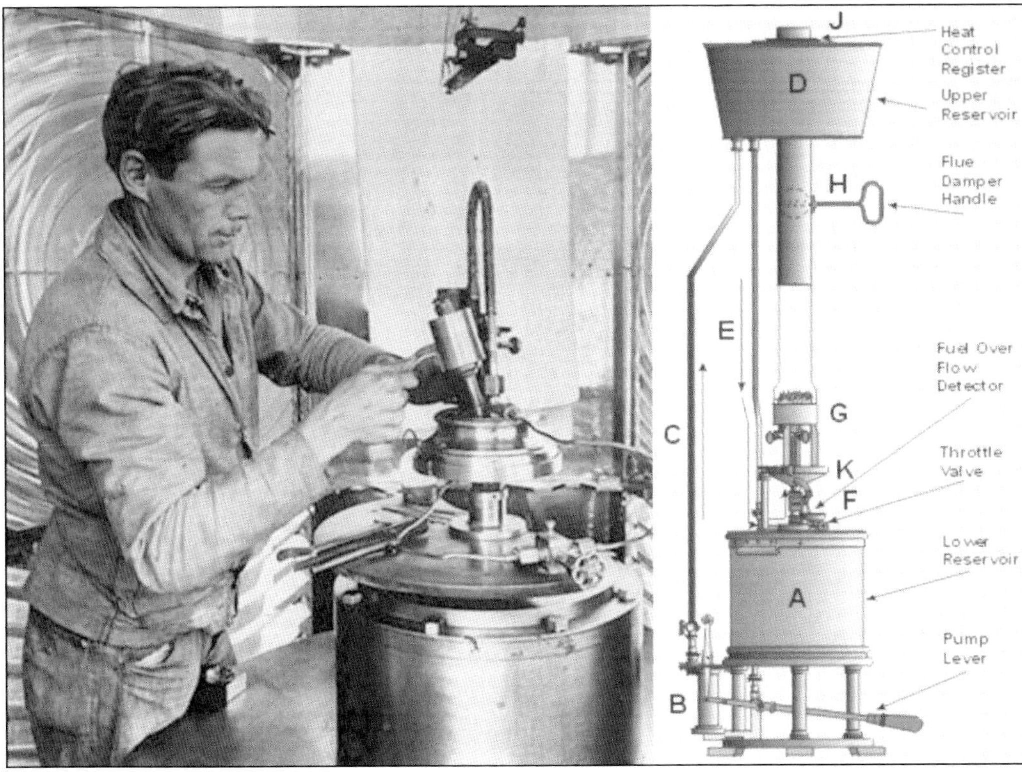

As lighting technology advanced, moderator lamps were replaced by more reliable hydraulic lamps in which keepers could pump oil from a lower reservoir in the base to an upper reservoir, from which gravity would feed oil to the wick all night. One popular model was invented by lighthouse engineer George Meade, who later became a general in the Union army and commanded forces at the Battle of Gettysburg. (USLHS.)

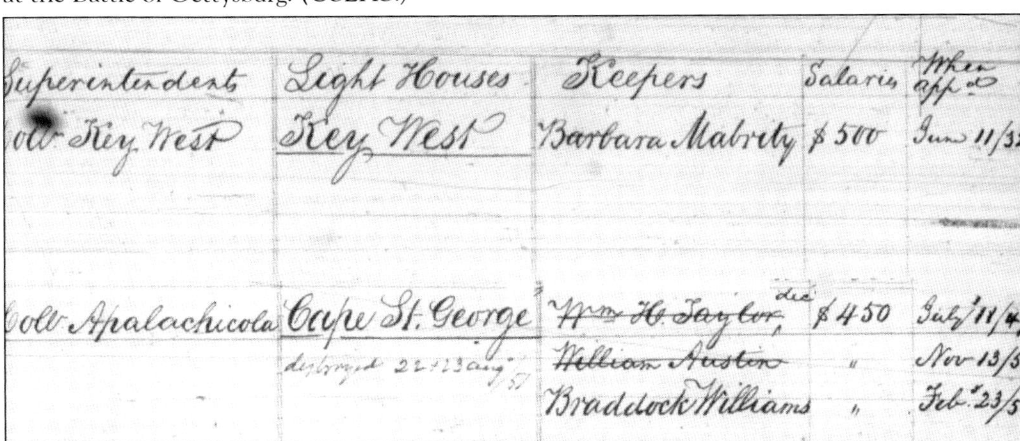

Superintendent	Light Houses	Keepers	Salaries	When app.
Coll. Key West	Key West	Barbara Mabrity	$500	Jun 11/32
Coll. Apalachicola	Cape St. George	~~Wm. H. Taylor~~ dec.	$450	July 11/4[illegible]
	destroyed 22 & 23 Aug. /51	~~William Austin~~	"	Nov 13/5[illegible]
		Braddock Williams	"	Feb. 23/5[illegible]

A keeper's register maintained in the fifth auditor's office noted the names and salaries of lighthouse keepers. This 1852 page notes that Braddock Williams was hired at an annual salary of $450. His name is listed on the same page as a famous female keeper, Barbara Mabry of Key West. Note that she was paid $500 a year. The Lighthouse Service may have been the first federal agency to hire women on a routine basis, even though most assumed the duties when their husbands, the prior keepers, had died. (National Archives and Records Administration.)

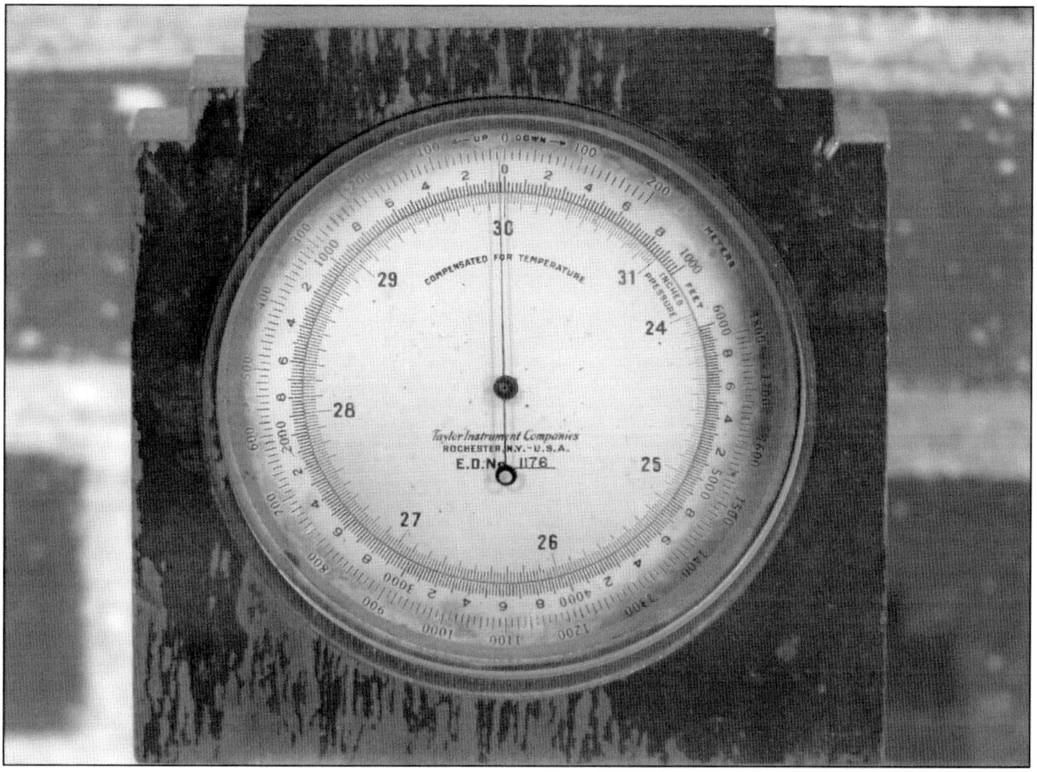

Most lighthouse keepers used barometers, such as this one owned by keeper Walter Roberts Jr., to help predict changes in the weather. Later, keepers also recorded air and water temperature. (SGLA.)

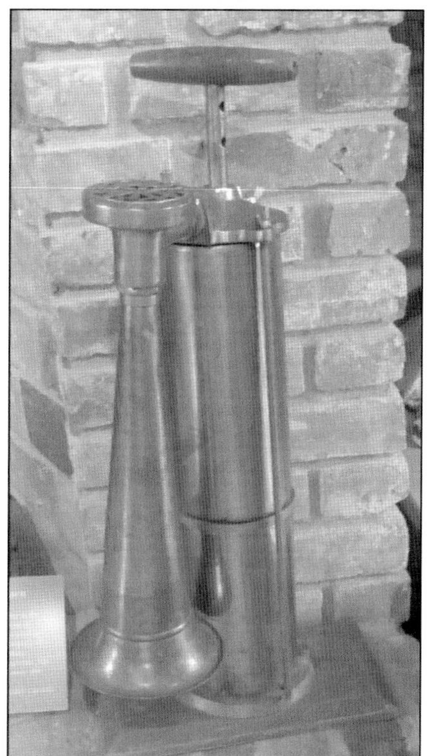

Fog becomes very dense around St. George Island in the winter, making navigation difficult. The light station never installed a permanent fog horn, but a brass hand-pumped signal such as this one in the lighthouse museum may have been used. (SGLA.)

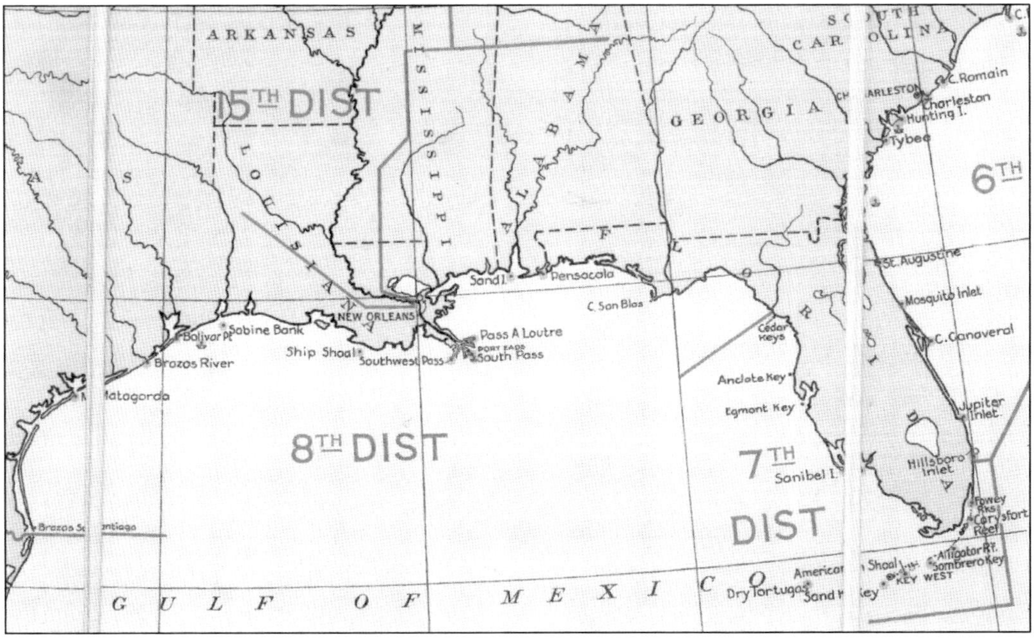

The lighthouse board operated from 12 districts that each had a superintendent and an engineer, one of whom made quarterly inspections. Cape St. George was at times supplied by the 7th district in Key West, and sometimes by the 8th district in Port Eads, New Orleans. Keepers were required to file reports with the district superintendent, who in turn reported to the lighthouse board, which remained in the Treasury Department until 1910. This map is from the 1881 Annual Report of the US Lighthouse Board. (USCG.)

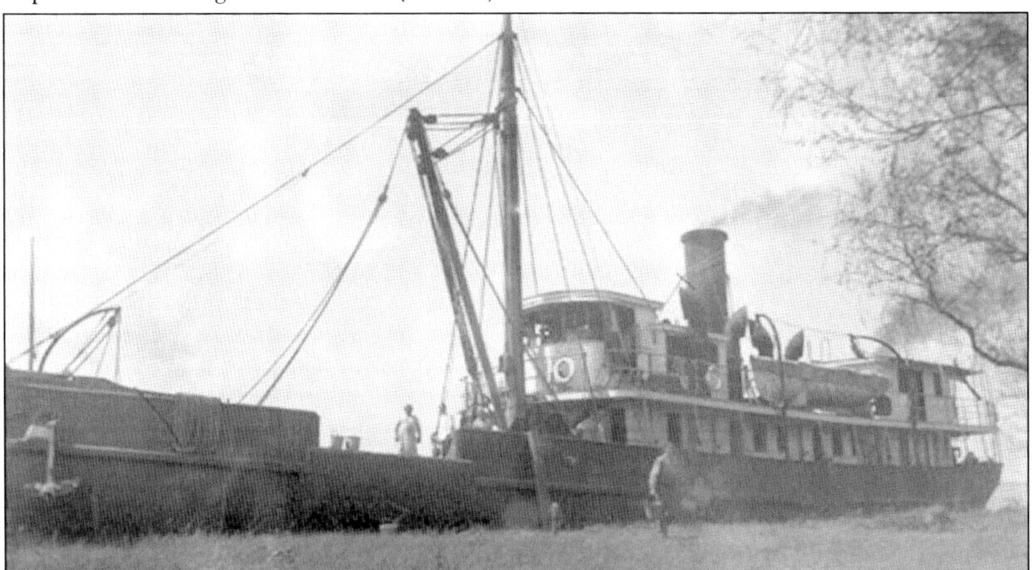

Each lighthouse district set up a supply depot and maintained at least one supply ship (lighthouse tender) that delivered supplies a minimum of once a year. The *Camellia*, one of the tenders that supplied Cape St. George, is shown here unloading supplies. These ships also served as buoy tenders. The cranes and low area on the deck were used when buoys needed to be cleaned or replaced. (USCG.)

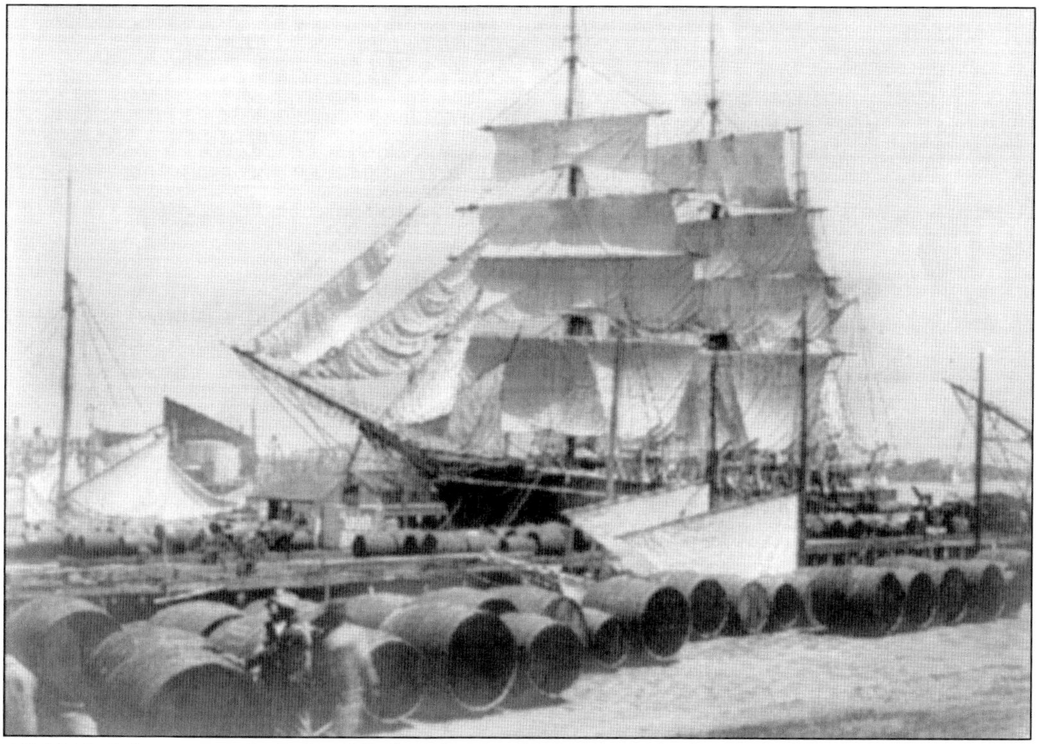

All US lighthouses used whale oil before the Civil War. Most was brought to ports in New England like this one and then shipped to lighthouses around the United States. (NYPL)

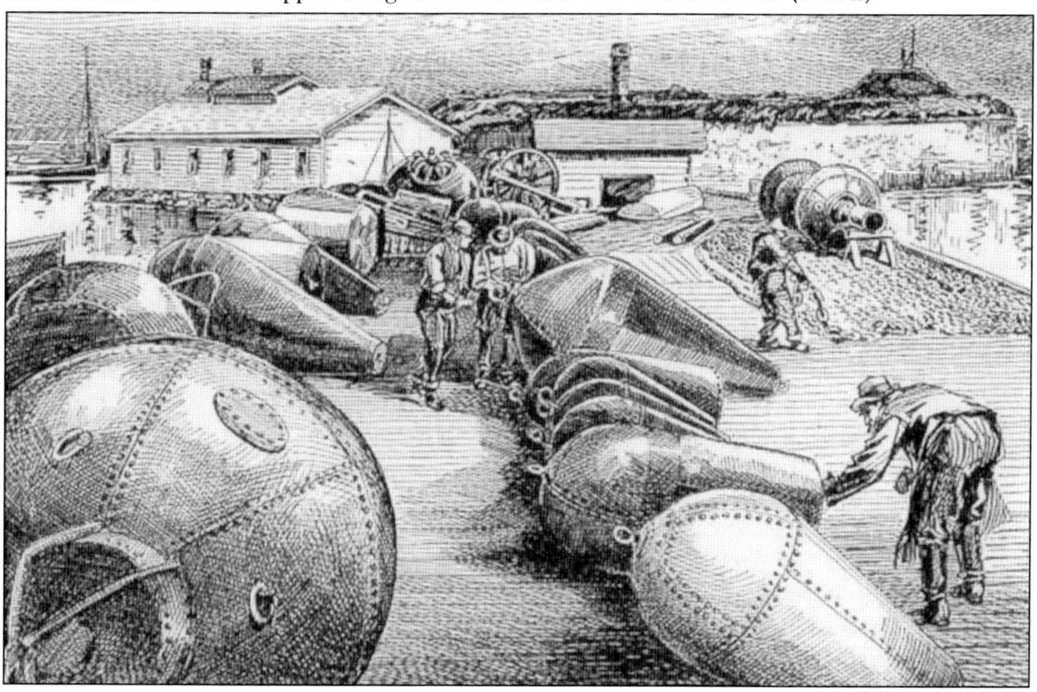

A 19th-century lighthouse supply depot is depicted here, with men working on metal buoys that would later be used to mark shipping channels. (USLHS.)

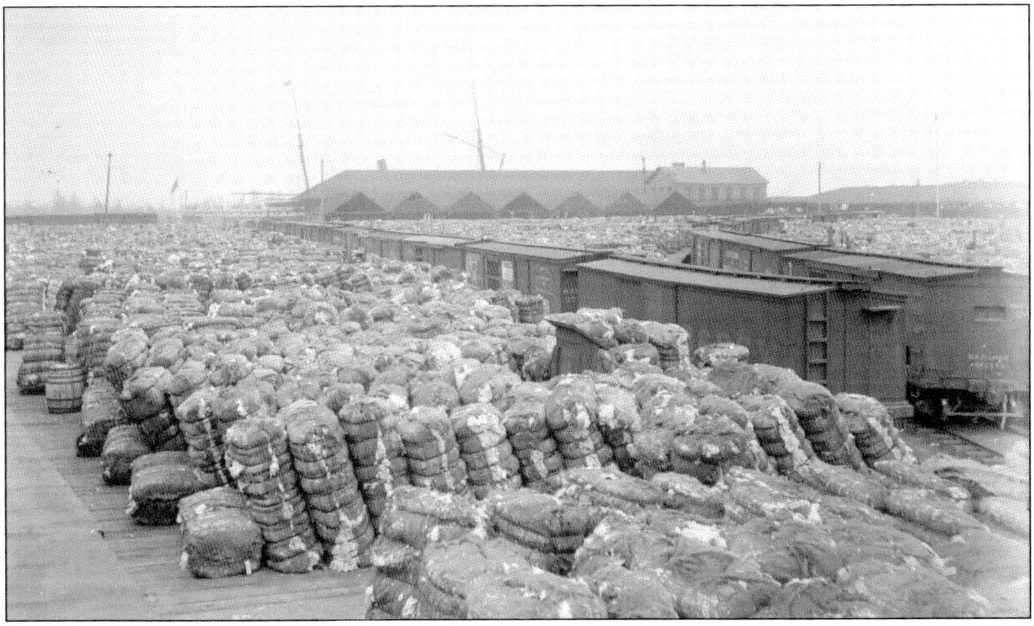

Cotton shipping by rail diminished steamboat traffic down the Apalachicola River, and the economy suffered after the Civil War. This image shows cotton bales ready to be shipped over the Southwestern of Georgia Railway to the port of Savannah. (LOC.)

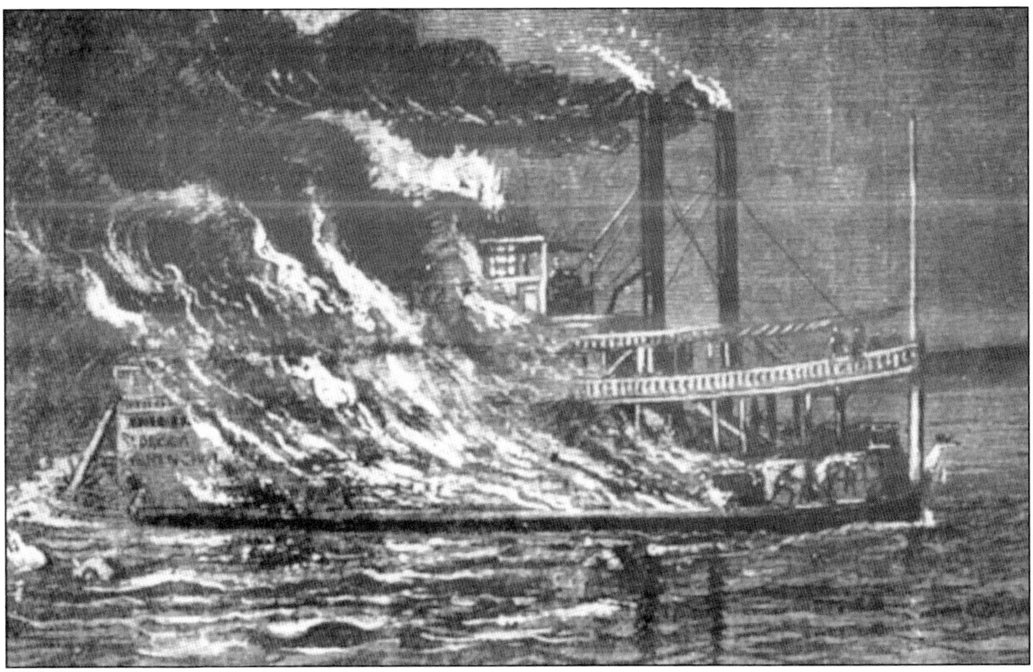

Traffic down the Apalachicola River also decreased owing to steamboat wrecks in the river channel. This lithograph shows the wreck of the steamer *Rebecca Everingham* as depicted in the *Daily Graphic* of New York. (LOC.)

Four

The Civil War in Apalachicola Bay

In 1860, the only residents on St. George Island were the families of lighthouse keeper Braddock Williams, his wife Sarah, the assistant keeper James Albert Williams, and his wife Lucretia. They lived together in the two-story keeper's dwelling with its lower story of brick and upper wood-framed loft. Shipping patterns through West Pass had started to change. Much more cotton was being grown upriver; however, some of the cotton was being spun into cloth in the mills of Columbus, and much was being shipped by railway to Savannah. Fewer shipments of products from New Orleans were arriving because farmers up the Apalachicola and Chattahoochee Rivers could purchase goods from merchants in Savannah. Increasingly, the channel up the river was blocked by steamboat wrecks.

The population of Apalachicola and the rest of Florida included nearly equal numbers of free persons and African slaves, and in the year Abraham Lincoln was elected president, even the lighthouse keepers probably knew that war was imminent. When the Civil War broke out, the Gulf Squadron blockaded Apalachicola Bay and almost totally blocked cotton shipments from upriver. Commerce evaporated, citizens joined the army or moved, steamboats rotted at the wharves, and the economy of Apalachicola suffered tremendously. With a serious loss of population, the town would need to reinvent itself after the war.

Several skirmishes occurred around Apalachicola Bay as Union blockaders seized cotton shipments arriving from upriver, and the Confederate forces converted the Columbus Iron Works and nearby mills into factories for shipbuilding and military supplies. Braddock Williams stayed on as Confederate lighthouse caretaker, but he and the customs collector were discharged when commerce terminated. Williams was sent to nearby Cape San Blas lighthouse after the war, but returned to Cape St. George in 1868 to continue the Williams family's remarkable record of service.

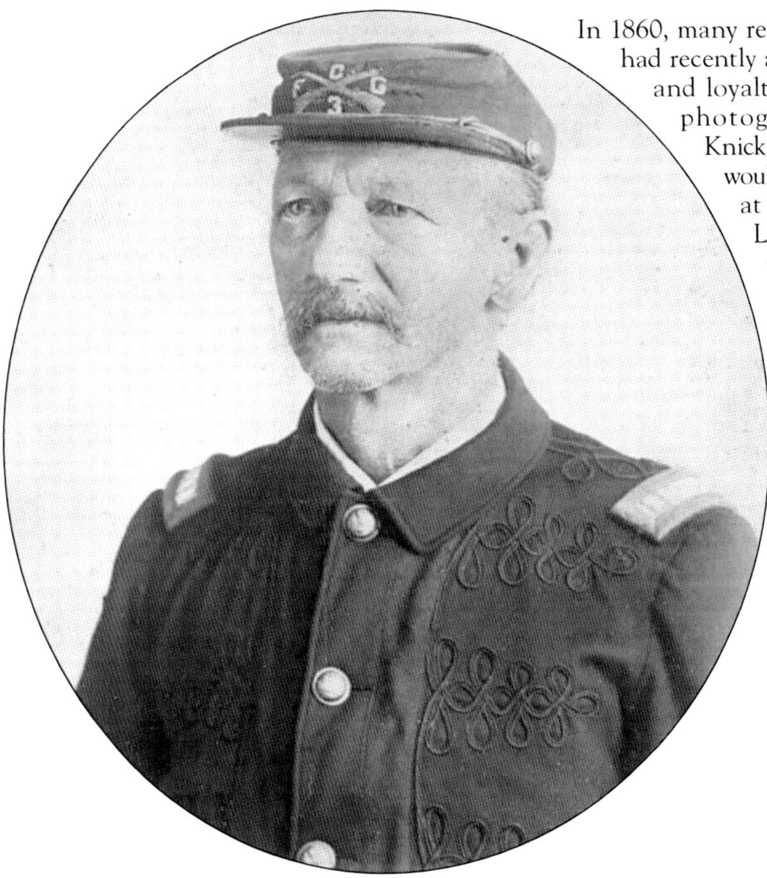

In 1860, many residents of Apalachicola had recently arrived from the North, and loyalties were divided. This photograph shows Robert Knickmeyer, whose son William would serve as assistant keeper at the Cape St. George Lighthouse after the war was over. Although Robert had been born in Germany, he enlisted in the Confederate army in Apalachicola and fought in campaigns from Vicksburg and Chickamauga to the Battle of Atlanta. (SGLA.)

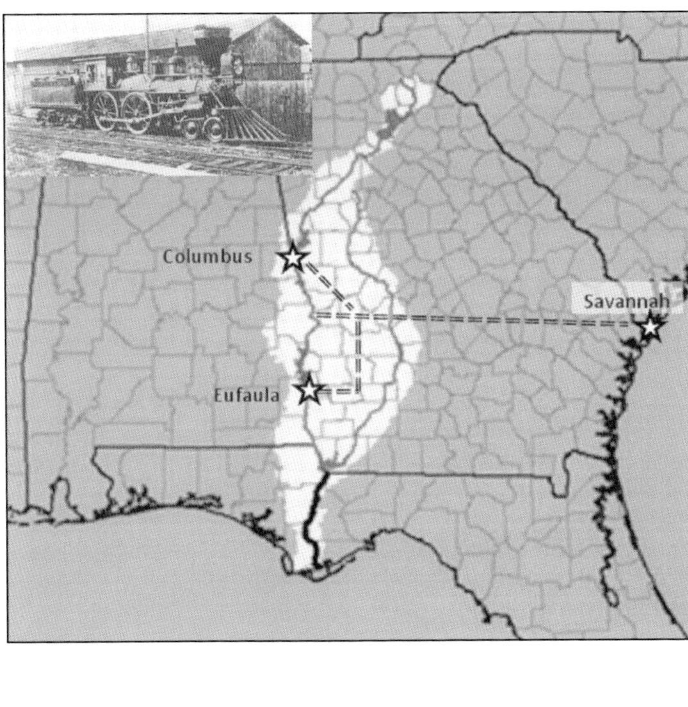

The Civil War began in an era of massive railroad construction that greatly affected commerce in Apalachicola. During the 1850s, the Georgia Southwestern Railroad built lines into the Chattahoochee and Flint River valleys that connected Eufaula, Alabama, and Columbus to the deepwater port at Savannah. Although cotton was still being shipped down the Apalachicola River, farmers in the tri-river valley had new options for shipping their produce and could also purchase farm implements and supplies locally. (LOC.)

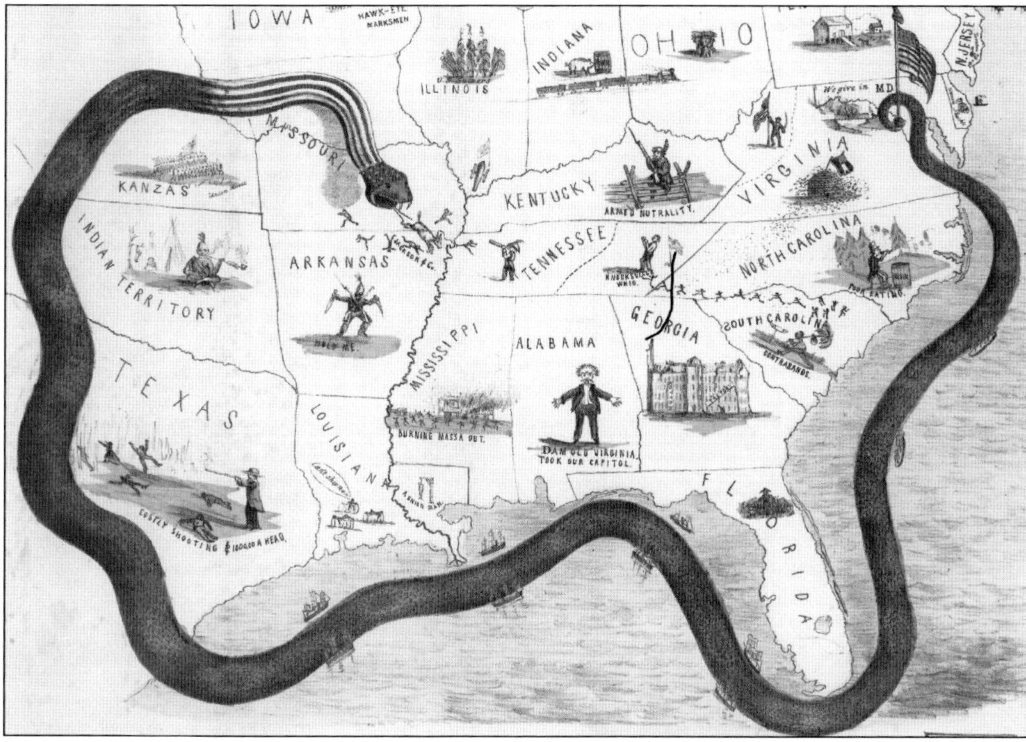

In 1861, the United States imposed a blockade of the Confederacy from the mid-Atlantic to the Gulf of Mexico. Called the Anaconda Plan, or General Scott's Great Snake, the Gulf Blockading Squadron effectively stopped shipping from Apalachicola. (Drawing by Joseph Elliott, LOC.)

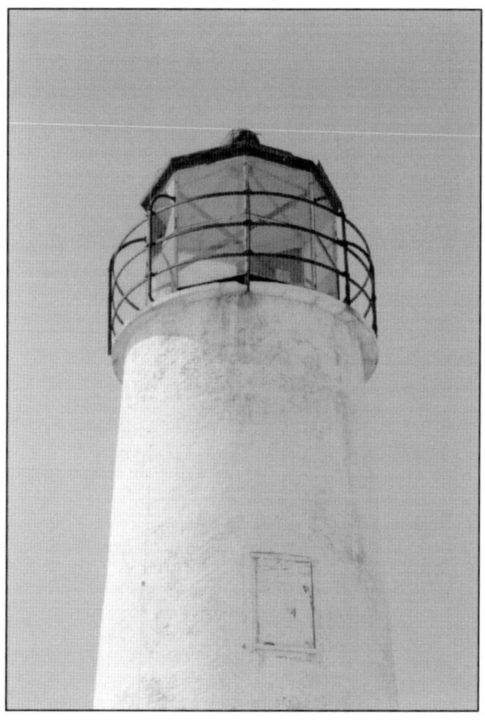

The lamp was removed from the 1852 lighthouse on Cape St. George during the Civil War and it stood vacant, as shown here, except when occupied by the Union navy. The Confederate superintendent of lights retained Braddock Williams as caretaker at a reduced salary but then sent a work crew to remove the Fresnel lens and lamps, which were taken to Eufaula, Alabama, for the duration of the war. (LOC.)

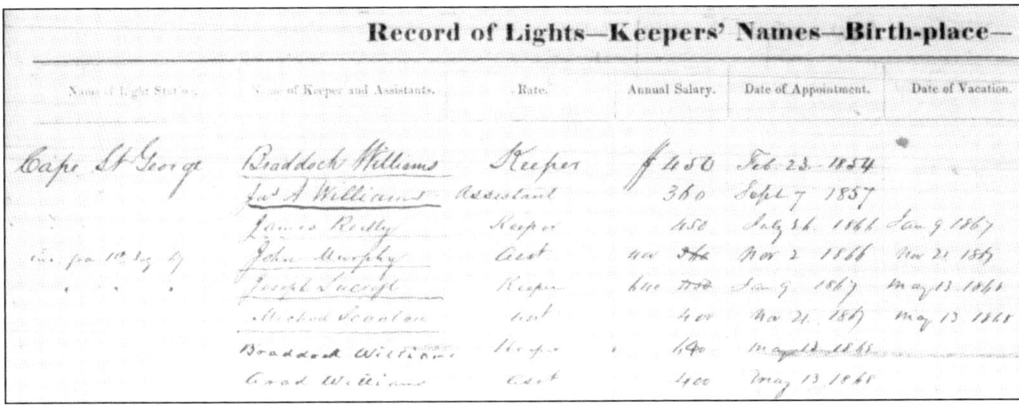

Record of Lights—Keepers' Names—Birth-place—

Name of Light Station.	Name of Keeper and Assistants.	Rate.	Annual Salary.	Date of Appointment.	Date of Vacation.
Cape St George	Braddock Williams	Keeper	$450	Feb 23. 1854	
	Jas A Williams	Assistant	360	Sept 7 1857	
	James Reilly	Keeper	450	July 26. 1866	Jan 9 1867
[illegible]	John Murphy	Asst	400 [illegible]	Nov 2 1866	Nov 21 1867
	[illegible]	Keeper	640 [illegible]	Jan 9 1867	May 13 1868
	Michael Scanlon	Asst	400	Nov 21. 1867	May 13 1868
	Braddock Williams	Keeper	640	May 13 1868	
	[illegible] Williams	Asst	400	May 13 1868	

The keeper's register from the Department of Treasury lists Braddock Williams as keeper and James A. Williams as assistant keeper before the Civil War broke out. There is a gap during the war until 1866, when James Reilly relit the light. Reilly resigned, and Braddock and his sons were hired again in 1868. (SGLA.)

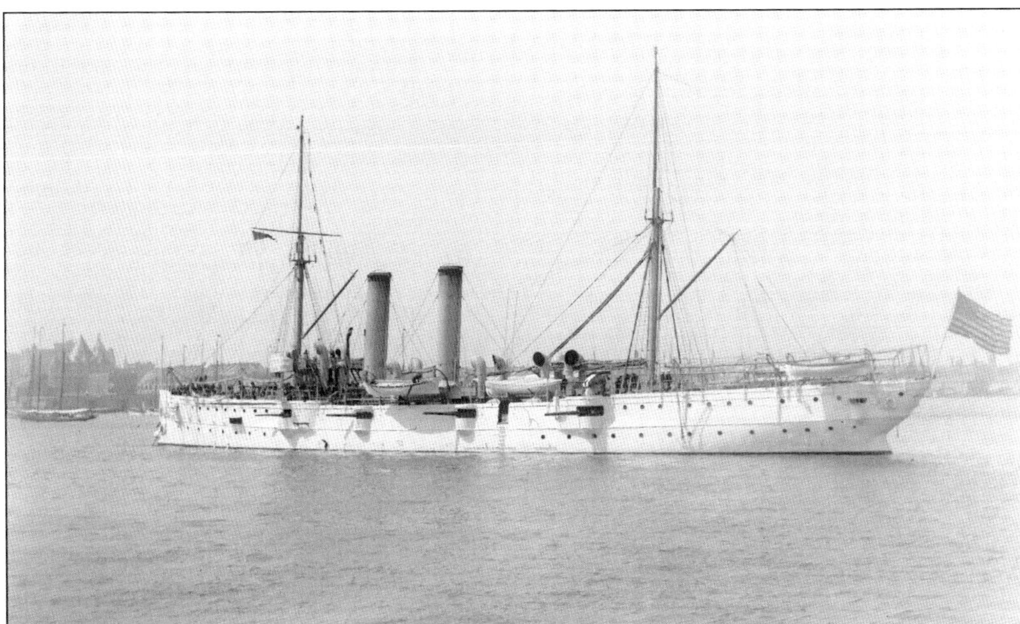

The USS *Montgomery* was one of the formidable warships assigned to the East Gulf Blockading Squadron near Apalachicola Bay. However, most federal warships were too large to negotiate the shoals and oyster bars in the bay, so most often, raiding parties were sent upriver in small boats to challenge Confederate blockade runners. (LOC.)

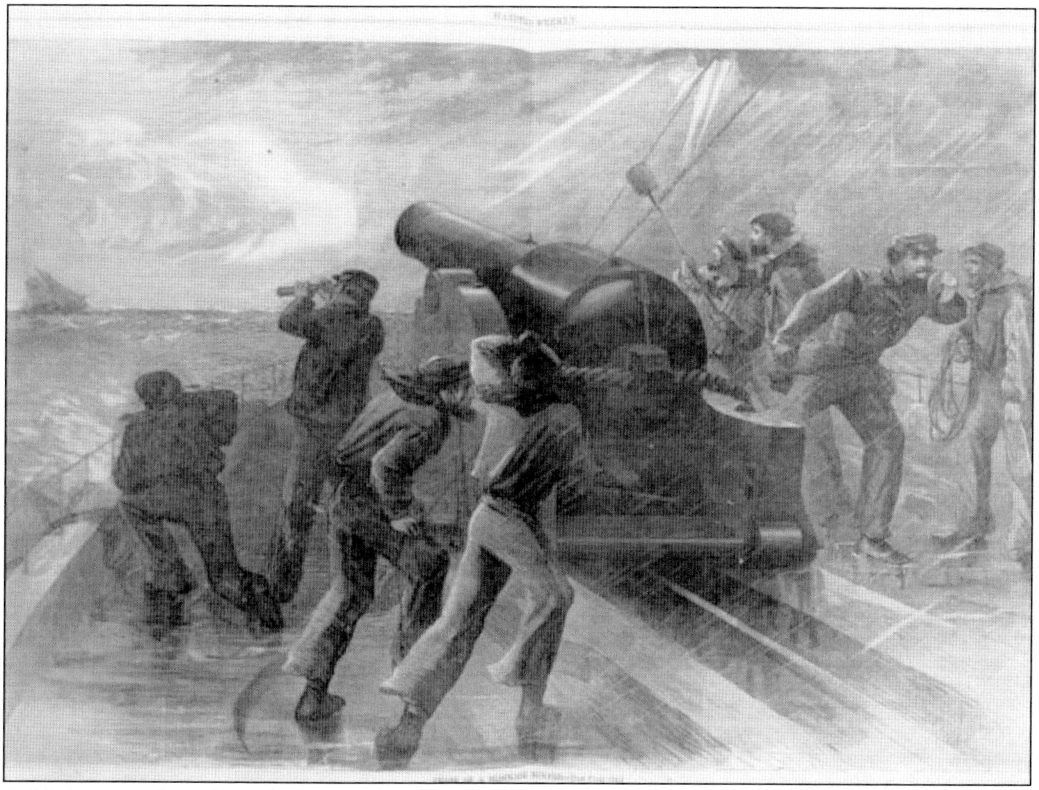

A Union naval gunboat fires at a Confederate blockade runner, such as the ones that attempted to ship Georgia cotton from the Apalachicola River to neutral countries, where it could be exchanged for armaments. (SAF.)

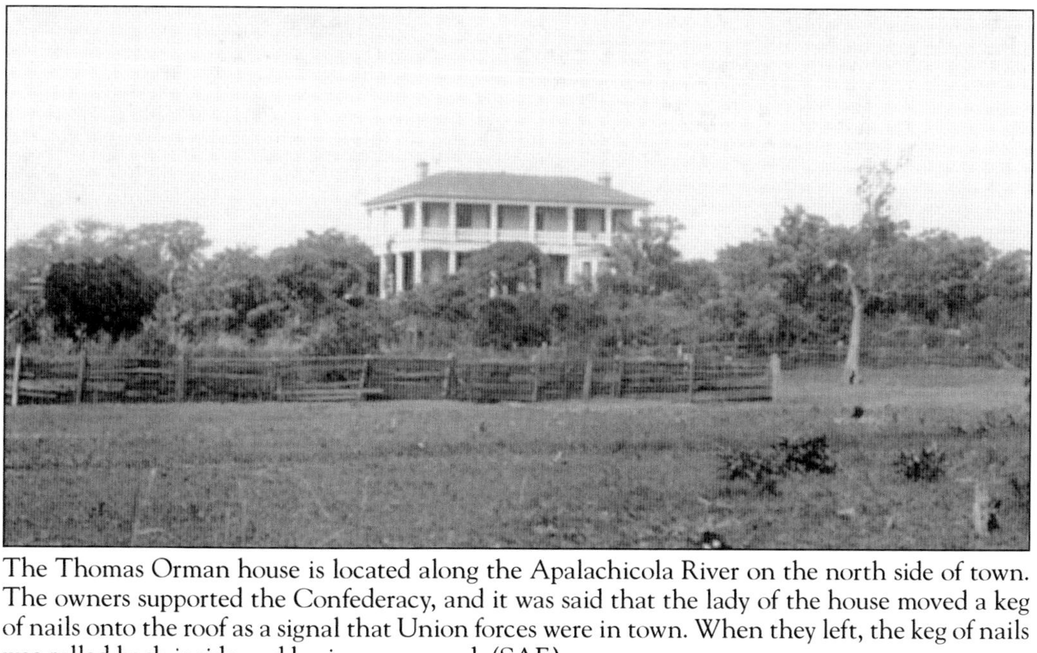

The Thomas Orman house is located along the Apalachicola River on the north side of town. The owners supported the Confederacy, and it was said that the lady of the house moved a keg of nails onto the roof as a signal that Union forces were in town. When they left, the keg of nails was rolled back inside and business resumed. (SAF.)

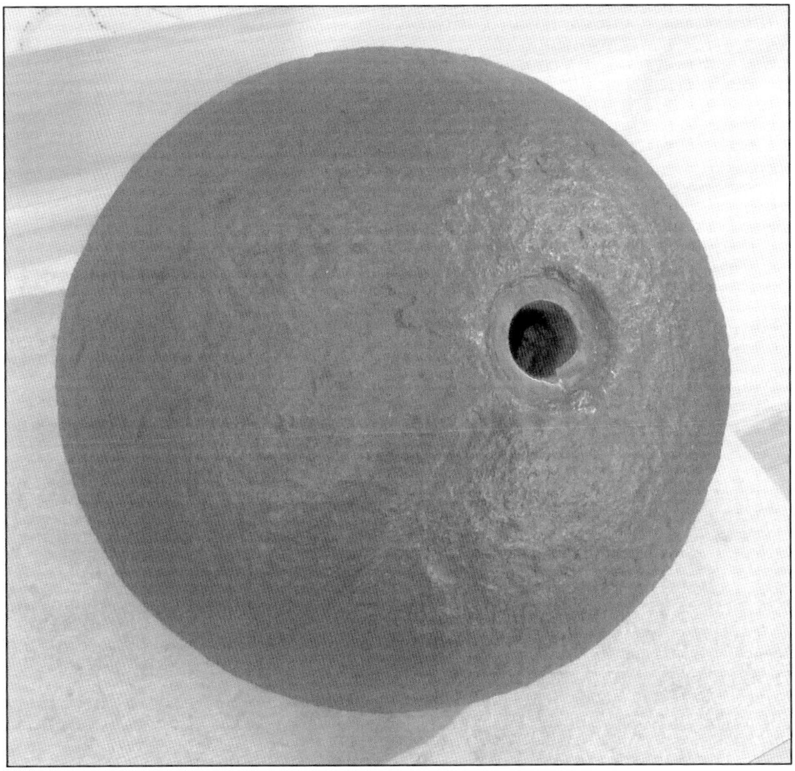

Union naval forces at times occupied the lighthouse on Cape St. George, which was a good vantage point to watch shipping. This unused exploding shell from a nine-inch Dahlgren gun, which weighs over 80 pounds, was found at the west end of St. George Island by a fishing guide. (SGLA.)

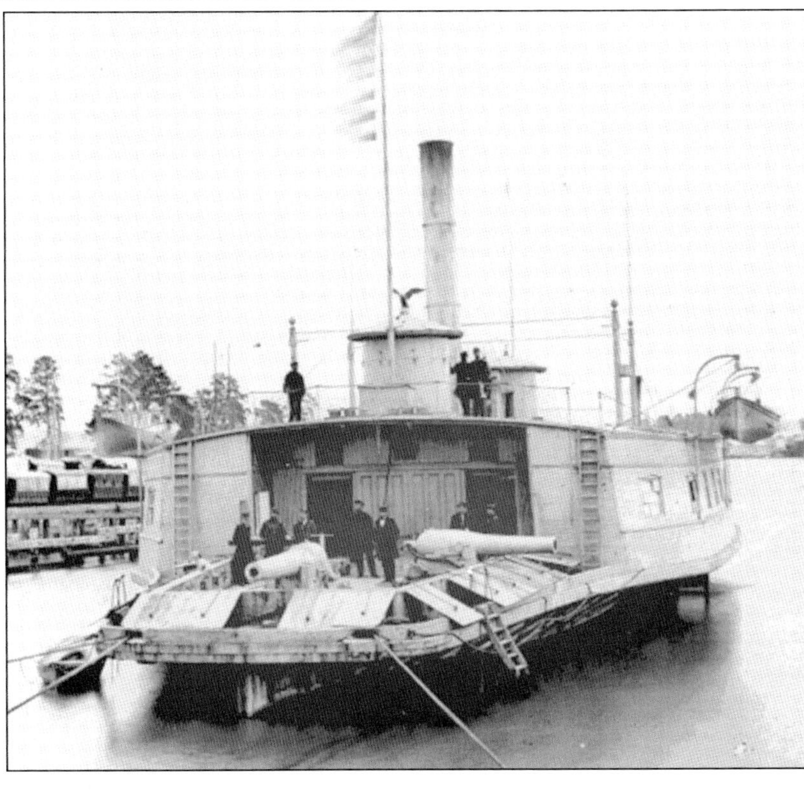

During the Civil War, the US Navy mounted Dahlgren guns on merchant marine ships that were converted to wartime use. This photograph shows two Dahlgren guns mounted on a Fort Henry–class steamboat of the kind that was stationed outside Apalachicola Bay. (LOC.)

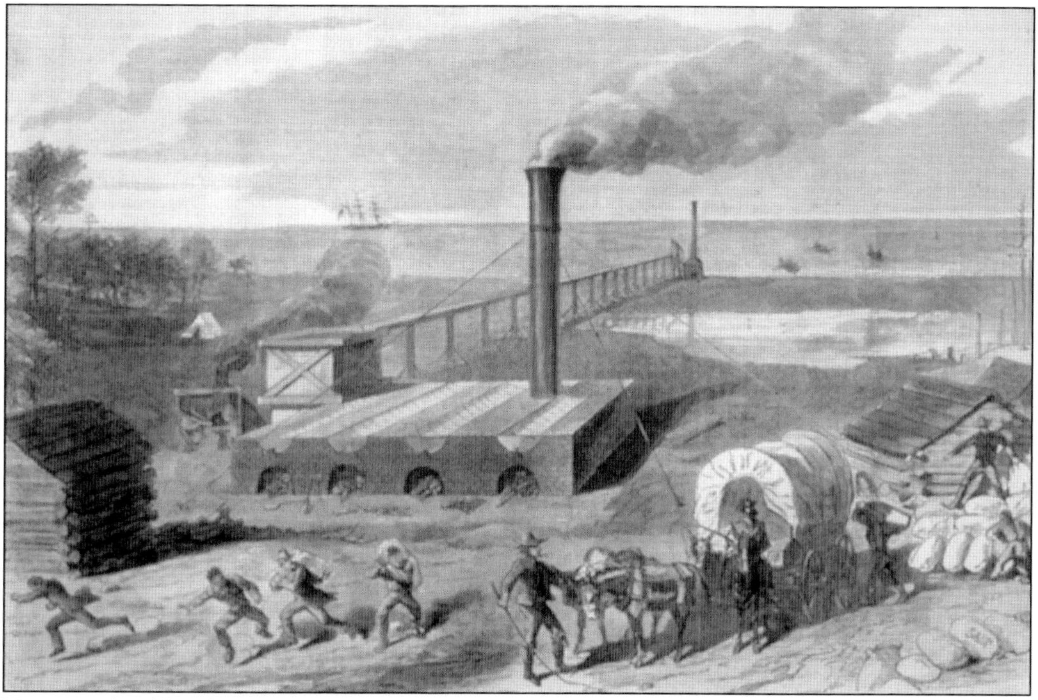

No major land battles were fought near Apalachicola Bay. However, salt made from seawater was used to preserve beef for Confederate troops. This painting shows an attack by the Union navy on a Confederate salt-making plant along the Gulf of Mexico. Saltworks used during the war have been documented from Cape San Blas to St. Marks, Florida. (SAF.)

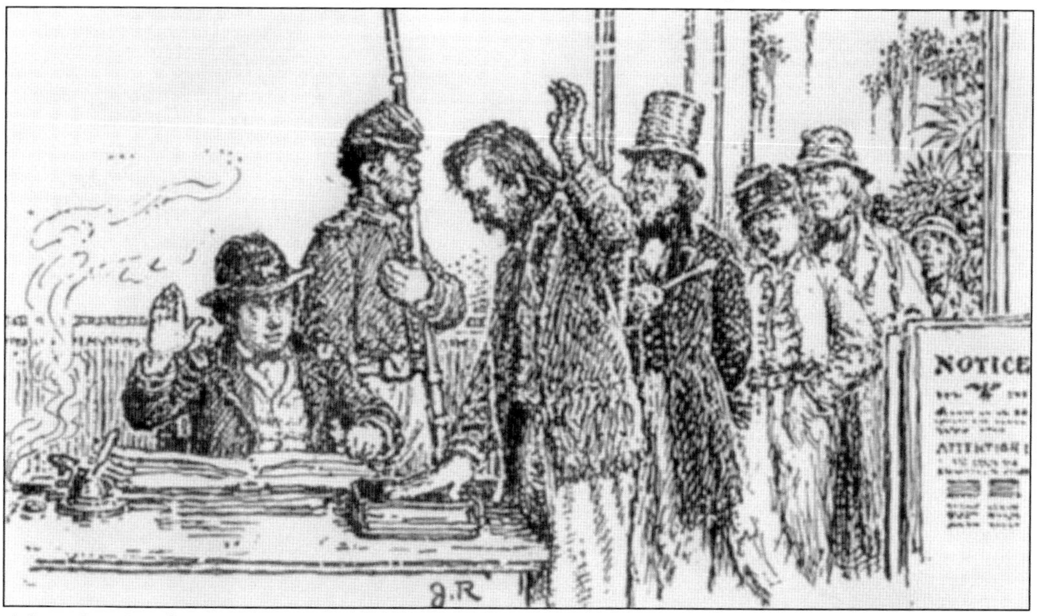

After the Civil War, many Confederate veterans were paroled in Apalachicola and sought civilian employment, but the population of the town was less than a third of its prewar level. Cotton shipping resumed briefly, but that business failed as railroads increasingly claimed that trade. (SAF.)

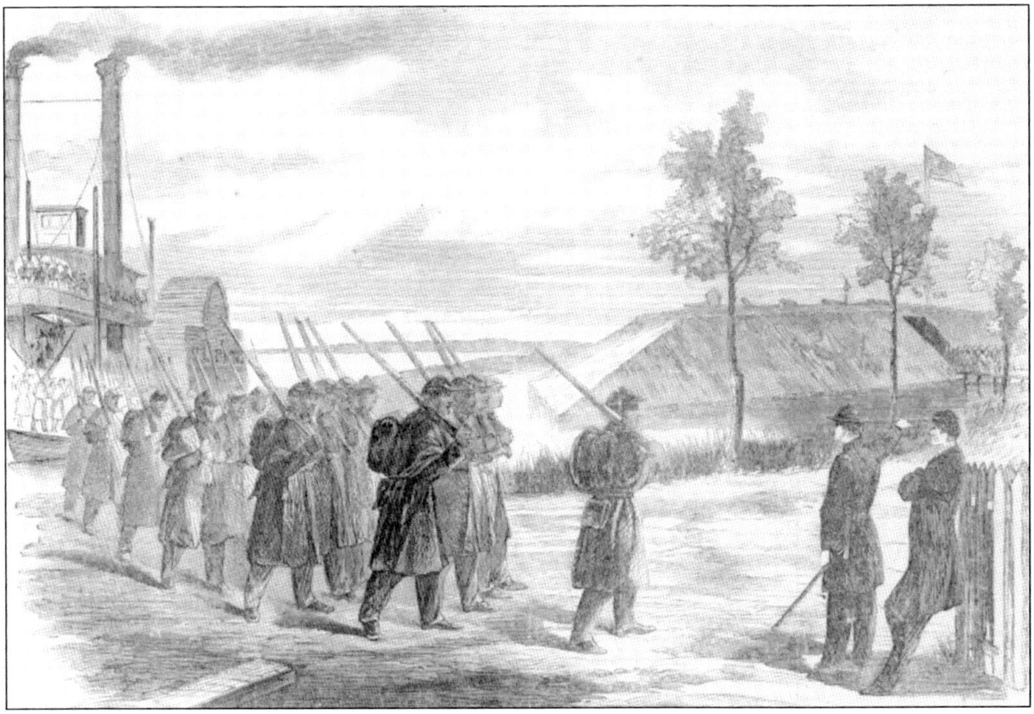

For the first year after the war, Apalachicola was occupied by a detachment of Union Negro troops, and business in the town was managed by the Freedmen's Bureau. Once all existing cotton had been shipped, various businessmen opened sawmills and lumber companies, and the town returned to civilian control (LOC.)

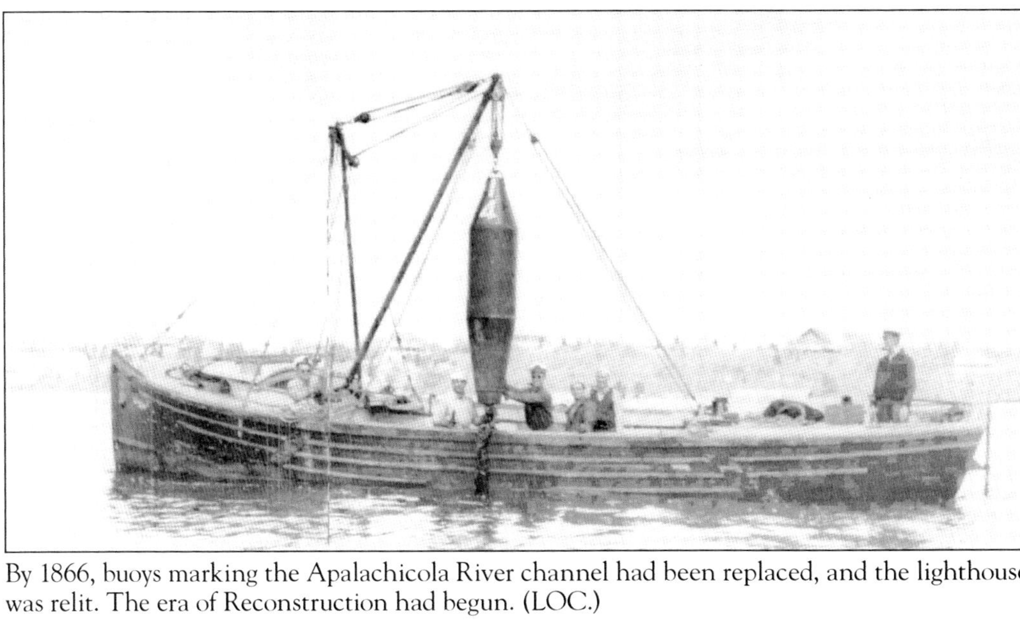

By 1866, buoys marking the Apalachicola River channel had been replaced, and the lighthouse was relit. The era of Reconstruction had begun. (LOC.)

Five

Lighthouses and Commerce During Reconstruction

With its economy destroyed, the population of Apalachicola fell to about 1,800 residents by the end of the Civil War. Very little agricultural land was available in Franklin County, and the future would depend on shipping lumber. New methods for canning and the availability of commercial ice machines would enliven the seafood industry within 20 years.

The lighthouse was relit in 1866 and was soon reassigned to the care of Braddock Williams and his sons. For about one year, cotton shipping returned to its prewar levels, but that business failed when a railroad was extended from Savannah to Bainbridge, Georgia. The Freedmen's Bureau sold unclaimed land to northern entrepreneurs, who soon established lumber mills that focused on making railroad ties for the new transcontinental railways and burgeoning railroad systems throughout the Southeast.

Steamboat traffic resumed on the Apalachicola, Chattahoochee, and Flint River system, but never reached its prewar levels. As canning factories and new ice plants were built, the seafood industry began to grow. Outbound ship traffic through the passes that define St. George Island primarily hauled lumber; arriving ships brought goods for sale in Apalachicola and along the river.

To facilitate navigation, an extensive system of lights and marked channels was built, and additional light keepers were needed to maintain the bay lights. After a hurricane destroyed the lighthouse at Dog Island next to East Pass on Apalachicola Bay, the new Crooked River Lighthouse was constructed on the mainland near Carrabelle.

The US Lighthouse Board set new standards for lighthouse keepers, and required that they be able to read and write and possess mechanical skills. Hiring gradually shifted from the local superintendent of lights at the customs houses to the district superintendents and engineers in the lighthouse districts. The board preferred to fill vacancies by transferring existing keepers from other locations or by hiring former seamen, who were accustomed to keeping night watches. Detailed instructions to lighthouse keepers were published, and dapper blue uniforms were issued after 1883. Keepers maintained daily logbooks with weather observations, daily activities, and unusual events such as storms and shipwrecks.

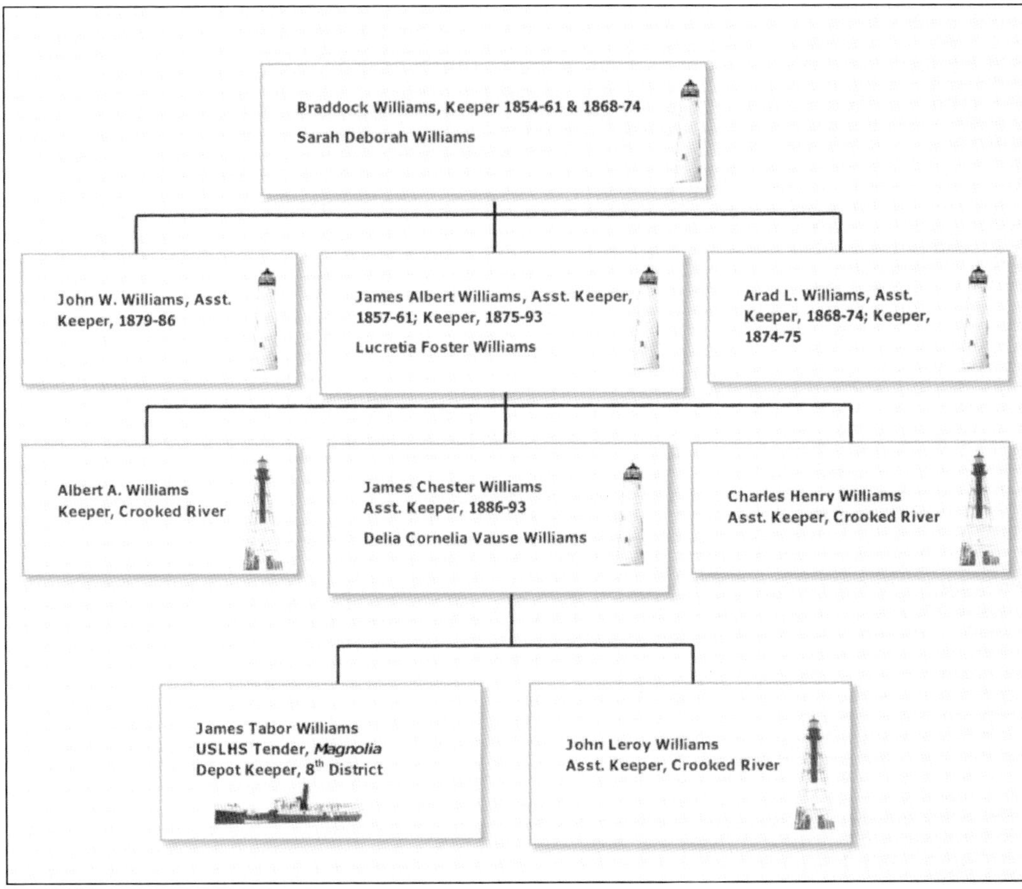

An engineer who arrived at Cape St. George in 1865 to inspect damage to the lighthouse reported that he was met by the old caretaker, presumably Braddock Williams. After Braddock's reappointment in 1868, four generations of Williams men (pictured on page 10) served at the lighthouses of Apalachicola Bay. This pedigree of the Williams lineage of lighthouse keepers shows their ratings and dates of service. Service at Cape St. George is indicated by the conical brick lighthouse, and Crooked River is depicted by a steel-frame tower. James Tabor Williams served as radio operator on the US lighthouse tender *Magnolia* and as a deputy superintendent at the Port Eads Lighthouse Depot near New Orleans. These four generations of keepers served from 1854 to 1939, which may vie for the longest service of any lighthouse family. (JLH.)

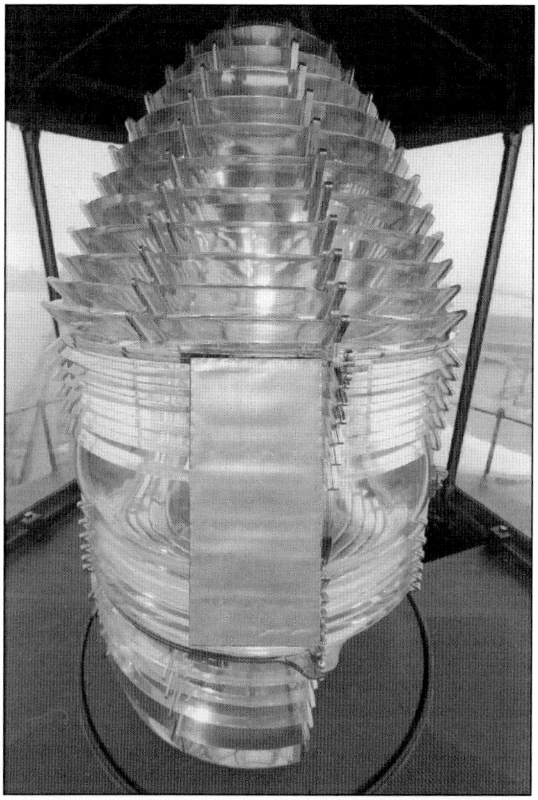

When the third-order Fresnel lens was returned to the Cape St. George Lighthouse after the Civil War, one of its glass panels was broken. No panel was available to replace it, and a reflective metal door was installed. Before the war, the lighthouse was said to light the horizon in the gulf and the bay. However, the metal door blocked light on the side of the tower that faced Apalachicola and created a dark angle that interfered with navigation in the bay. Despite frequent requests, the lens would not be replaced until 1888. (JLH.)

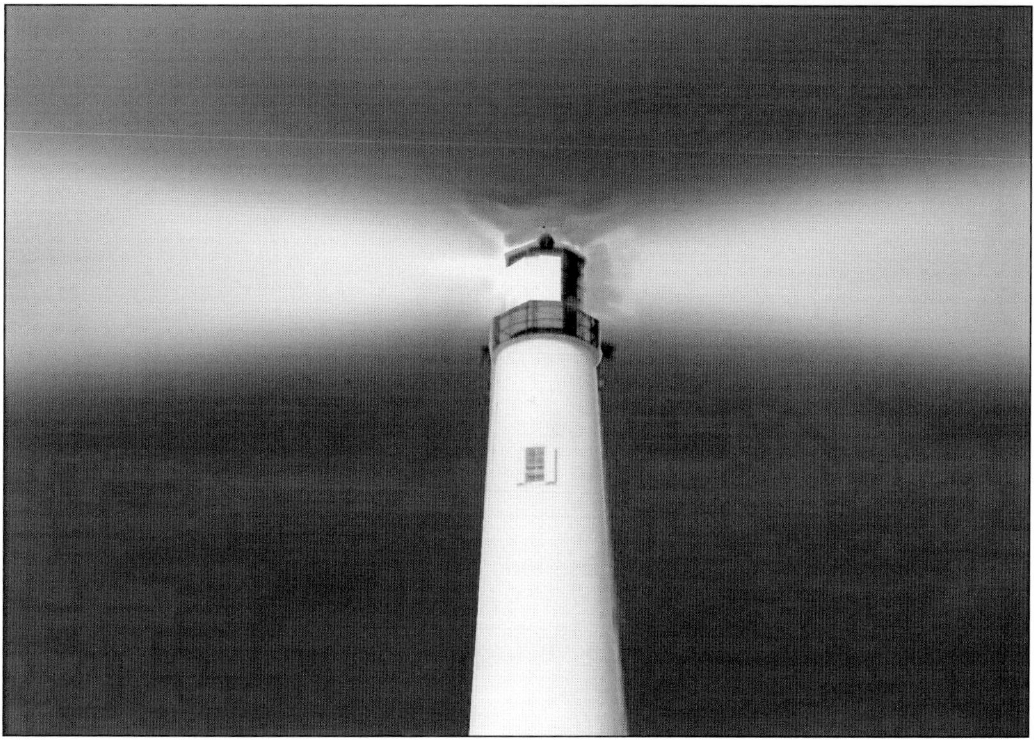

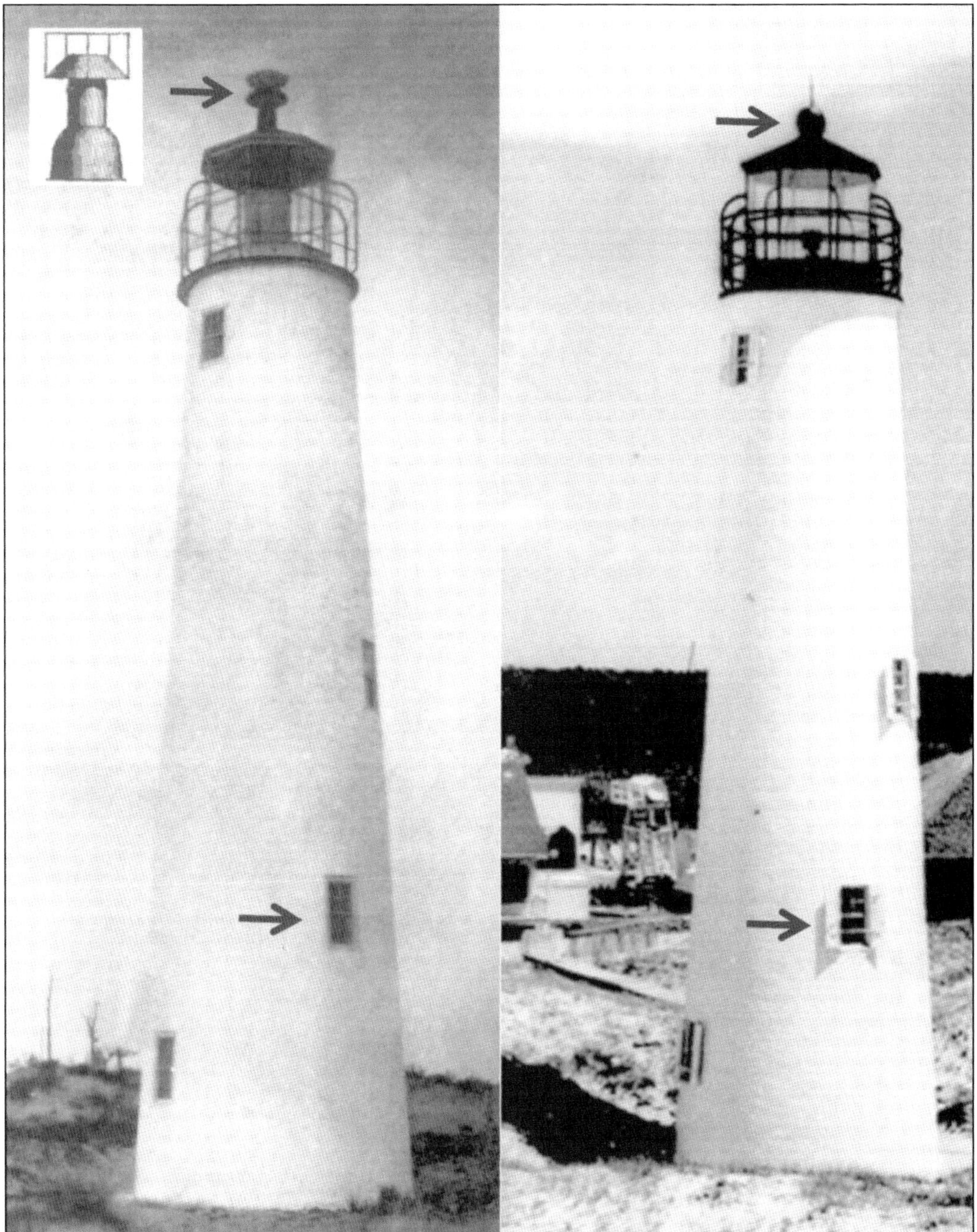

Other repairs or changes in the lighthouse tower were made after the Civil War, as shown in this before-and-after comparison. Heat from the oil lamp was removed from the 1852 lighthouse by a cylindrical device called an Emerson Patent Ventilator (left). Whether replaced due to damage from the war or a hurricane, all later photographs show a copper ball vent with a lightning rod mounted on top (right). There is no record of when the ventilation system was changed. In addition, shutters were added sometime after the war (lower arrows). (JLH.)

The US Lighthouse Board required that the Cape St. George Lighthouse be painted twice each year. Keepers typically rigged up scaffolding to paint the tower using ropes and planks, or made a crude seat called a bosun's chair. This unsafe system led to the only accidental death at the Cape St. George Lighthouse. In 1874, Braddock Williams requested that his son Arad A. Williams take over as keeper. The 76-year-old Braddock became the assistant keeper. Unfortunately, in 1875, Arad died in a fall while he was white-washing the tower. (SGLA.)

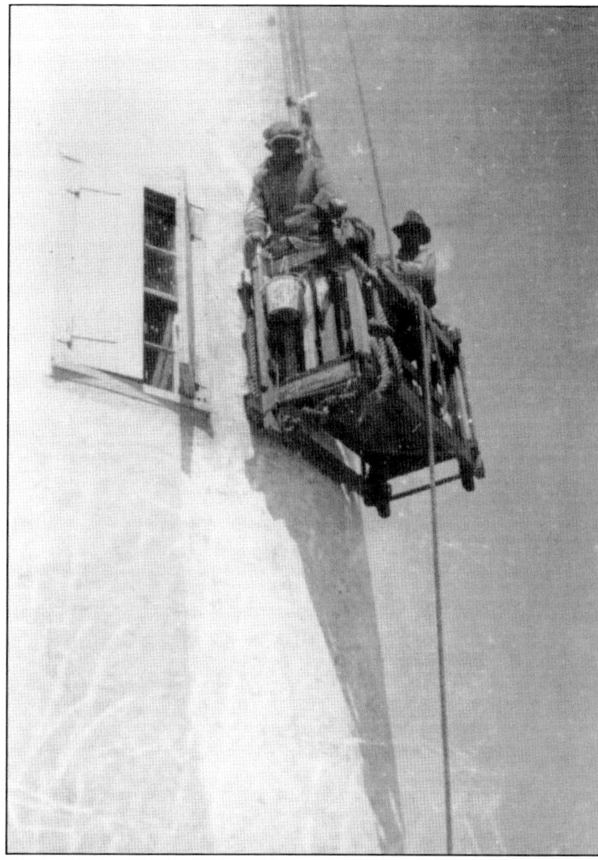

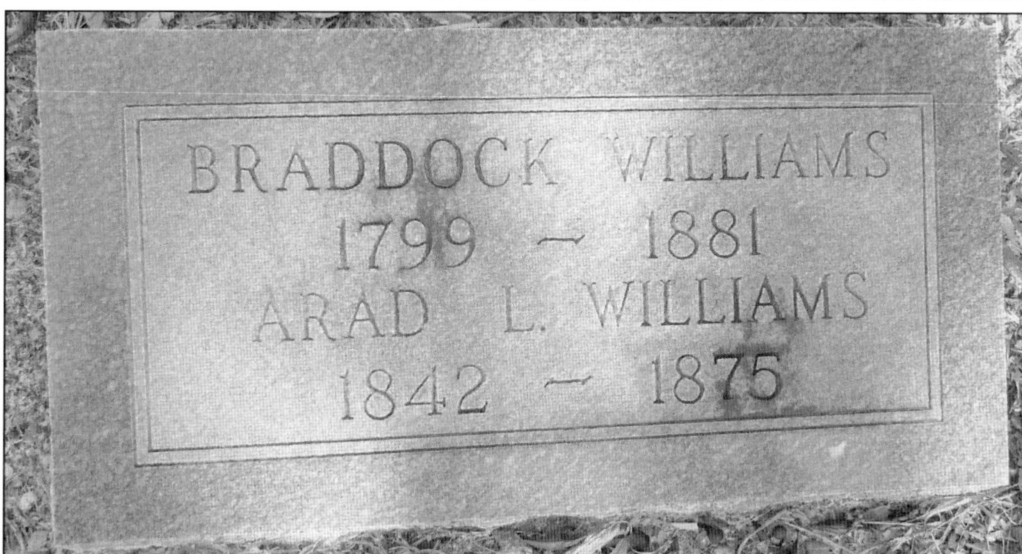

With no medical help available on Cape St. George, Arad Williams died before a doctor could be summoned. He was buried in Chestnut Cemetery in Apalachicola. Six years later, Braddock also died and was buried near his son. The original wooden markers are badly decayed, and family members recently placed this granite marker commemorating the two lighthouse keepers. (JLH.)

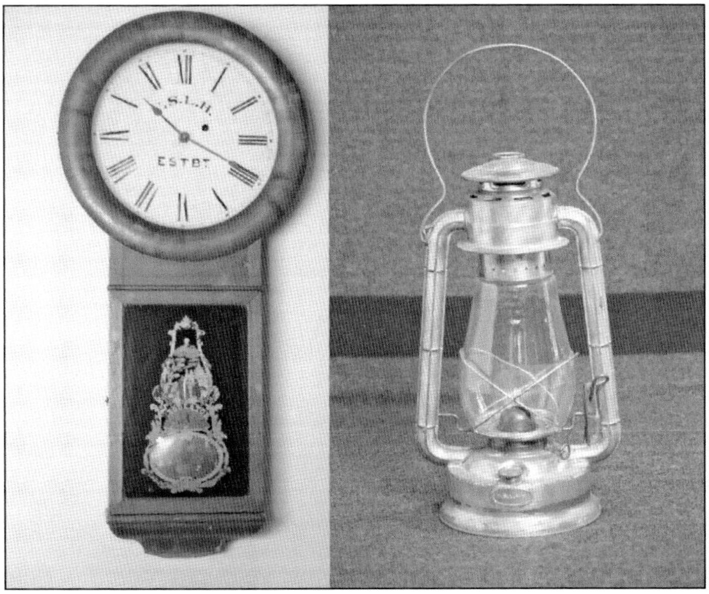

Because much of the work at the lighthouse took place at night, the two essential tools needed by every keeper and assistant were a wall clock (left) and service lantern (right). Hand-carried oil lamps like this Dietz model were used until the 20th century. Friction matches could be used to light lamps in the keeper's quarters but were regarded as too dangerous to use near kerosene. For many years, a small hand-lamp called a Lucerne was used to light the lamp in the lantern room. (USLHS.)

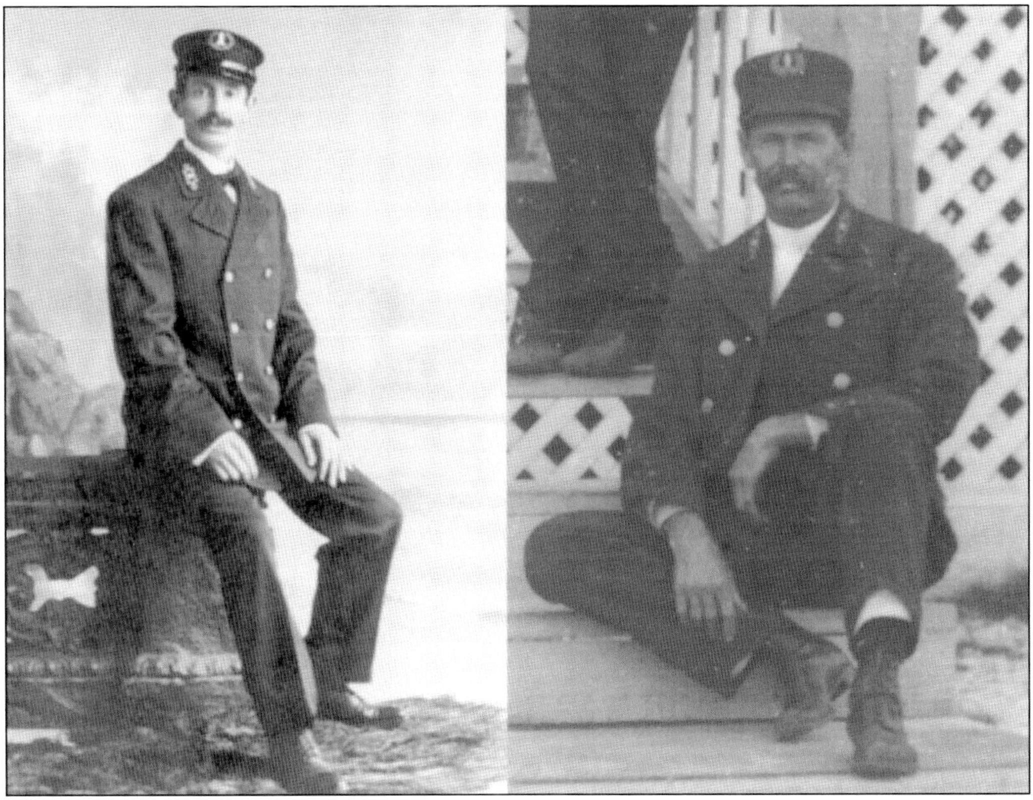

In 1883, the US Lighthouse Board designed regulation uniforms (as modeled by the unidentified keeper at left) with the intention of boosting the spirits of the corps of lighthouse keepers. The new caps displayed a lighthouse surrounded by a gold wreath, and the insignia on the lapel was a gold-bordered "K." At right, Charles Henry Williams displays the uniform during his service as head keeper at the Crooked River Lighthouse. (USLHS, SAF.)

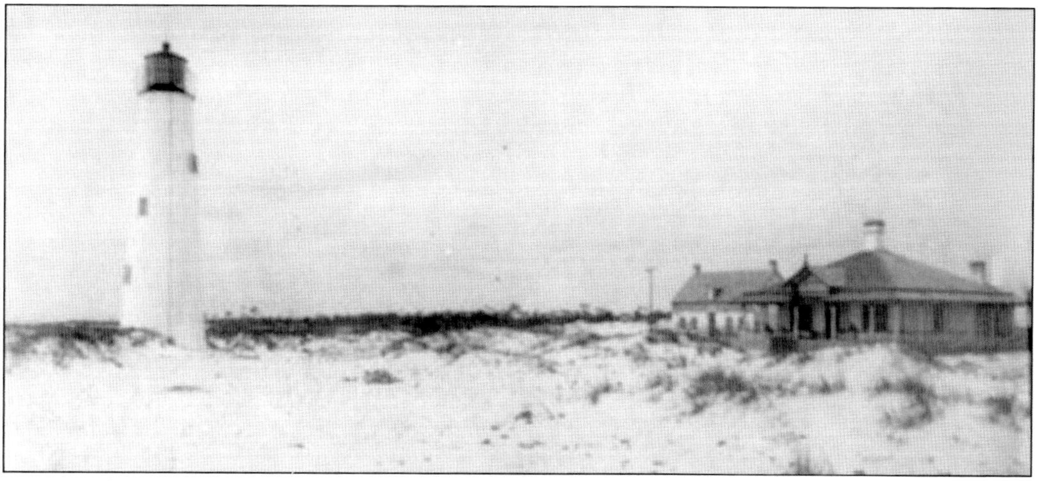

In 1878, the US Lighthouse Board approved funds for a larger single-story building that would house the families of all future keepers. Capt. Dave Ellis anchored a schooner named the *Spray* in the gulf and sent men and lumber ashore. The crew completed the new quarters in 50 days of hard work, taking only the Fourth of July off. Boardwalks were added to connect both dwellings to the lighthouse, and picket fences were installed. (SGLA.)

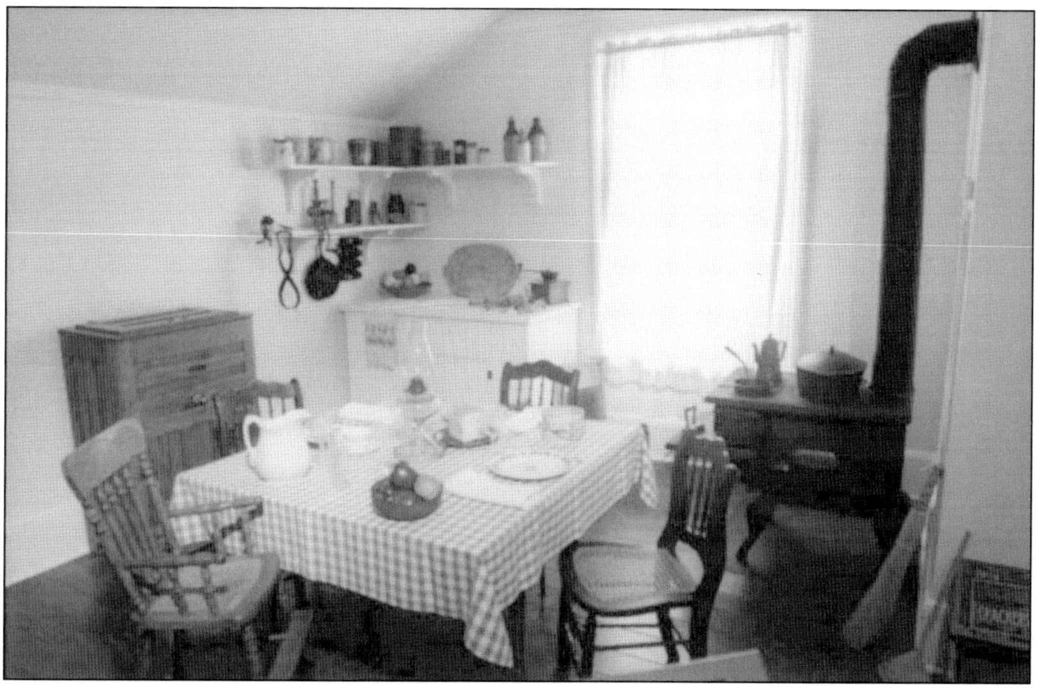

Interiors of keepers' quarters were always spartan. The buildings were heated by wood-burning fireplaces, and there was no electricity, running water, or refrigeration. Rainwater ran from the roof into a cistern, from which it was pumped by hand to reach the kitchen or washhouse. Cooking was originally done over a hearth by suspending pots from an iron trammel. Later, wood-burning stoves were installed. (USLHS.)

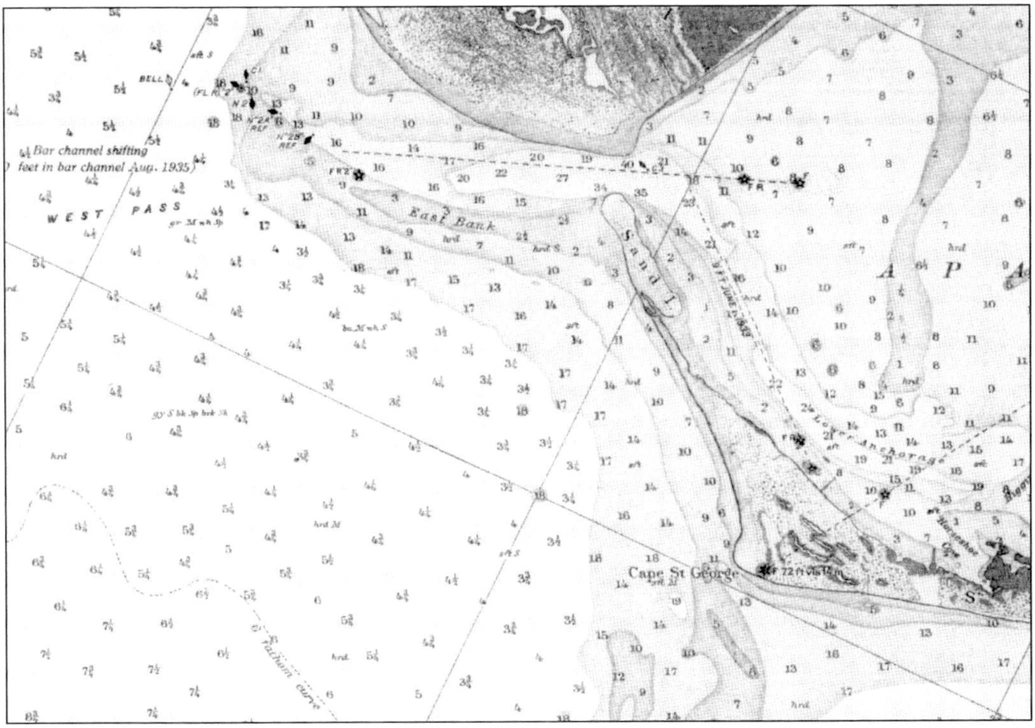

Besides taking care of the lighthouse, keepers serviced the lesser lights that mark the channels through West Pass (marked by star symbols) and three lights in Pilots Cove. Other lights were placed at the mouth of the Apalachicola River and at East Pass. (USGS.)

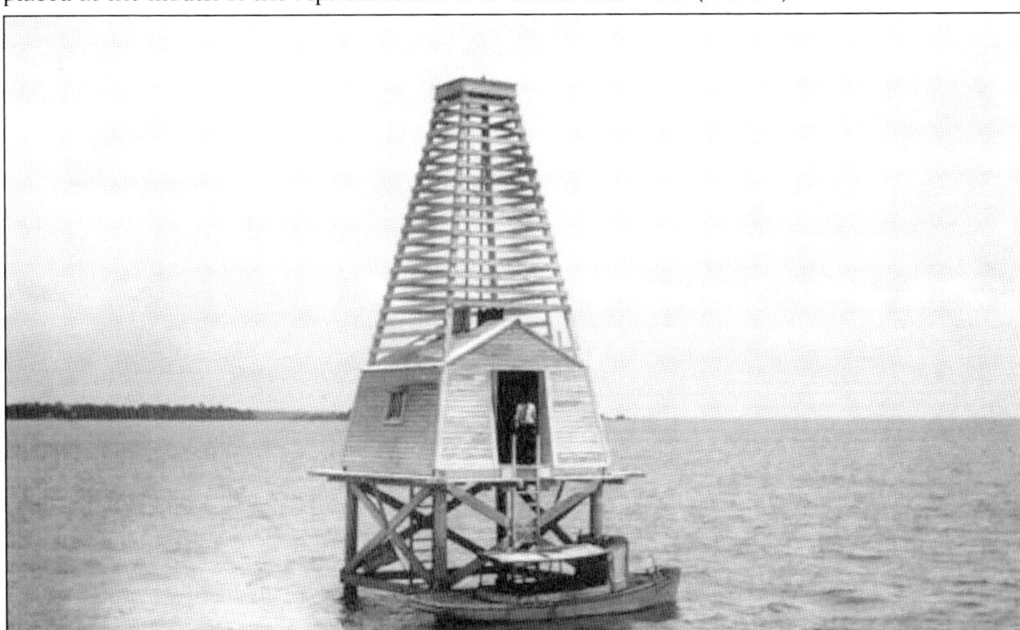

Some lights in the bay were placed atop large wooden pyramidal structures such as this one being tended by James C. Williams from his boat *Dixie*. These lights were probably constructed after kerosene was introduced around 1883. (SGLA.)

This is an example of a post light used by the US Lighthouse Establishment. (USLHS.)

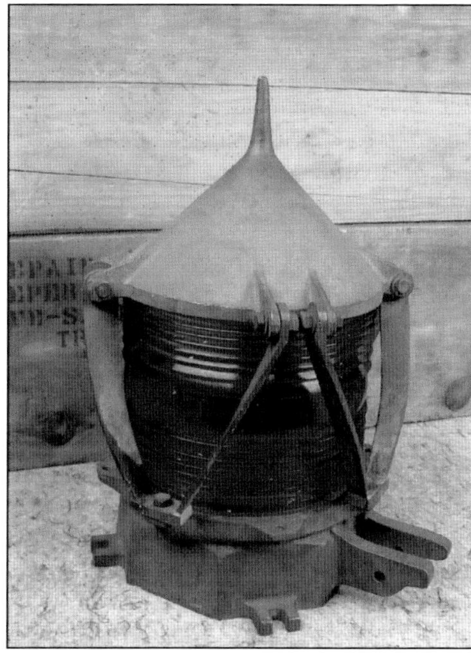

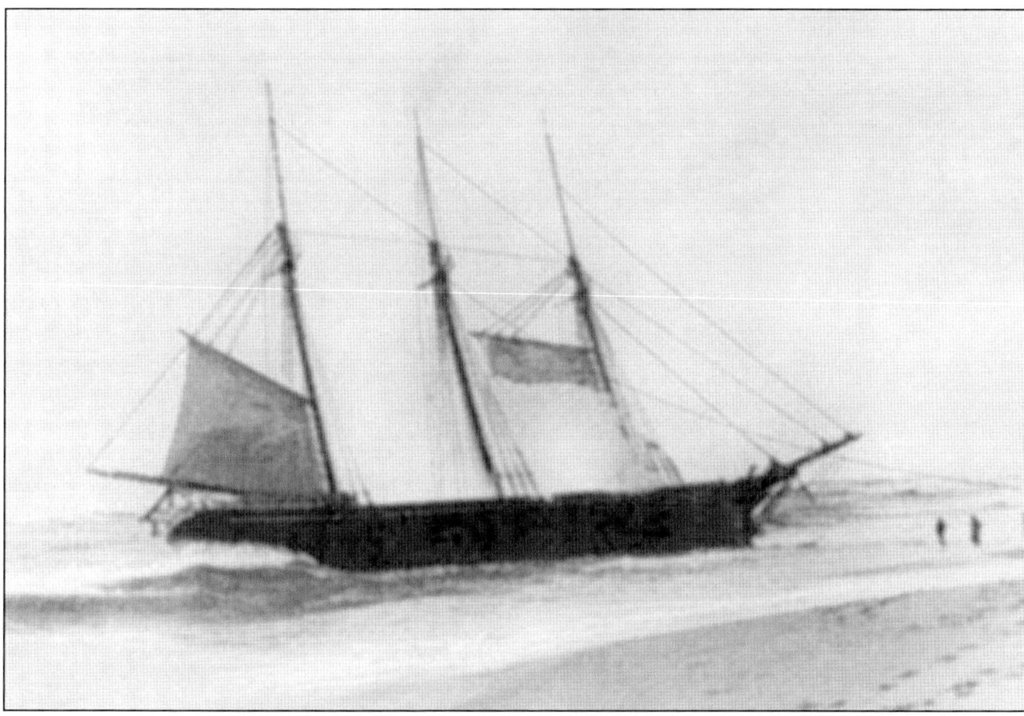

District inspectors always complimented the Williams family for running Cape St. George efficiently. Minor incidents occurred, such as waterfowl hitting the lantern and breaking a glass pane, a common experience at lighthouses. Perhaps the most serious incident occurred when a schooner named the *William Ebbits* ran aground in the bay in 1872 after delivering a load of fruit to Apalachicola. The captain said he could see the lighthouse and that the keepers were not at fault. (LOC.)

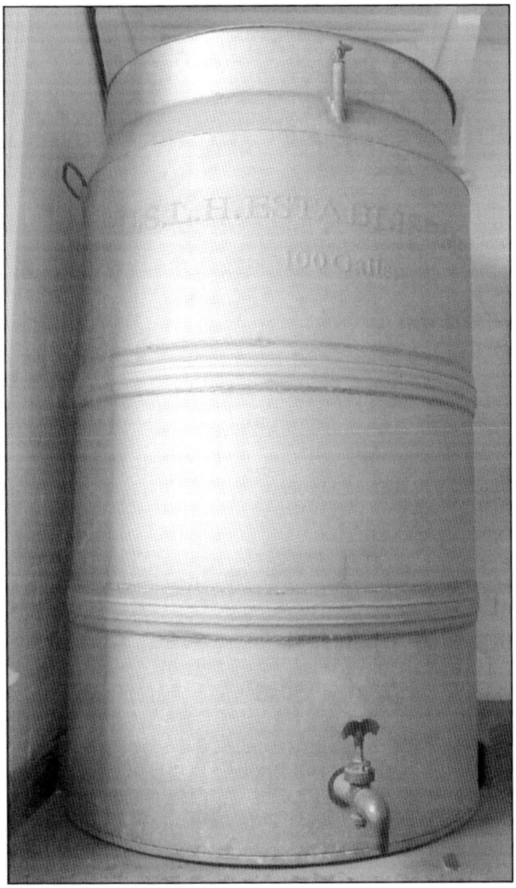

Whale oil, colza oil, and oil rendered from lard were not especially flammable, and were often kept in vats like this one inside the entryway to the tower. (JLH.)

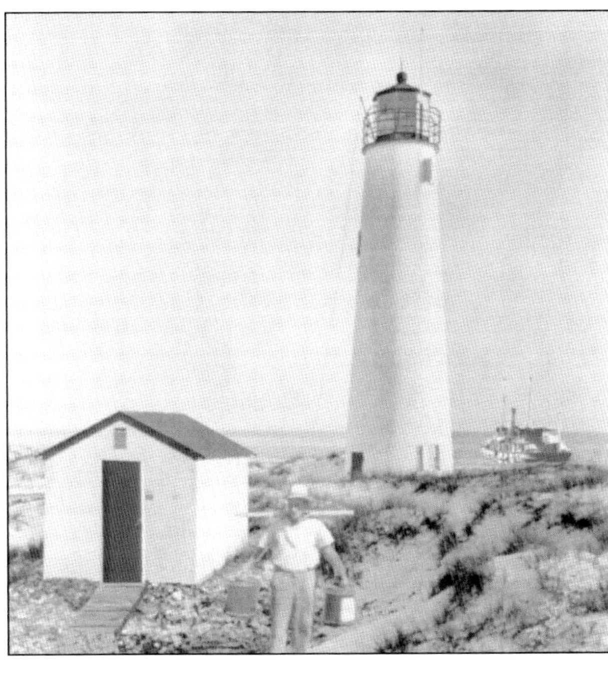

Because kerosene was more flammable than prior fuel oils, oil houses like this one were built around 1890. Here, a man from a supply tender carries two 5-gallon cans of kerosene ashore on a wooden yoke. (JLH, SGLA.)

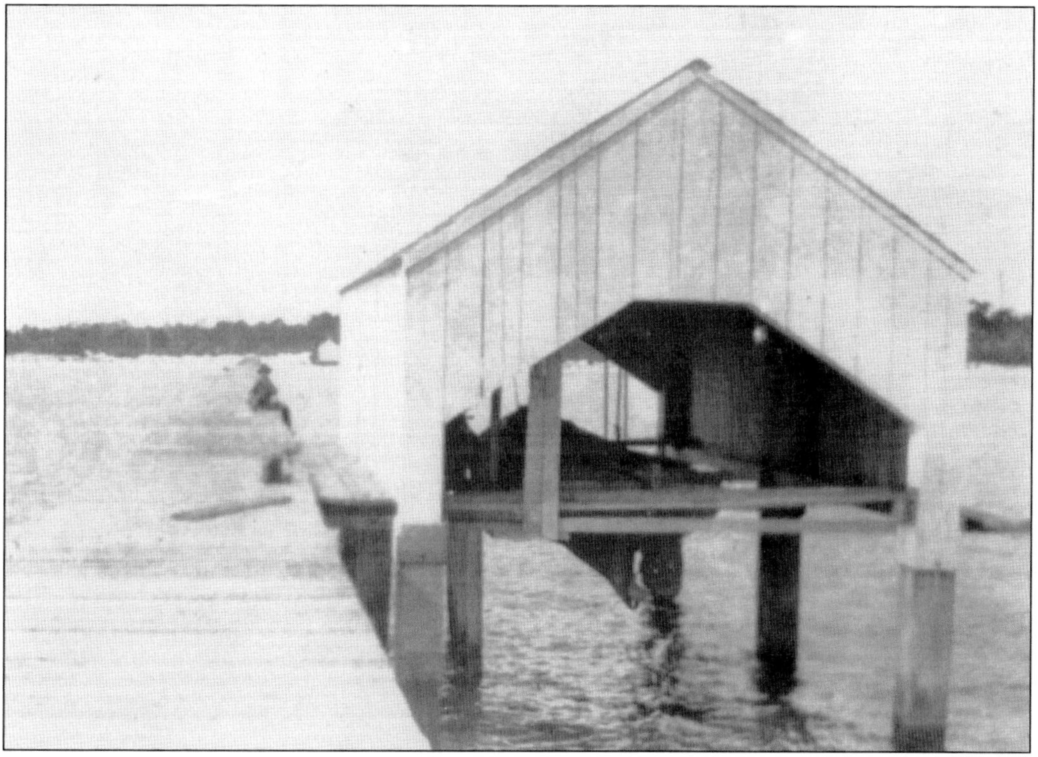

To facilitate the weekly trip to Apalachicola, a long dock was built in a cove on the bayside about a mile from the lighthouse reservation. Within a few years, a boathouse was added, and a winch and lift were installed so the keepers could hoist their boats out of the salty bay water. (SGLA.)

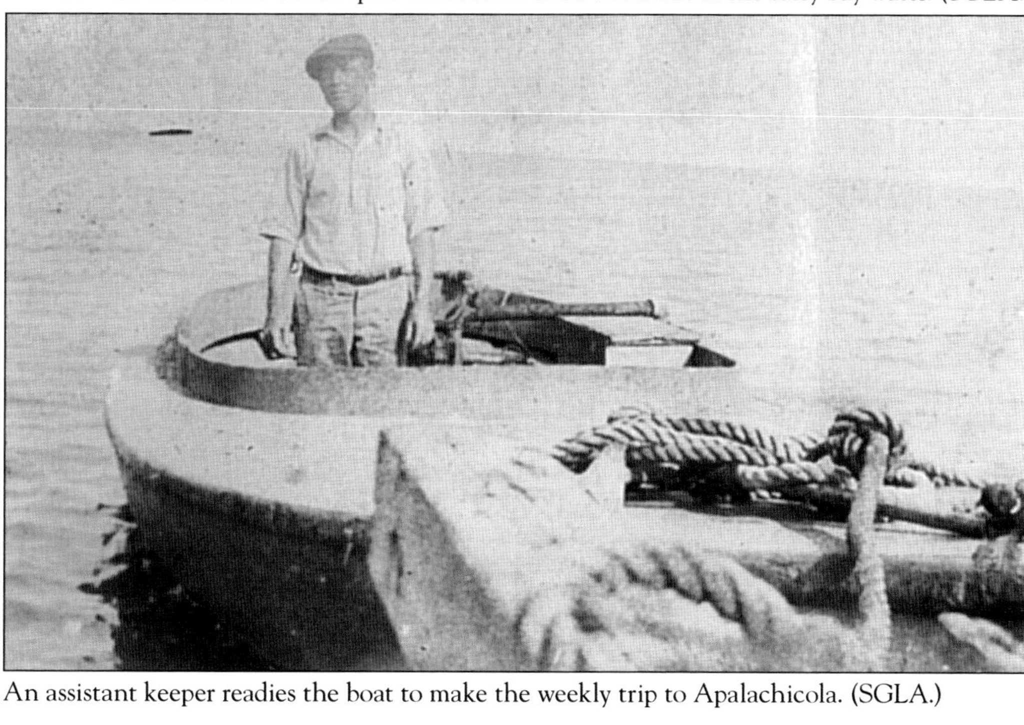

An assistant keeper readies the boat to make the weekly trip to Apalachicola. (SGLA.)

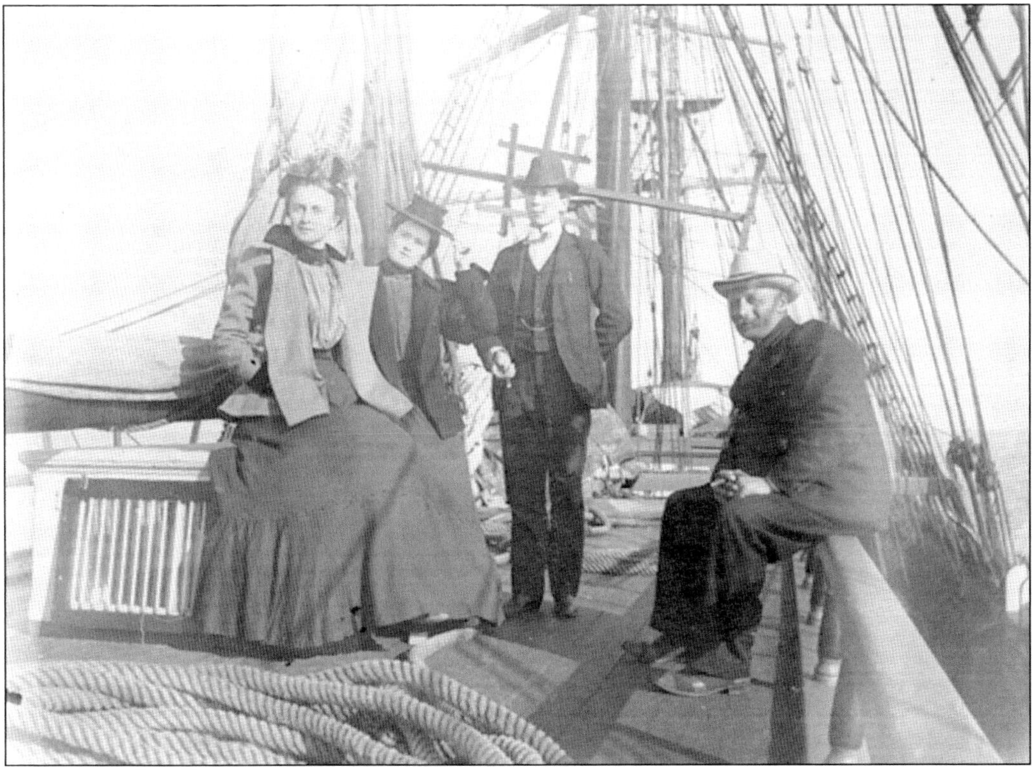

During the 19th century, no railroads had reached Apalachicola, and people traveled by horse and wagon on land, or by boat. Families from Apalachicola usually traveled by ferry along the coast or booked passage on passenger ships, like this one. (SAF.)

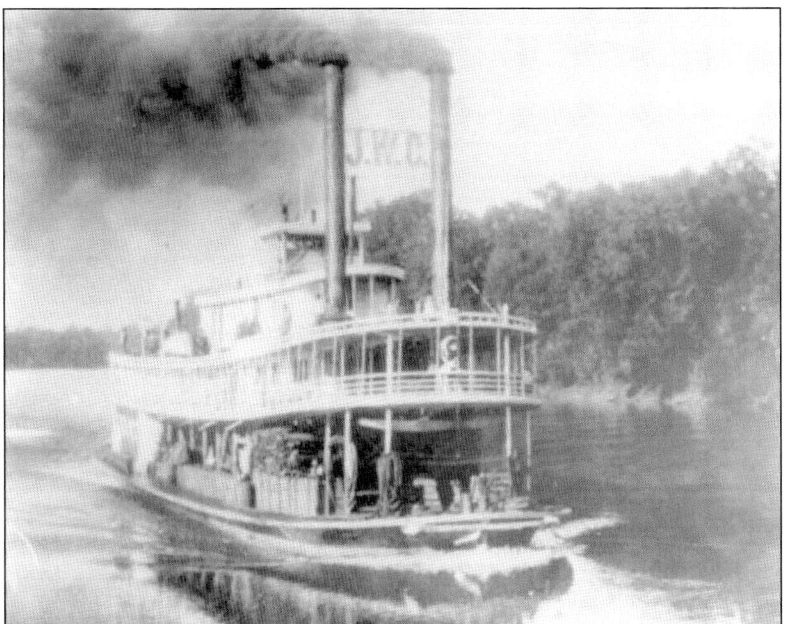

Turpentine and pine rosin were prepared from pine sap harvested in the vast forests of longleaf pine and slash pine that still grow north of Apalachicola. Here, a steamboat named the *Callahan* brings a load of naval stores downriver. (SAF.)

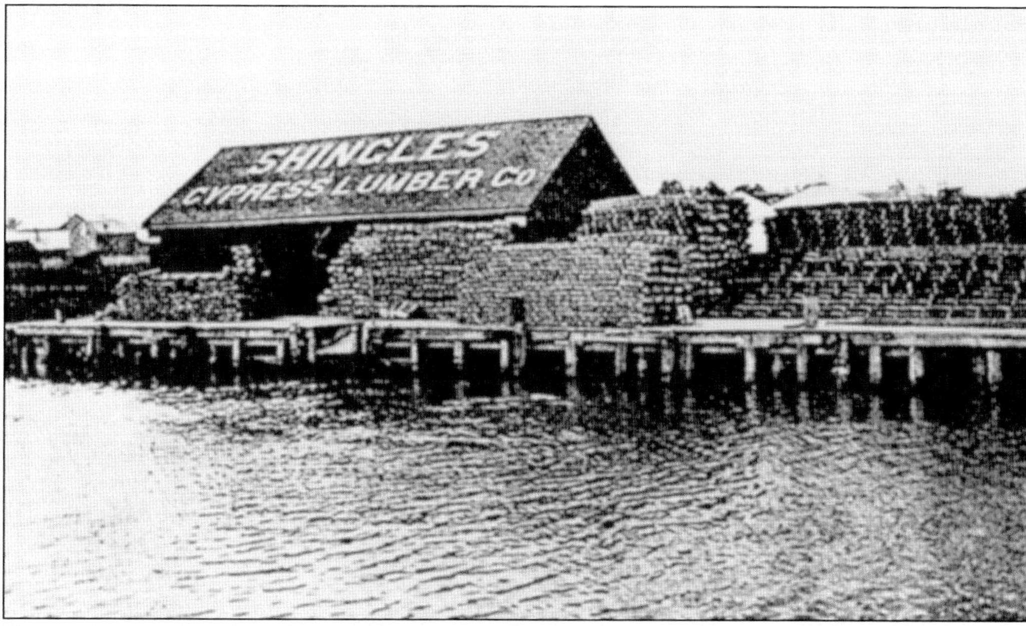

From 1870 to 1890, several sawmills were established in Apalachicola and Carrabelle. Lumber, railroad ties, and naval stores came to dominate shipping from Apalachicola Bay. The Cypress Lumber Company produced railroad ties, shingles, and millwork for home construction. (SAF.)

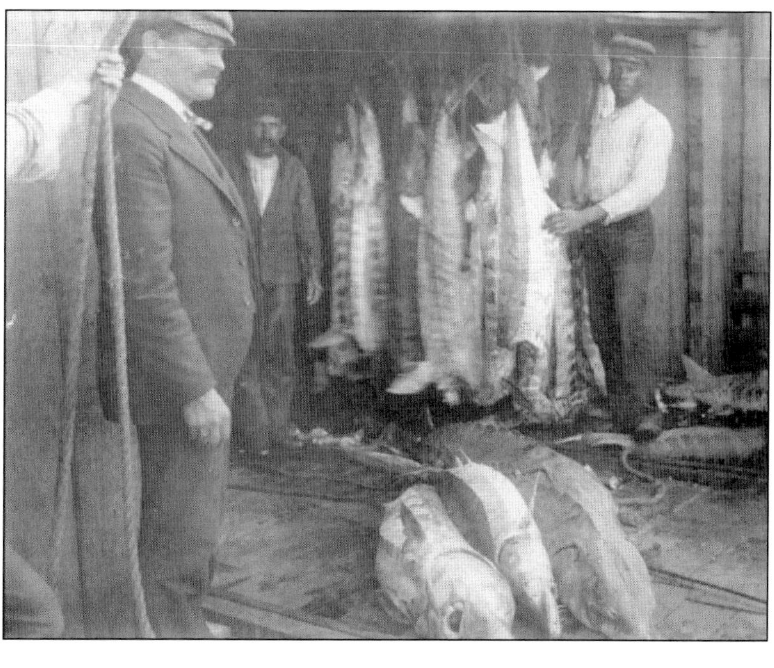

Apalachicola was rich in fresh seafood, from the sturgeon shown here to the abundant oysters, crabs, shrimp, and finfish in the river, bay, and Gulf of Mexico. However, no seafood industry could develop until there was a means to keep it fresh and transport it quickly. (SAF.)

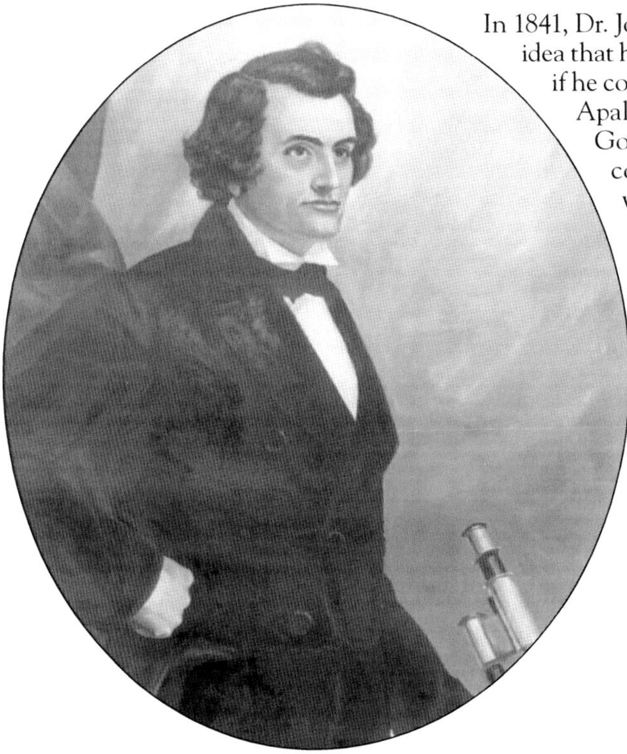

In 1841, Dr. John Gorrie became obsessed with the idea that he could cure patients with yellow fever if he could only keep them cool. Even though Apalachicola had no metal foundries, Dr. Gorrie managed to design and build a compressor that could condense air, which could cool water to the freezing point when the air expanded though a coil. He famously produced ice in Apalachicola in July 1850, and received a US patent for ice-making and refrigeration in 1851. (SAF.)

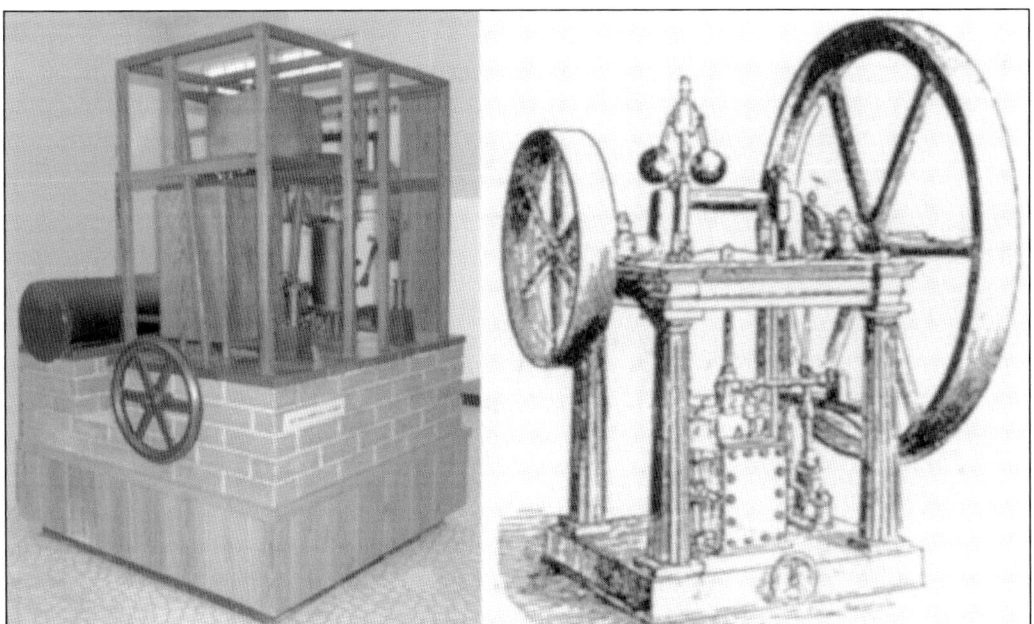

Dr. Gorrie paid a firm in Cincinnati to make his ice machine, at left. Note the large flywheel that runs the compressor. Ice machines require a source of power to run a drive belt for the flywheel, and the only one available to Dr. Gorrie was a steam engine, at right. Astonishingly, Dr. John Gorrie used steam power to make ice. Unfortunately, he died in 1855 before he was able to commercialize his invention. (JLH.)

In 1851, the Whiteside brothers moved to Apalachicola and heard about Dr. Gorrie's ice machine. Samuel Judd (right) probably met Dr. Gorrie. George Henry and Thomas (at left) worked at the Columbus Iron Works during the Civil War and knew that the ironworks began making commercial ice machines after the Civil War. The brothers purchased these machines and shortly founded commercial ice companies. (SAF.)

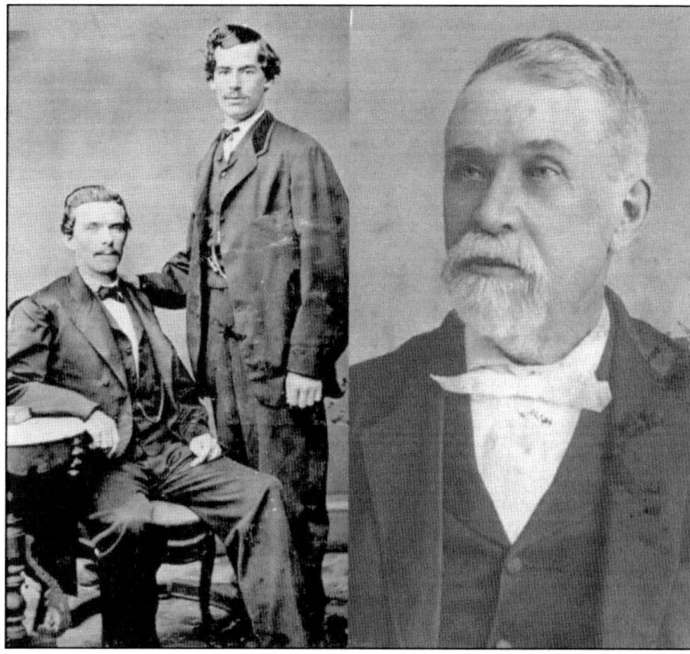

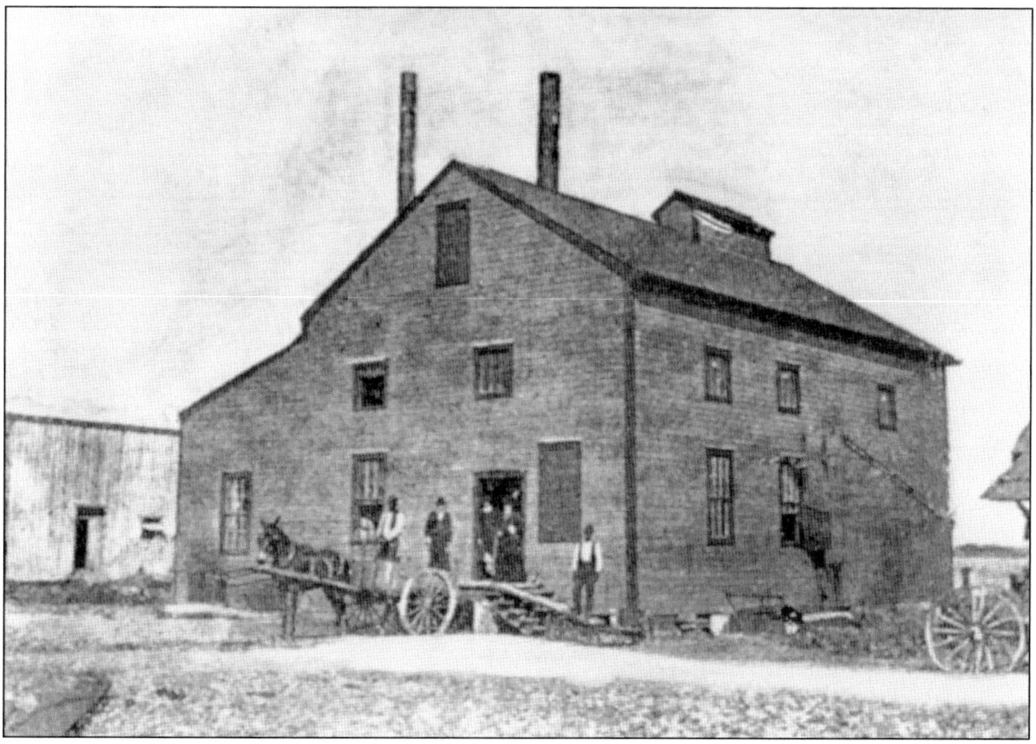

In 1885, George Whiteside founded the Apalachicola Ice and Canning Company on Water Street, while his brother Samuel started the Gorrie Ice Manufacturing Company in Savannah. Their ammonia-based Stratton Ice Machines could produce tons of ice each day, and the Apalachicola Ice Company installed a sluice that could fill the holds of fishing boats with ice. Suddenly, it was possible to keep seafood fresh and pack it or can it for shipping long distances. (SAF.)

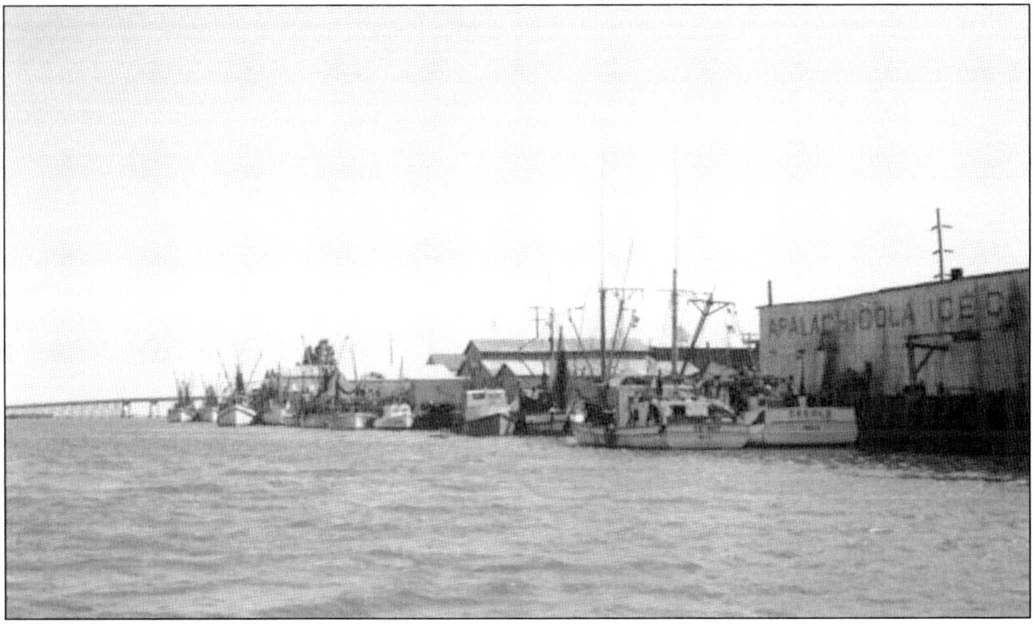

By 1890, the Cape St. George Lighthouse guided fishing boats as they navigated Apalachicola Bay and West Pass on the way to offshore fishing grounds. The fishing fleet, here tied up at the dock outside a more recent Apalachicola Ice Company, augmented the lumber industry as a major source of trade. By then, Columbus was a major railway head, but steamboats still carried goods up and down the river. (SGLA.)

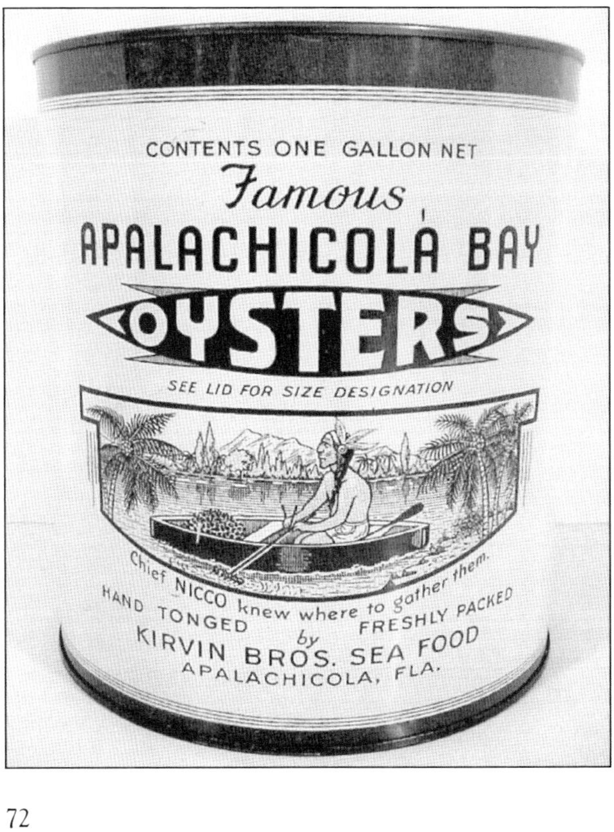

With ice available to keep finfish and shellfish fresh, several canning operations opened in Apalachicola during the 1880s and thereafter. In addition to packinghouses run by the Ruge and Tarantino families, the Kirvins operated an oyster canning plant and shipped their product in cans such as this one.

Six

Living at the Cape St. George Lighthouse

In 1893, the Williams family moved from Cape St. George to take care of the new Crooked River lighthouse and the bay lights around Eastpoint. The new head keeper at Cape St. George, Edward G. Porter, proved just as tenacious. He and his wife, Jo, lived at the light station for 20 years and raised six children during that time. In addition to the Porter family, assistant keeper Walter A. Roberts Sr. would also leave a legacy. His son Walter A. Roberts Jr. would later be promoted to head keeper, and then continue with the US Coast Guard at the Rear Range light near Port St. Joe.

Members of the Porter and Roberts families wrote memoirs that describe what it was like to live at Cape St. George. Pearl Porter Marshall was born in 1900 while her family was living at the light station. Her father loved Little St. George Island and purchased all the land outside the six-acre lighthouse station. Little St. George was still separated from the rest of the island by New Inlet, which did not close until after 1907. To supplement his income of $600 per month, Porter raised cattle and hogs, and the family raised a vegetable garden.

During Edward Porter's tenure, several severe hurricanes struck Apalachicola Bay. Keeper Porter convinced the US Lighthouse Service that his family required a storm shelter, and materials were delivered to build one in 1900. Neither the keeper nor his family could evacuate the island during such storms.

William Roberts, son of Walter Roberts Jr., also wrote a memoir about his family's three generations of service and a warm account of his childhood on Cape St. George. William Roberts donated many family implements and photographs to the St. George Lighthouse Association.

A railroad arrived in Apalachicola in 1907, and shipping declined as lumbering depleted the timber north of the town. An era ended when the last steamboat on the Apalachicola River stopped making its runs in 1927. Finally, World War II brought an end to the US Lighthouse Service as it had existed since 1852. In 1939, Pres. Franklin Delano Roosevelt merged the Lighthouse Service with the US Coast Guard. Although the two keepers at Cape St. George joined the Coast Guard and remained as the last real caretakers, technological changes during World War II ended the era of lighthouses as aids to coastal navigation.

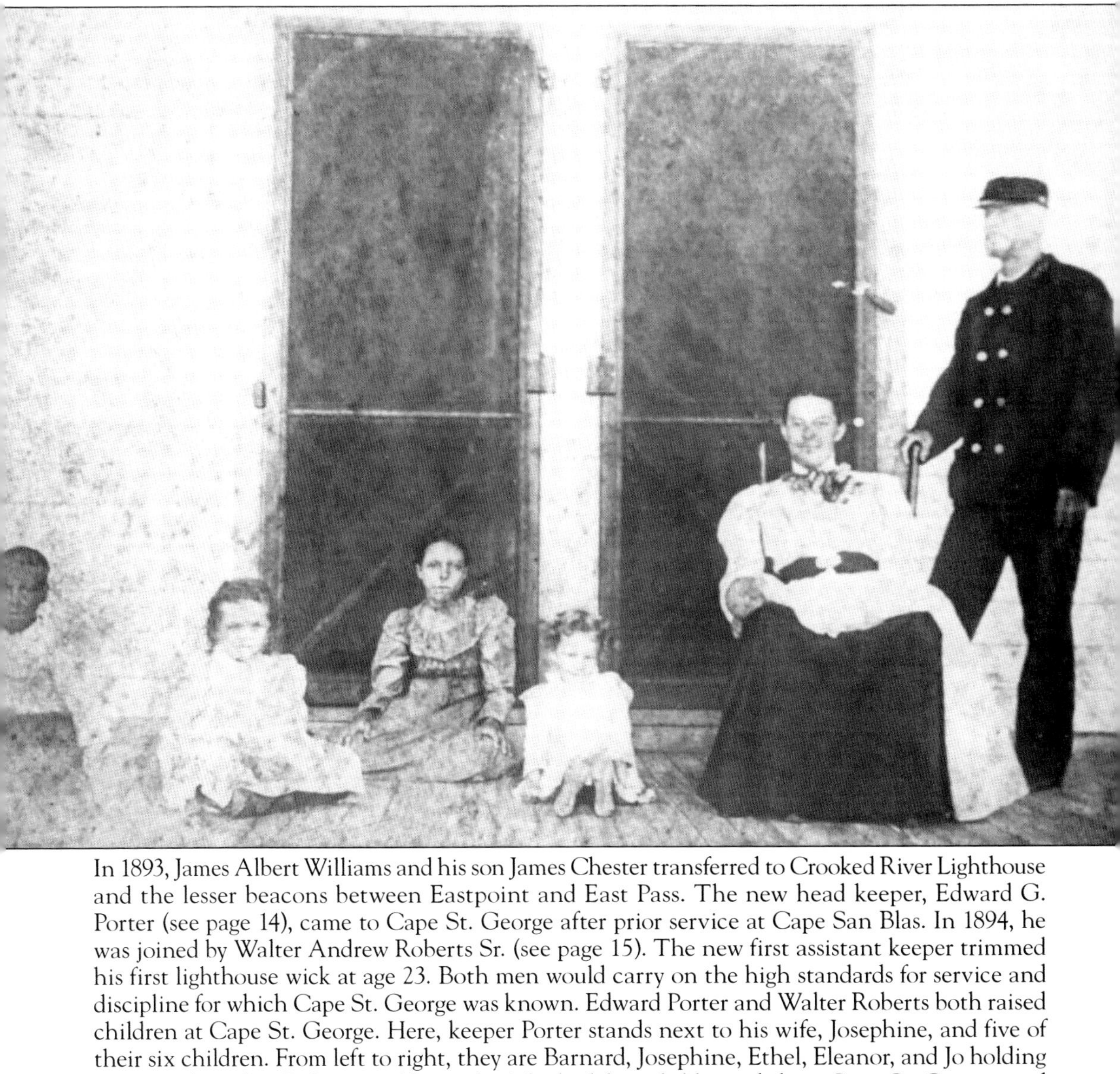

In 1893, James Albert Williams and his son James Chester transferred to Crooked River Lighthouse and the lesser beacons between Eastpoint and East Pass. The new head keeper, Edward G. Porter (see page 14), came to Cape St. George after prior service at Cape San Blas. In 1894, he was joined by Walter Andrew Roberts Sr. (see page 15). The new first assistant keeper trimmed his first lighthouse wick at age 23. Both men would carry on the high standards for service and discipline for which Cape St. George was known. Edward Porter and Walter Roberts both raised children at Cape St. George. Here, keeper Porter stands next to his wife, Josephine, and five of their six children. From left to right, they are Barnard, Josephine, Ethel, Eleanor, and Jo holding baby Pearl. Walter Roberts and his wife, Ada, had four children while at Cape St. George, and keeper Porter later hired a school teacher named Ida Rhodes to teach their 10 children. In most cases, the women and children were sent to Apalachicola during the school term. (SGLA.)

General duties at the lighthouse did not change. The keepers continued to carry five-gallon cans of kerosene up the 92 steps to the watch room, cleaned the lamp and lantern glass daily, and protected the Fresnel lens from sunlight by draping curtains from hooks on the lantern room wall. (SGLA.)

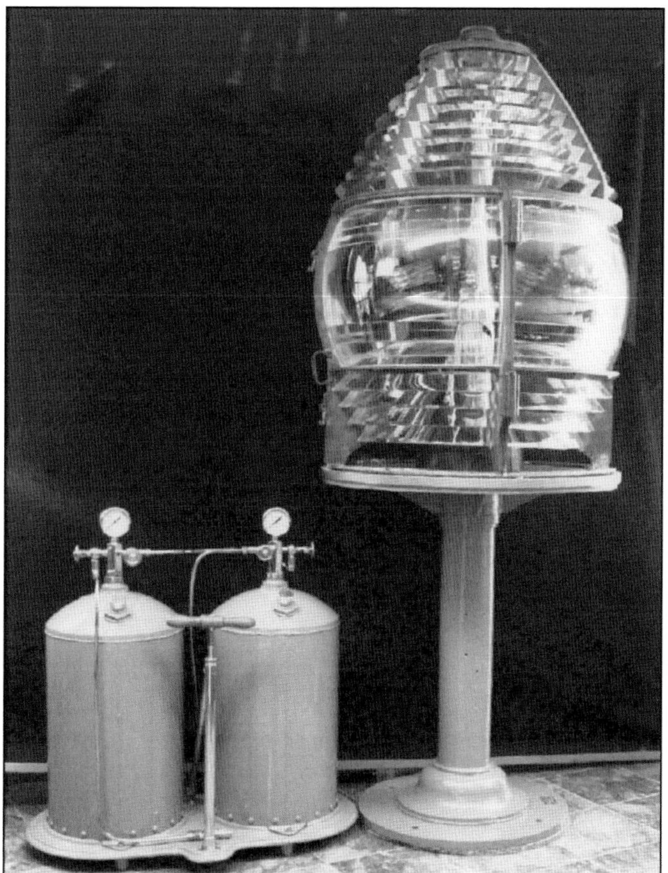

During Edward Porter's tenure as head keeper, the illuminating apparatus was changed from a lamp with wicks to an incandescent oil vapor lamp. The new device had a gas mantle made of cotton impregnated in rare earth salts, which produce an intense white light. Like camp lanterns, the fuel reservoir was pressurized by pumping a handle similar to a bicycle pump. The new lanterns could run most of the night with only an occasional check. (St. Augustine Lighthouse & Maritime Museum.)

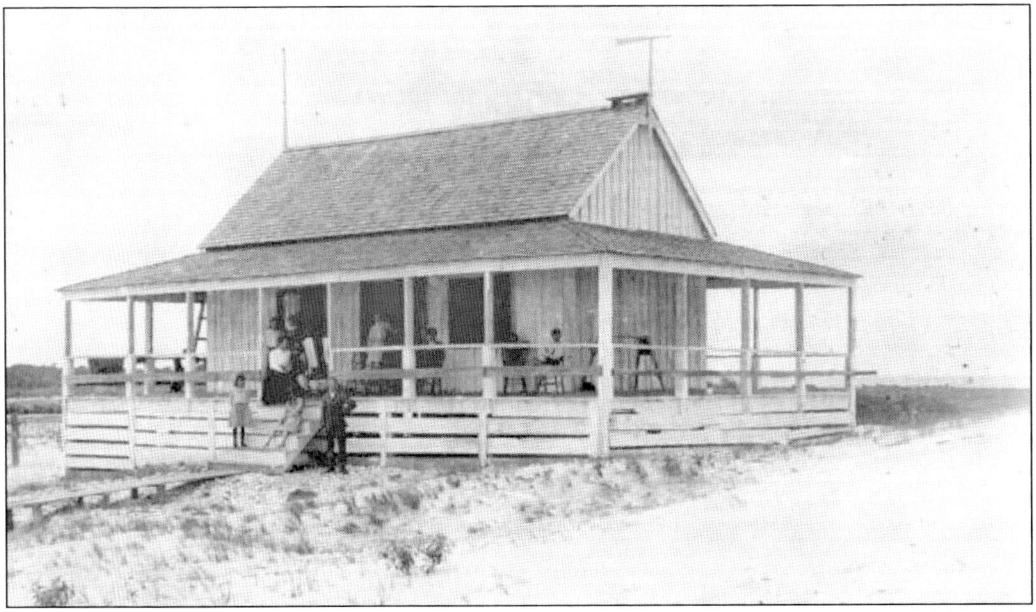

In 1900, the district superintendent agreed to provide materials so Edward Porter could build a storm house partway between the lighthouse and the bay. Having undergone several severe storms during his first six years, the keeper rightfully wanted a safer place for his family to stay during hurricanes. Shortly thereafter, he also built a cottage near the boat dock that he would rent or loan to visitors. Visitors were never allowed to stay overnight at the light station without written permission from the district superintendent. (SAF.)

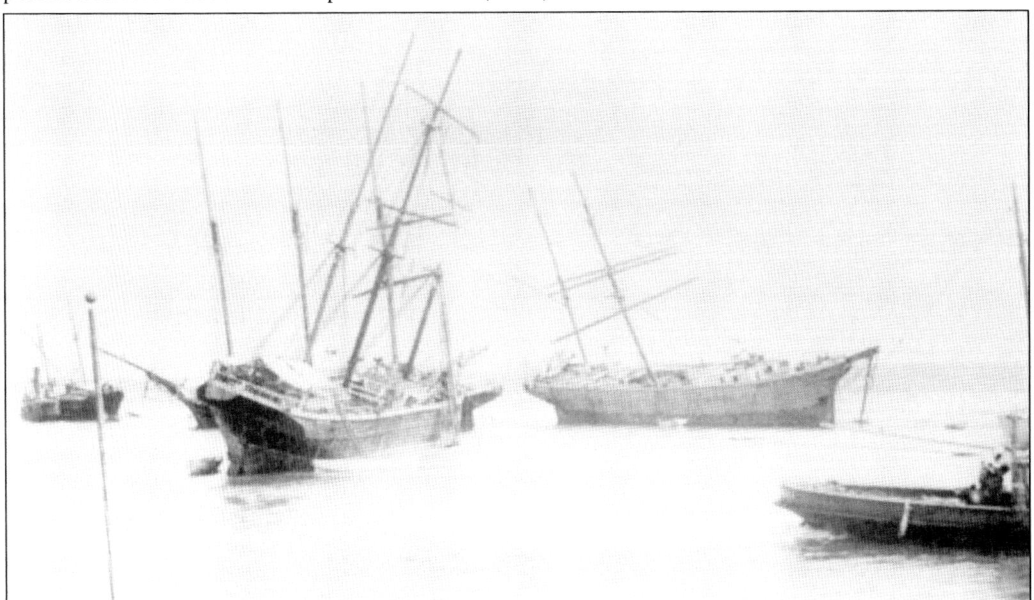

The storm house was badly needed. This image shows several ships that were washed ashore on St. George Island by the hurricane of 1899. During a later storm, Pearl Porter remembered that even after the storm passed, seawater had surged beyond the lighthouse and covered the picket fence around the dwellings. The keeper had to remain in the rocking tower and keep the lamp lit until the storm was over. (SAF.)

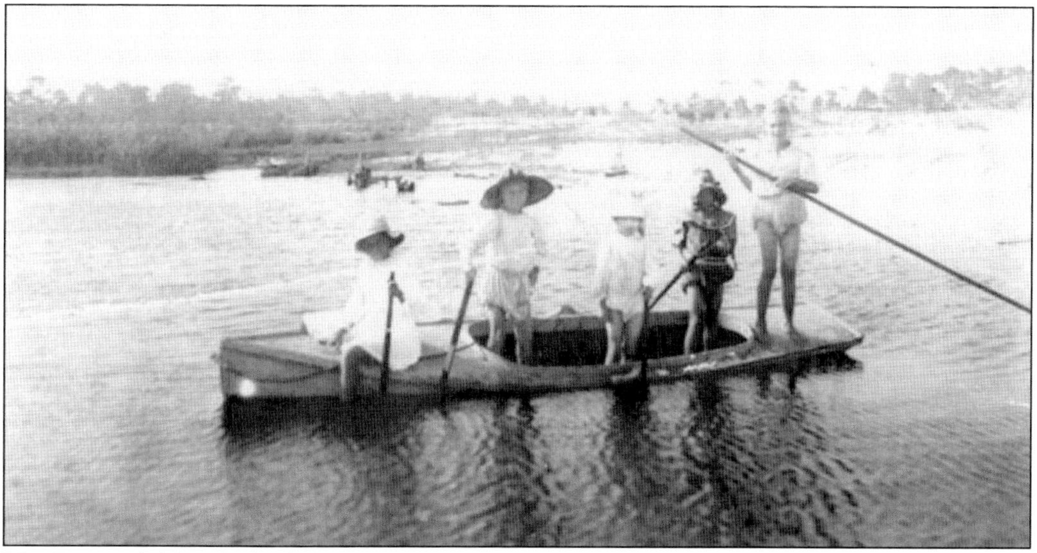

The Porter children helped their parents care for the livestock and the vegetable garden and did chores around the living quarters. However, they also found creative ways to have fun. In about 1906, a photographer from Apalachicola took this picture of, from left to right, Josephine Porter, Hazel Knickmeyer, Pearl Porter, Eleanor Porter, and Rosa Montgomery poling a rowboat in a pond near the lighthouse. (SGLA.)

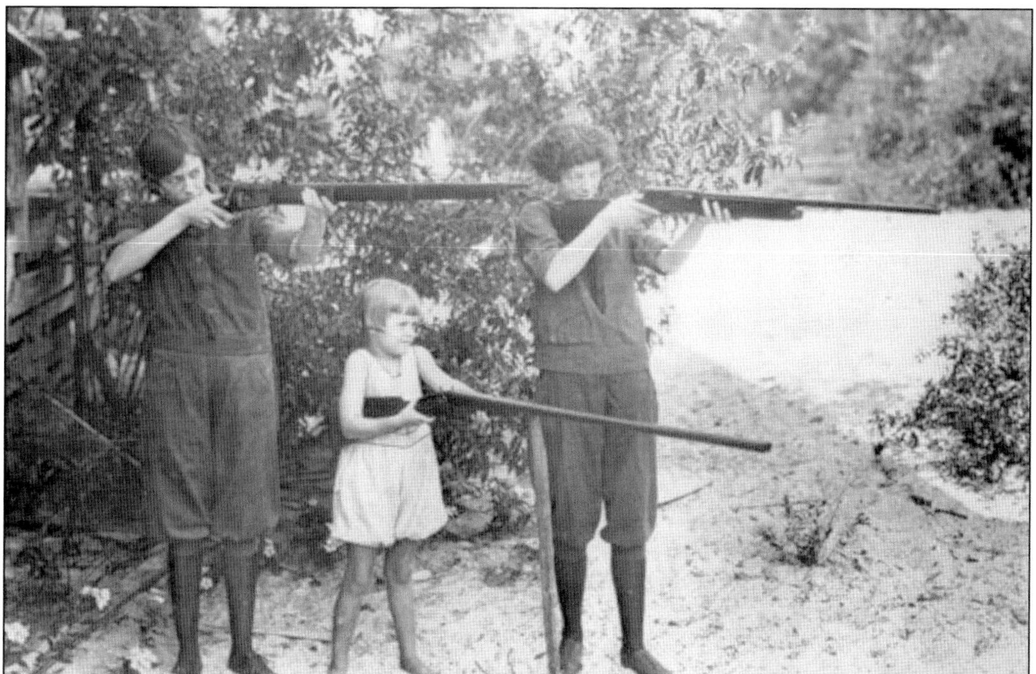

After her father died, Pearl Porter lived with her mother in a cottage near the dock. In 1924, she married Herbert Marshall, who later became sheriff of Franklin County. He gave her a 16-gauge shotgun, and she tried her hand at duck hunting. Here, Bess Marshall Porter, her daughter Mary Virginia Porter, and Pearl Porter Marshall pose with firearms. Note the large stick propping up the shotgun Mary Virginia is aiming. (SGLA.)

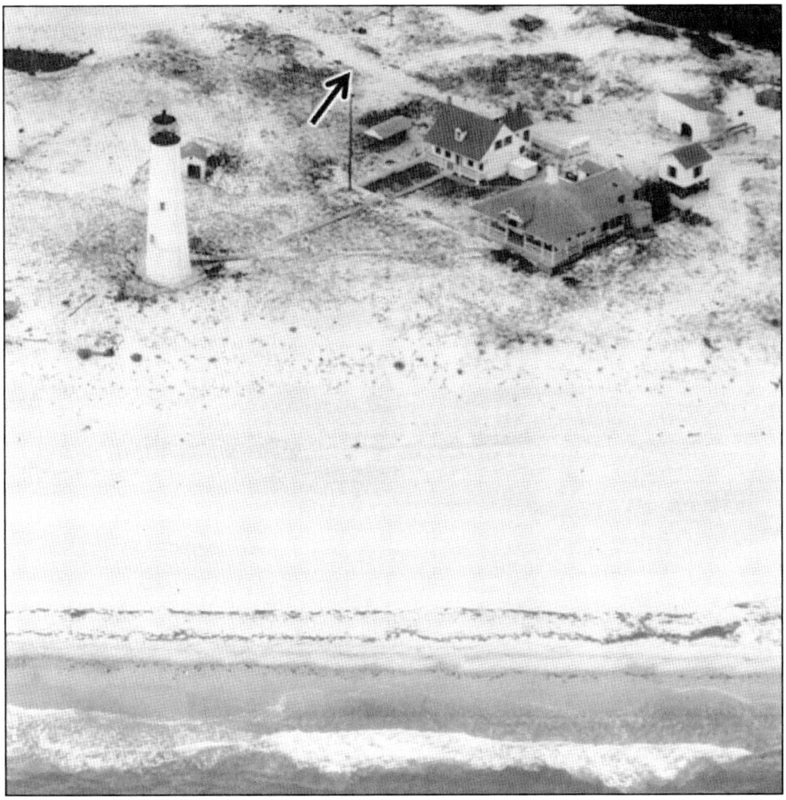

The trip to the boat dock started when the keeper hitched a horse and wagon to travel over the sand road indicated by the arrow in this aerial photograph of the Cape St. George Light Station. (USCG.)

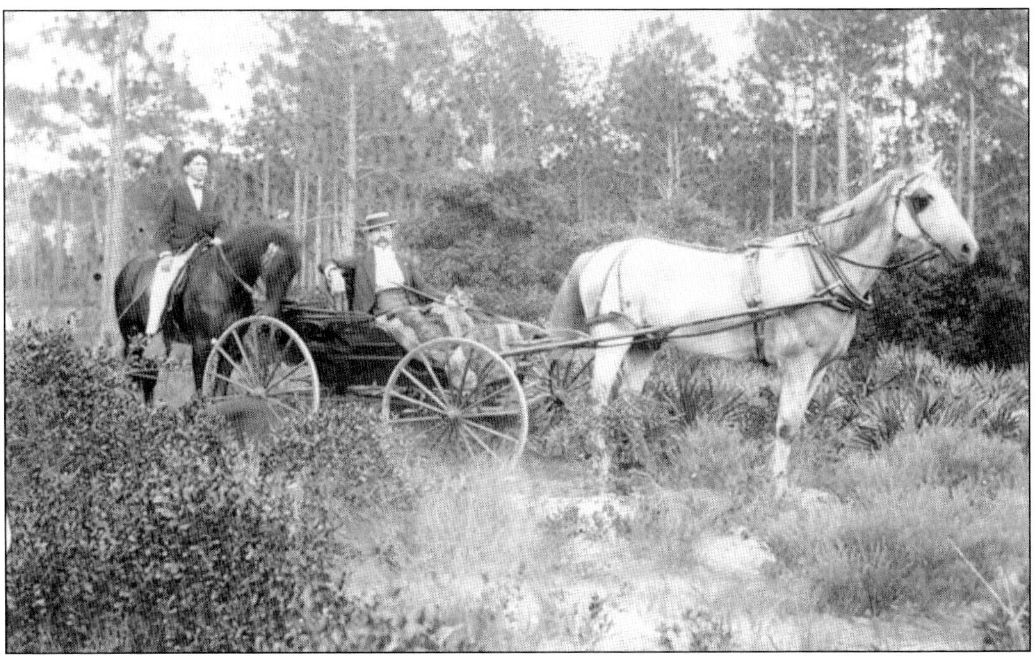

Travel over the sand road on the island, as well as elsewhere around Apalachicola, required a horse and wagon until the Coast Guard furnished a jeep during World War II. The first tarmac-paved road on the mainland was not completed until 1935. (SAF.)

Although keepers were expected to wear their blue uniforms when on duty, they were allowed to wear fatigues when painting or doing heavier labor. David D. Silva Sr., who became assistant keeper in 1913 and head keeper in 1917, displays his work clothes in the photograph at left. In the c. 1920 image at right, Silva wears his formal uniform. The son of immigrants, Silva served as assistant keeper from 1913 to 1917 and then as keeper until 1932. The Silva family used large quantities of garlic, and it was said that ship captains would call out, asking if they were off the coast of Italy. (SGLA.)

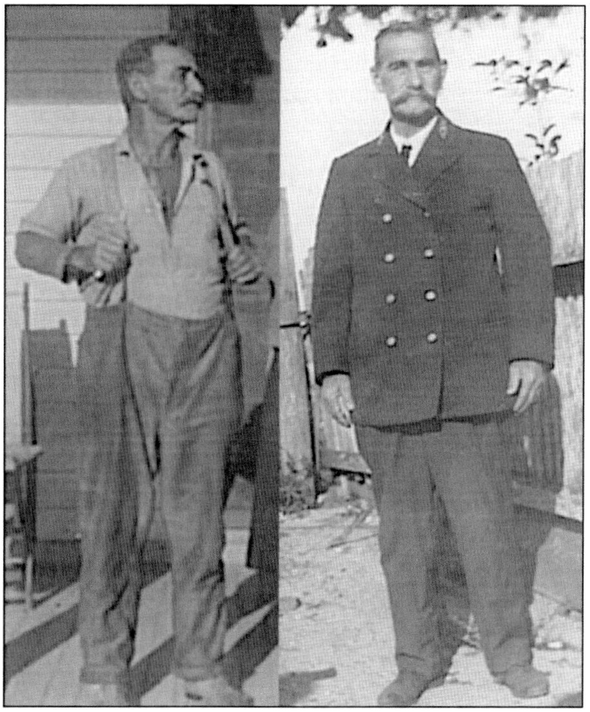

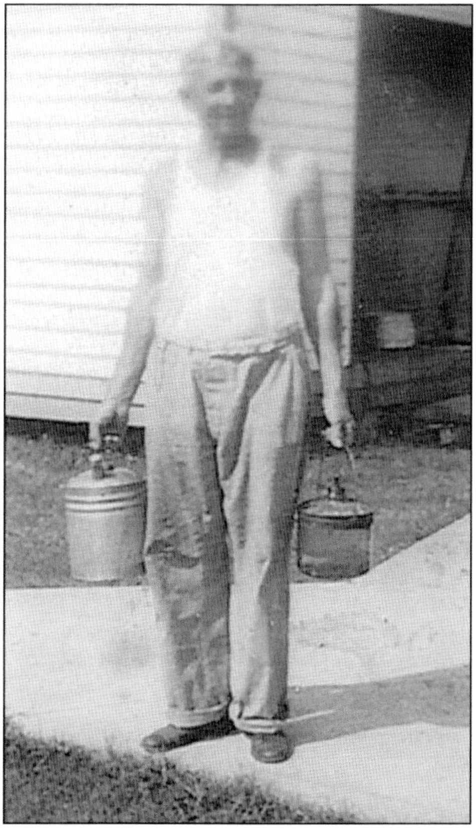

The most common daily chore at the Cape St. George Lighthouse was lugging three- to five-gallon cans of kerosene up the lighthouse stairs to replenish the lamp reservoirs. In this photograph from about 1923, assistant keeper Louis Buras starts his journey. (SGLA)

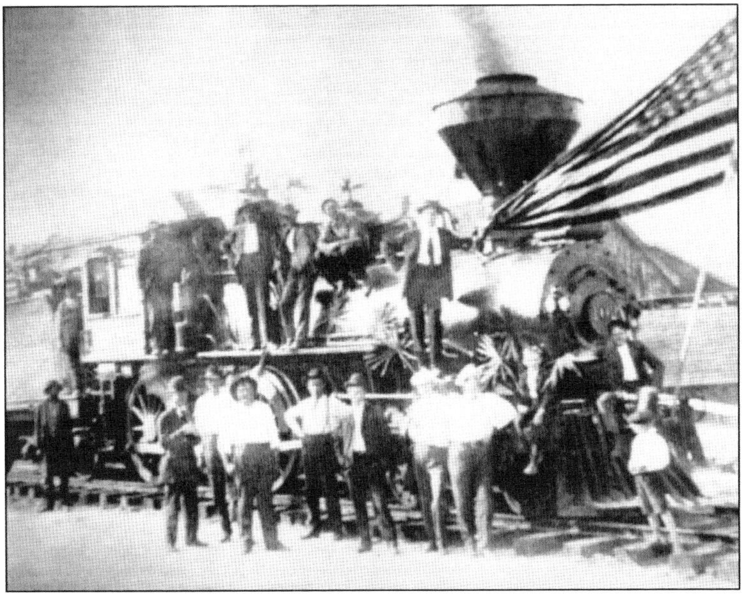

During Edward Porter's years at Cape St. George, transportation up the Apalachicola River changed permanently. On April 30, 1907, the Apalachicola Northern Railroad completed a rail line to the lumber yards and docks of Apalachicola. The train would revolutionize the speed of transportation and create new destinations for the seafood industry. (SAF.)

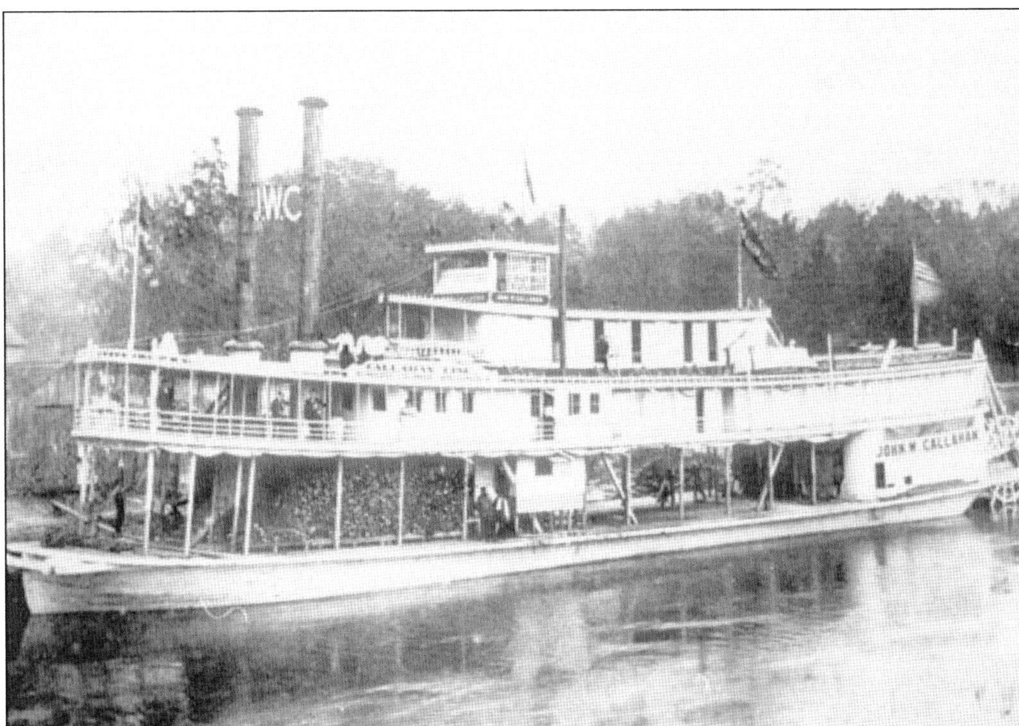

Only 20 years after the railroad came to town, the last steamboat completed its final run down the Apalachicola River. Capt. Tom Corley had the last first-class pilot's rating on the river, and operated the *John W. Callahan*, shown here. The last steamboat down the river was the *Callahan Jr.*, owned by Tri-State Navigation. (SAF.)

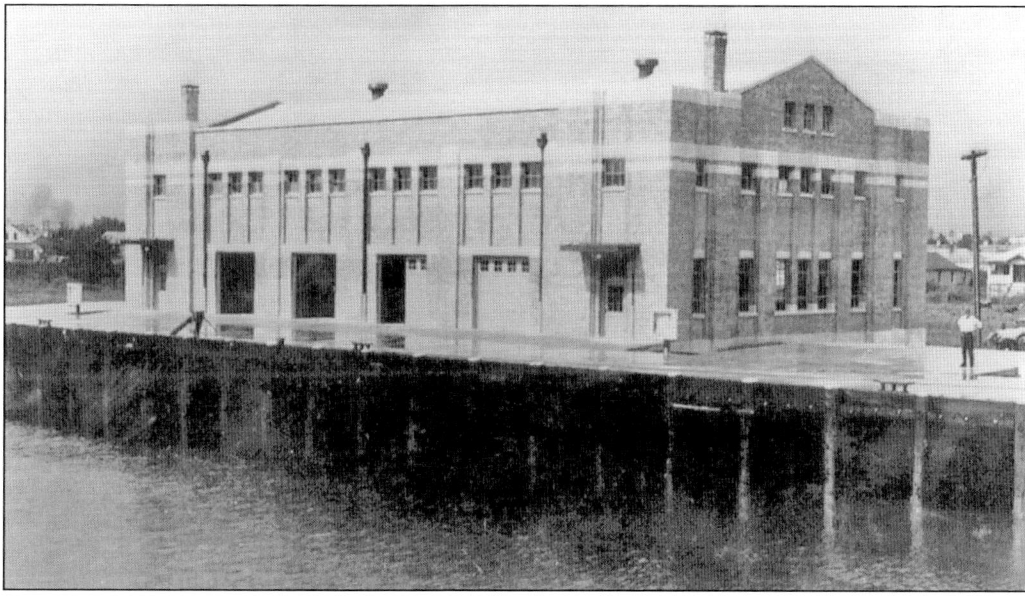

Cape St. George was supplied at various times from supply depots in Lighthouse District 7 at Key West, Mobile, or Port Eads, Louisiana. After 1910, lighthouse administration was transferred to the Department of Commerce. Thereafter, Cape St. George was supplied by the Port Eads depot in District 8 near New Orleans, shown here. (USLHS.)

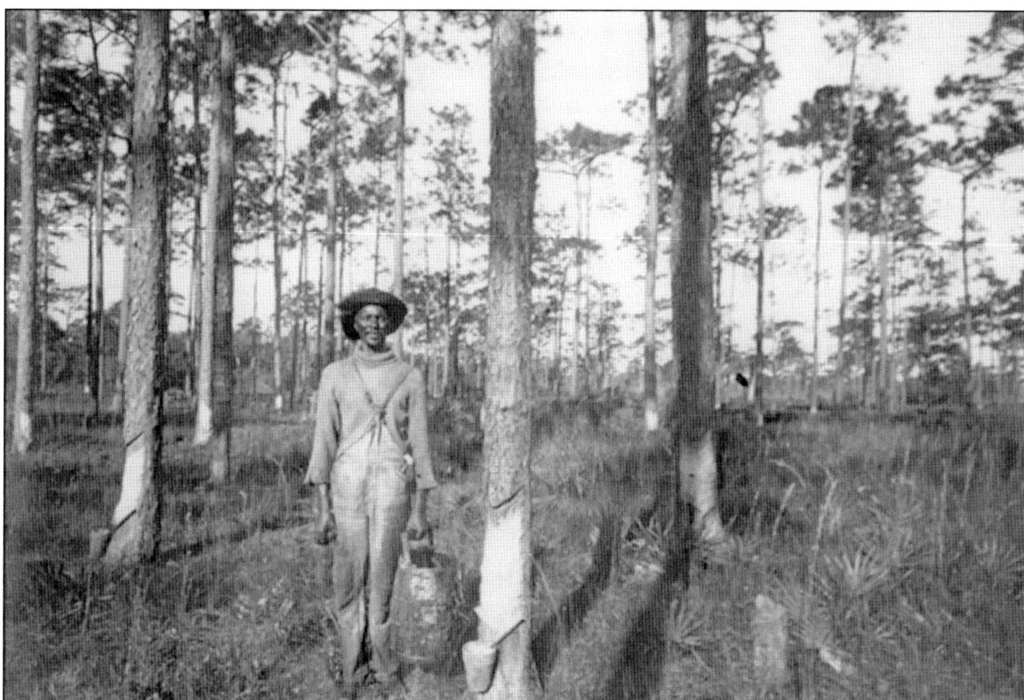

Beginning in 1912, H.L. Oliver leased Little St. George Island for the purpose of collecting turpentine. Later, C.C. Land leased St. George Island for collecting turpentine and raising cattle. Most of the larger slash pines on the island show cat-faced scars cut by men, such as this worker, who collected pine sap for the naval stores industry. (SAF.)

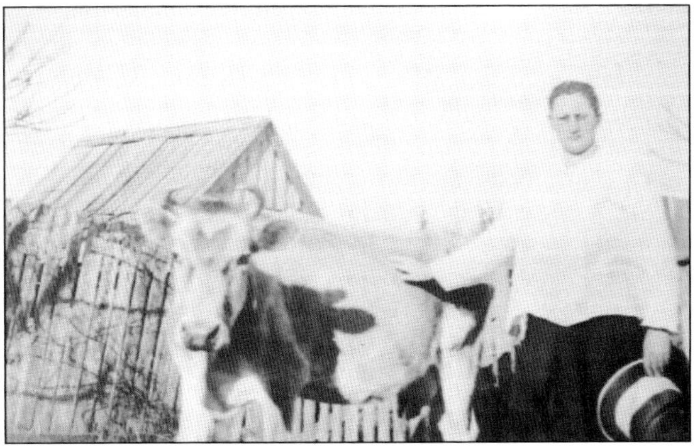

Edward Porter purchased most of Little St. George Island and raised cattle to provide milk for his children and to supply the Porters' butcher shop in Apalachicola. Later, C.C. Land also raised cattle on the island and allowed the lighthouse keepers to select a milk cow for their daily use. Here, Ornamae White, the daughter of keeper Sullivan White, poses next to one of the milk cows. (TC/MM.)

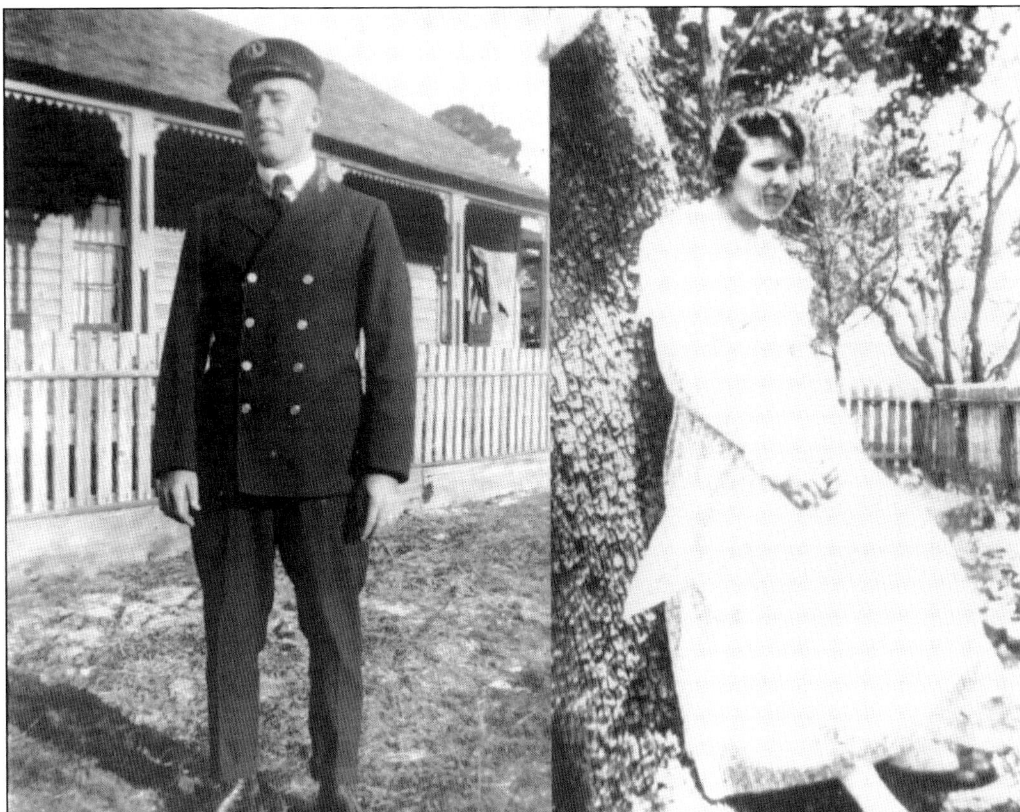

Walter A. "Pete" Roberts Jr. became assistant keeper at Cape St. George in 1925 and keeper in 1931 after relocating from Pensacola. He and his wife, Bessie Pryor Roberts, raised four children at Cape St. George. During their tenure, a stove and refrigerator that operated on kerosene were installed, and a telephone line was run to Cape St. George from Apalachicola by way of St. Vincent Island. When the US Lighthouse Service was merged with the US Coast Guard, Roberts enlisted and served as chief petty officer at the St. Joseph Bay Rear Range Light from 1938 to 1952. (SGLA.)

Children at Cape St. George always helped their parents with work around the lighthouse and dwellings. Here, Walter III and his younger brother, William, help their parents with gardening chores. Later, William would recall that his dad taught him the meaning of doing a job right the first time, responsibility, honesty, and loyalty. (Roberts family collection, SGLA.)

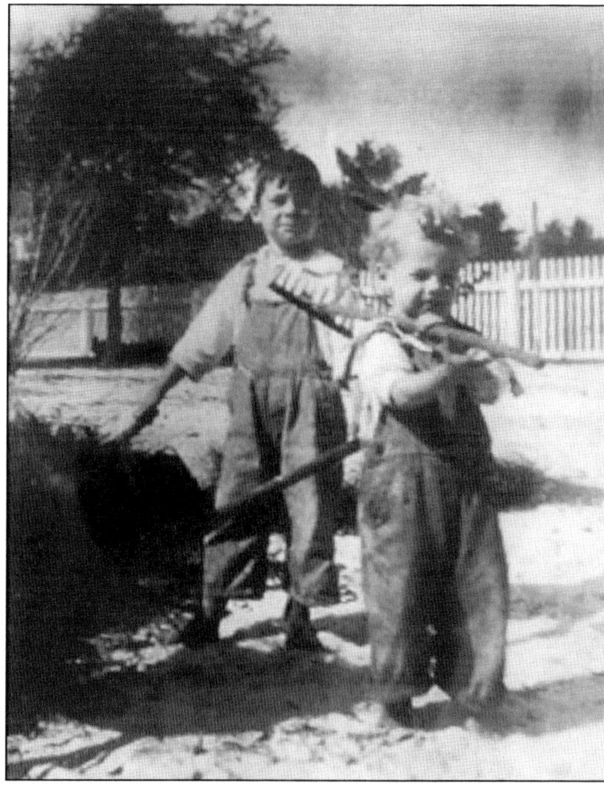

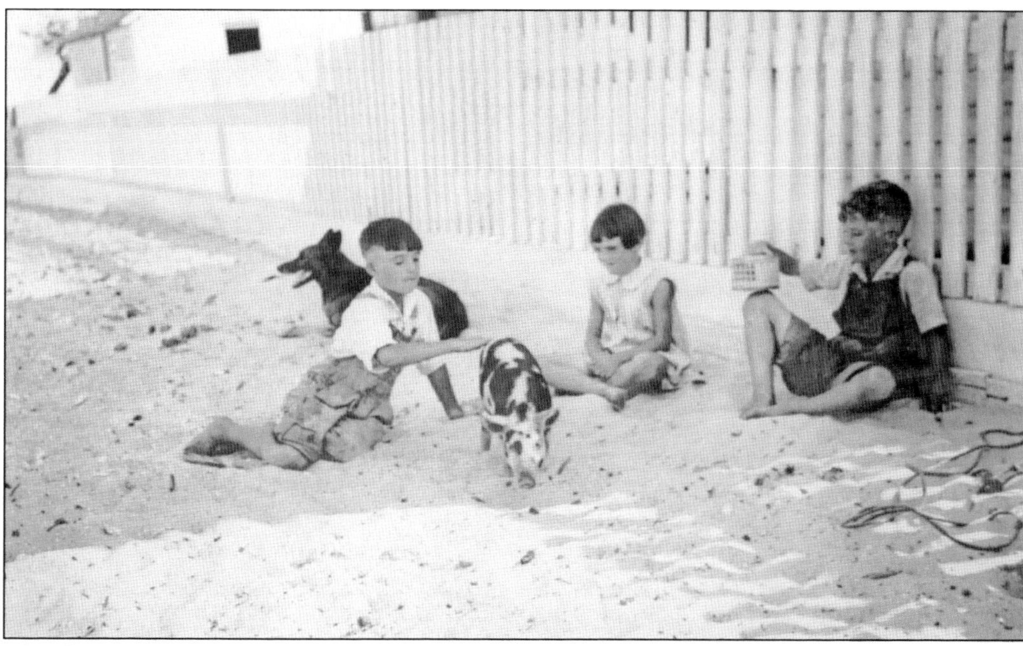

The three oldest Roberts children (William, Elizabeth, and Walter III) rest next to the picket fence with their pet German shepherd Trixie and a pig they caught in the woods. Alice the pig probably descended from the hogs that Edward Porter brought to the island along with horses, cows, goats, and chickens. (Roberts family photos, SGLA.)

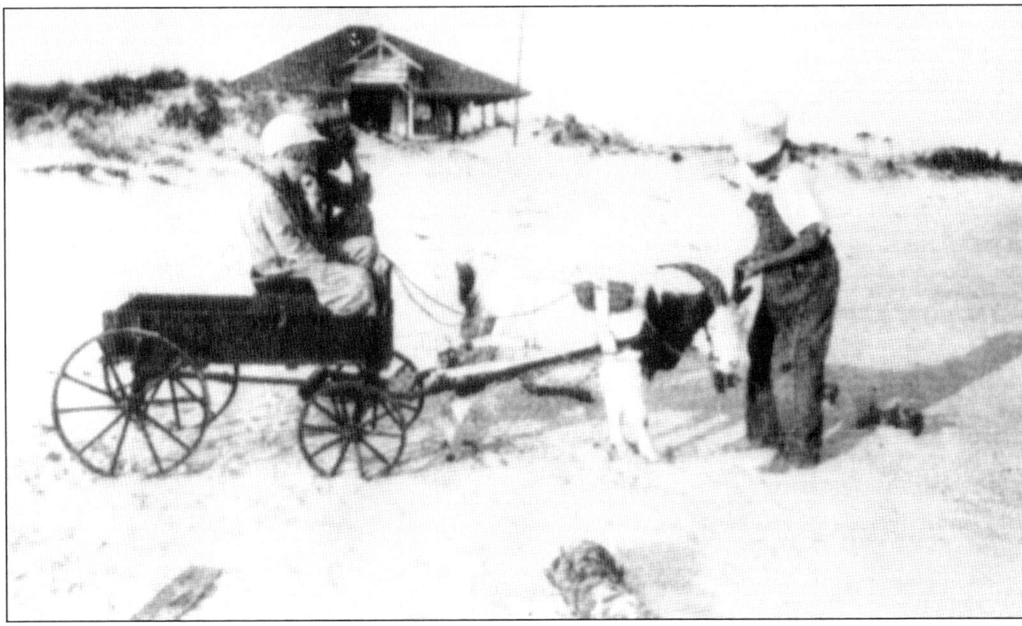

Keeper Walter Roberts purchased a red pony cart from the Montgomery Ward catalog, but their old pony Prince would not pull it. Roberts took Trixie the German shepherd to Sand Island, where a herd of goats still roamed. Trixie picked out Billy from the herd, and the billy goat soon loved to pull the cart. Keeper Roberts always returned the goat to the herd when the children went to school in Apalachicola in the fall and brought it back each spring for the next four years. (Roberts family photos, SGLA.)

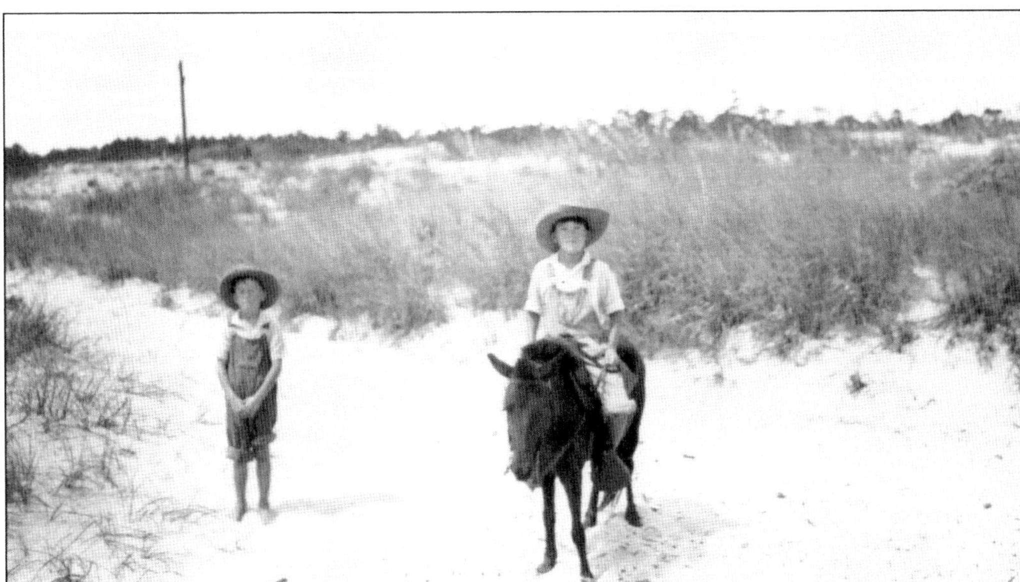

William Roberts recalled that his father would often ask him to ride with him by wagon over the sand road to the bay in order to take care of the horses during the weekly trip for mail and supplies. Here, William watches as his brother Walter III sits astride their old pony Prince. (SGLA.)

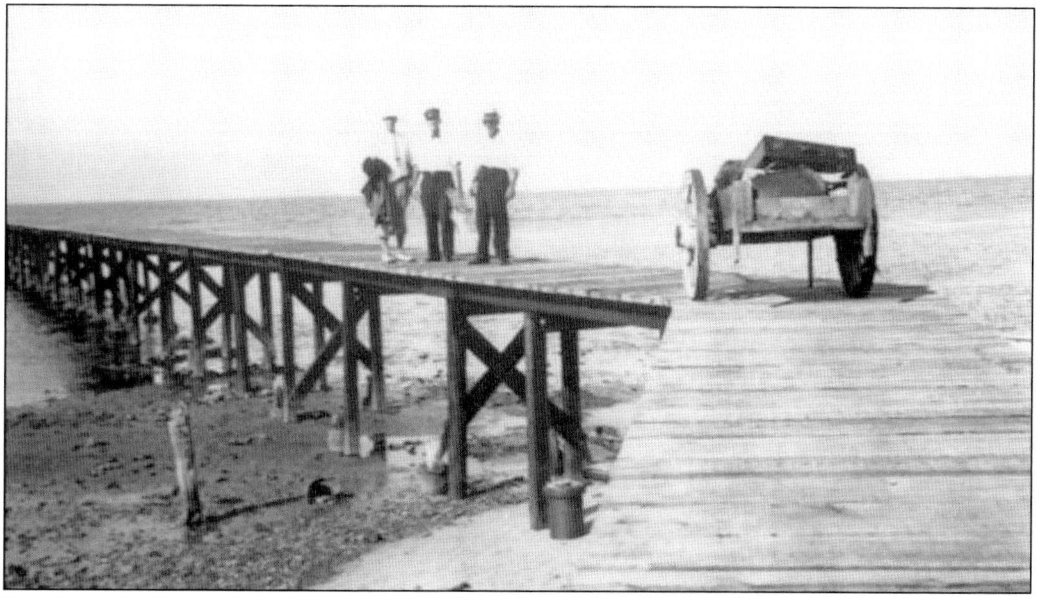

The boat dock at Pilot's Cove was a T-shaped, 900-foot boardwalk with a boat launch and hoist. Supplies delivered to the dock had to be loaded onto a wagon. Usually, Old Neb would be turned loose while the keepers made the trip and then hitched up again for the mile-long trip home. (SGLA.)

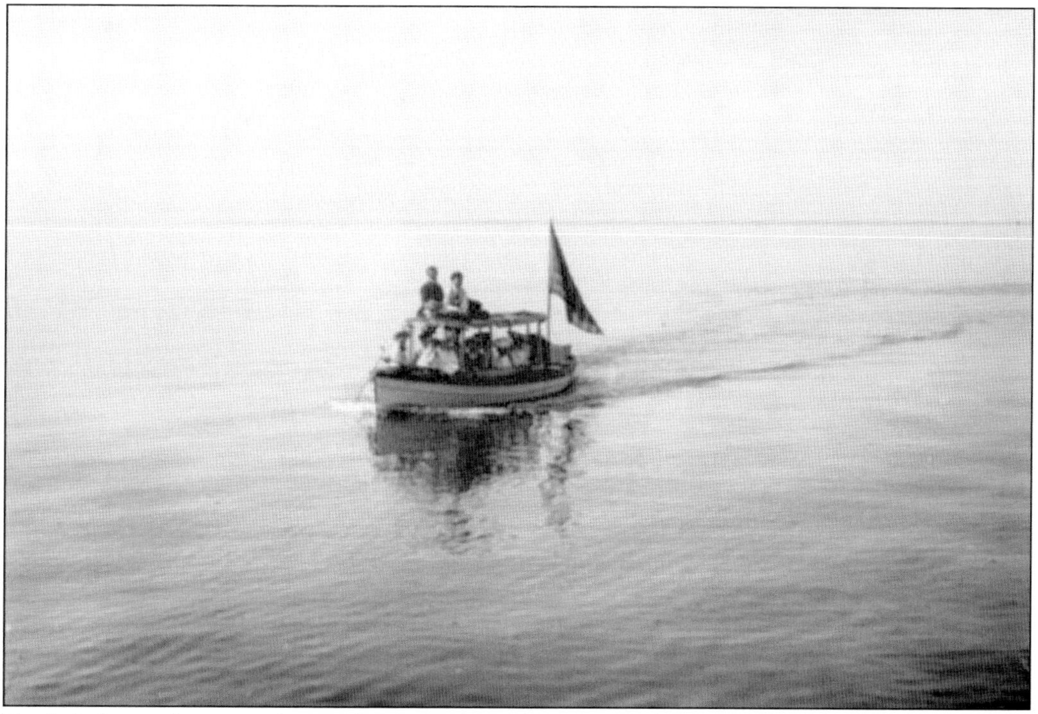

For lighthouse keepers, the availability of gasoline-powered marine engines was an immense help. Sometime after 1910, Cape St. George replaced or refitted its single-masted sailboat with a motor-powered launch. The one shown here was used by keeper J.C. Williams to ferry people from the mainland to destinations around the bay. (SAF.)

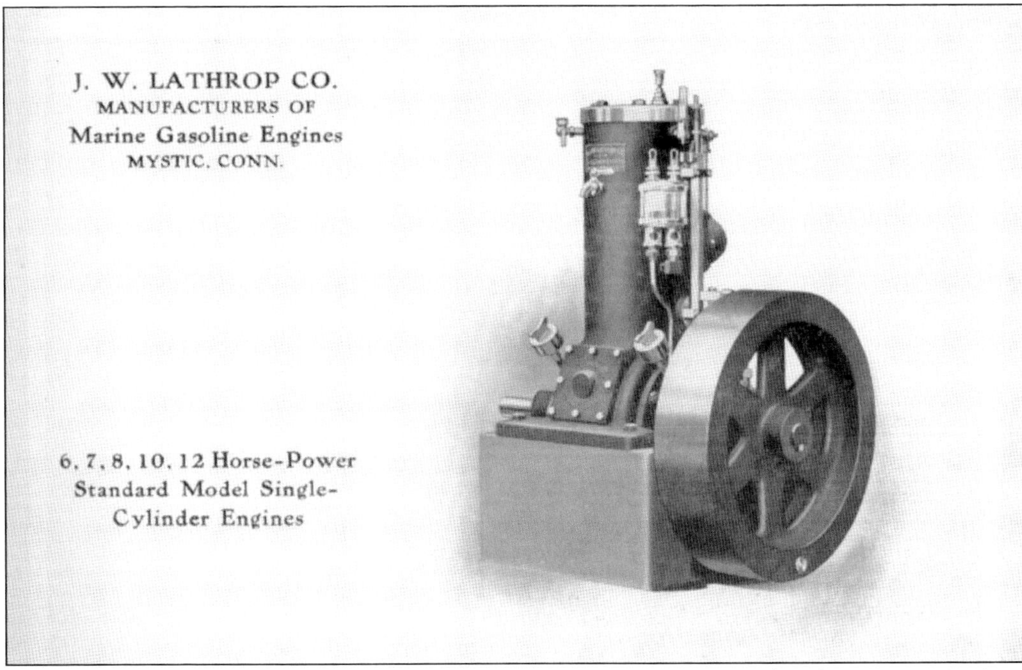

The motor launch at Cape St. George was powered by a gasoline-powered six-horsepower Lathrop engine similar to the one shown in this advertisement.

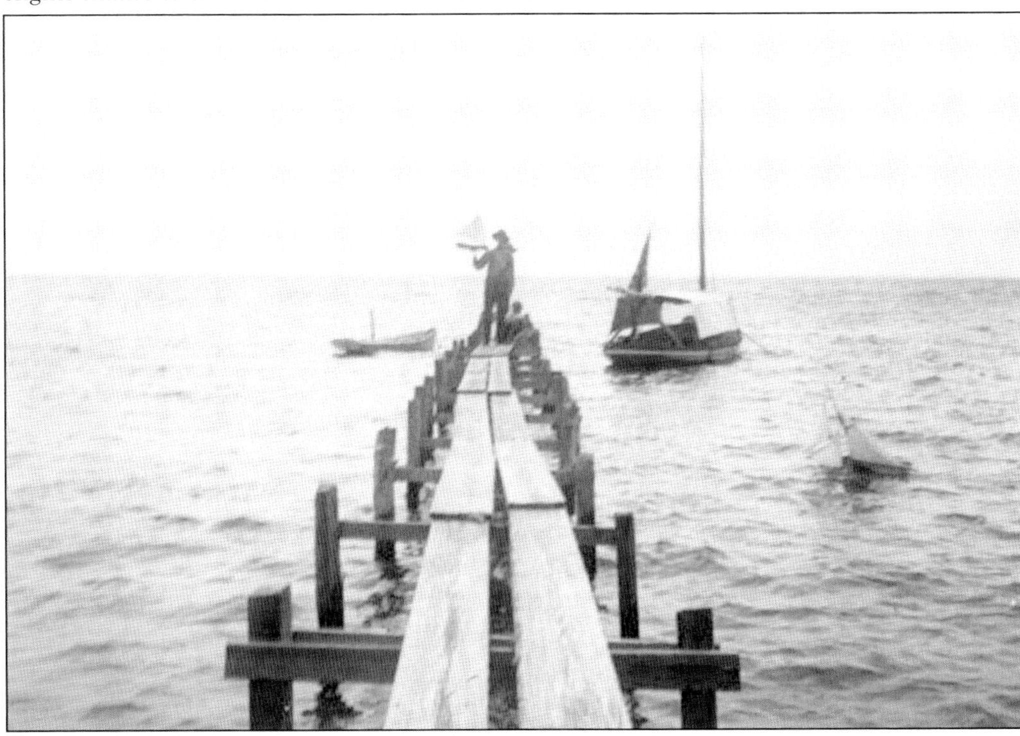

While their father, the keeper, was gone to Apalachicola, the Roberts boys would usually either fish or sail the wooden boats the men had made for them. This collection of wooden boats belonged to James C. Williams, keeper of range lights and bay lights near Apalachicola at the time. (SAF.)

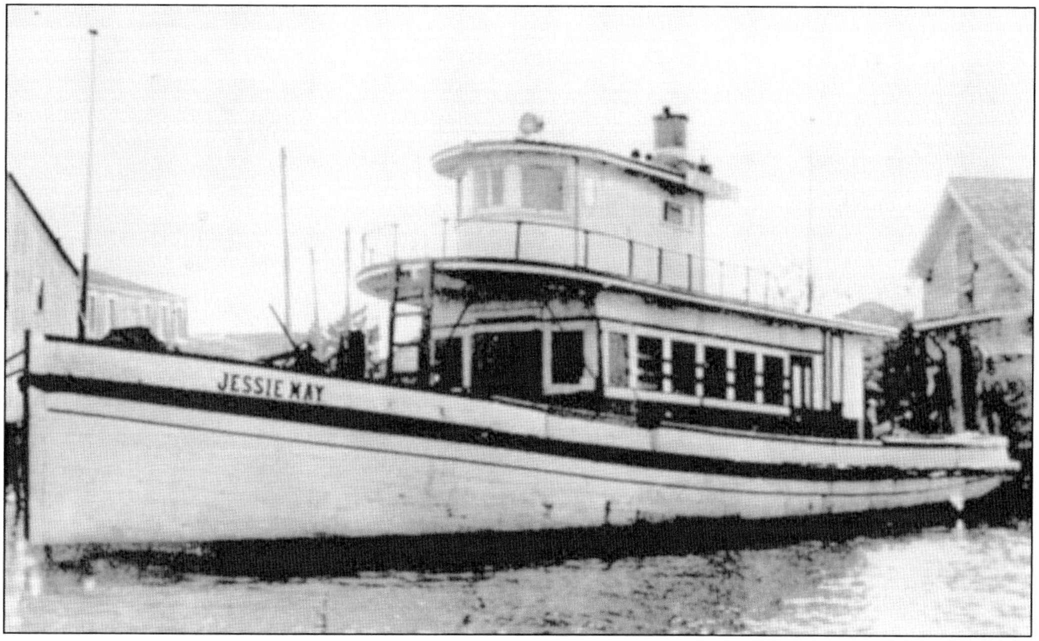

During the 1920s, Apalachicola steamboat captain Andrew L. Wing began a ferry service that ran to Eastpoint and the train depot in Carrabelle but also made two weekly excursions to St. George Island. This image shows his boat the *Jessie May* taking on passengers at the landing in Apalachicola. (SAF.)

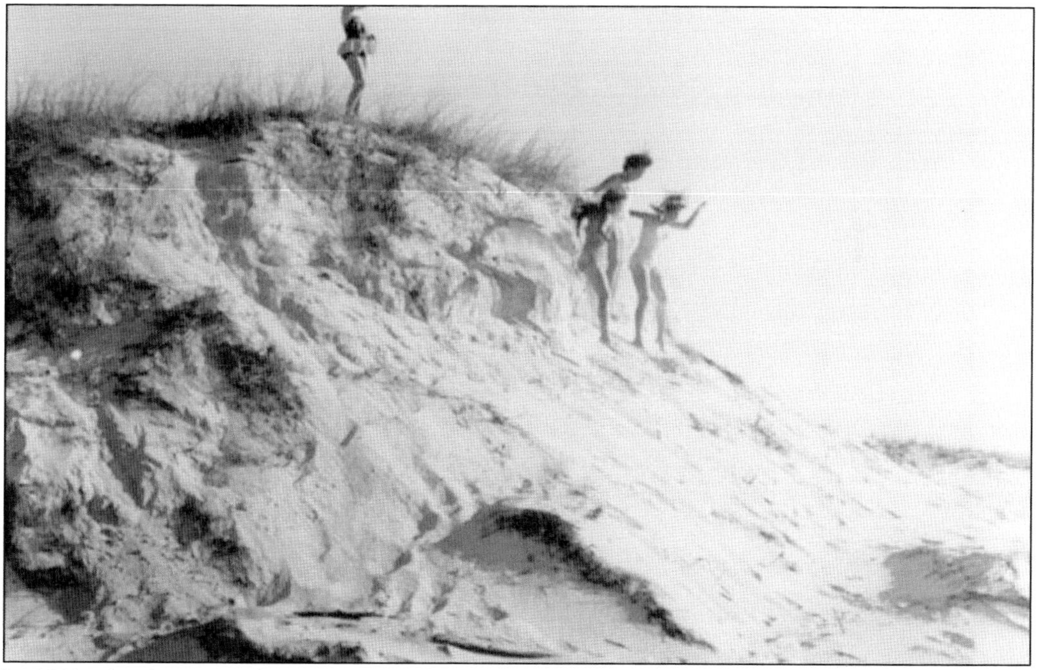

In 1911, a banker named George Saxon built a small hotel on "big" St. George Island that became a popular destination for beachgoers. Residents of Apalachicola frequently took Captain Wing's ferry or private boats to the island to bathe in the surf, fish, or jump from the dunes, as shown here. (SAF.)

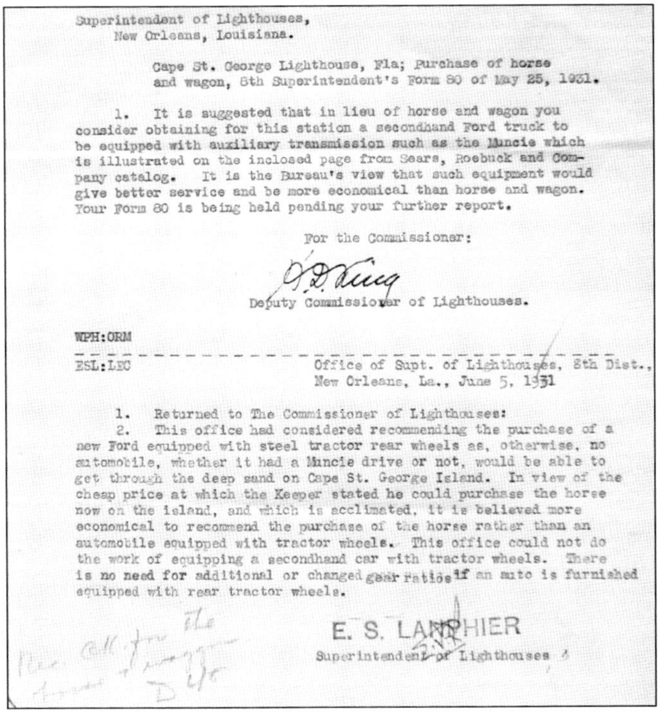

Superintendent of Lighthouses,
New Orleans, Louisiana.

Cape St. George Lighthouse, Fla; Purchase of horse and wagon, 8th Superintendent's Form 80 of May 25, 1931.

1. It is suggested that in lieu of horse and wagon you consider obtaining for this station a secondhand Ford truck to be equipped with auxiliary transmission such as the Muncie which is illustrated on the inclosed page from Sears, Roebuck and Company catalog. It is the Bureau's view that such equipment would give better service and be more economical than horse and wagon. Your Form 80 is being held pending your further report.

For the Commissioner:

O. D. King
Deputy Commissioner of Lighthouses.

WPH:ORM

ESL:LEC

Office of Supt. of Lighthouses, 8th Dist.,
New Orleans, La., June 5, 1931

1. Returned to The Commissioner of Lighthouses:
2. This office had considered recommending the purchase of a new Ford equipped with steel tractor rear wheels as, otherwise, no automobile, whether it had a Muncie drive or not, would be able to get through the deep sand on Cape St. George Island. In view of the cheap price at which the Keeper stated he could purchase the horse now on the island, and which is acclimated, it is believed more economical to recommend the purchase of the horse rather than an automobile equipped with tractor wheels. This office could not do the work of equipping a secondhand car with tractor wheels. There is no need for additional or changed gear ratios if an auto is furnished equipped with rear tractor wheels.

E. S. LANPHIER
Superintendent of Lighthouses

Although early automobiles could drive the beaches on St. George Island, they frequently became stuck in the sand. As shown in this memo, the lighthouse keepers turned down a request from the commissioner of lighthouses to replace Old Neb with a Ford automobile, and district superintendent Edward S. Lanphier agreed with the keepers. (SGLA.)

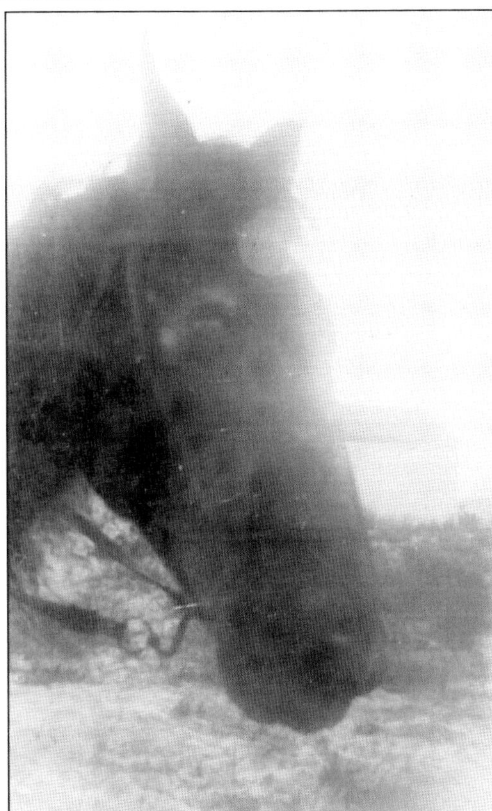

Old Neb, the lighthouse horse, was delighted to keep his job until he developed arthritis at the outset of World War II. He was well over 40 years old when he died. (SGLA.)

Seven

The Coast Guard Years and World War II

When Walter Roberts Jr. transferred to the St. Joseph Point lighthouse in 1938, Thornton K. Cooper was promoted to keeper. John W. Montgomery was sent from Cape San Blas to undertake duties as assistant keeper. However, when word came that the Bureau of Lighthouses would be transferred to the US Coast Guard in 1939, Cooper became unsettled. The gentle bachelor who had helped Walter Roberts make toys for his children killed himself, and left John Montgomery as acting keeper to deal with the aftermath. The US Lighthouse Service quickly transferred Sullivan R. White from Louisiana to assume duties as keeper.

After 150 years of operation under the Departments of Treasury and Commerce, the US Lighthouse Service ceased to exist. The Coast Guard gave all keepers a chance to enlist or resign. The keepers at Cape St. George both enlisted to serve during the coming war and were both assigned the rank of boatswain's mate first class; the Coast Guard did not have a rating of lighthouse keeper. The era of the Lighthouse Service that had begun in 1789 came to an end. Keepers White and Montgomery both carried forward their duties as they understood them, keeping up the light and the dwellings, the log books, and all necessary records.

During World War II, the Cape St. George Lighthouse was used as an observation tower, although a separate wooden structure was built nearby. The keeper and assistant keeper both had wives and young families, but they were shortly joined by servicemen who conducted beach patrols and guarded against German U-boats.

During the war, the US government leased St. George Island from its owners, Bill Wilson and Clyde Atkinson, to be used for D-Day landing practice for infantry stationed at Camp Gordon Johnston outside Carrabelle. The beaches were used for landing craft, dirigibles, and strafing practice. Visitors still occasionally find spent brass casings of .50 caliber ammunition.

World War II brought the development of accurate radio navigation called LORAN (Long Range Aid to Navigation), and the need to maintain lighthouses diminished. In 1949, the Coast Guard dismantled the reliable old Fresnel lens and installed an aero beacon that operated from a large electric battery. The aero beacon flashed at six-second intervals, unlike the fixed white light that had characterized the station since 1833. Daily care of the beacon was not needed, and crews simply checked the bulb and changed the battery every few months. After 1949, no one lived at the light station.

Sullivan White retired to Apalachicola, and John Montgomery moved on to other stations. He finished his service at Carysfort Reef Lighthouse in the Florida Keys. With no keepers maintaining the old living quarters, storms and wind-blown sand took their toll. Although the Cape St. George Lighthouse continued operating until 1994, the beach gradually eroded. After Bob Sikes Cut was dredged in 1954, neighboring St. George Island was permanently separated from Little St. George Island. St. George Island was developed for the growing tourist industry, and the abandoned lighthouse on Little St. George became a place for boaters' picnics.

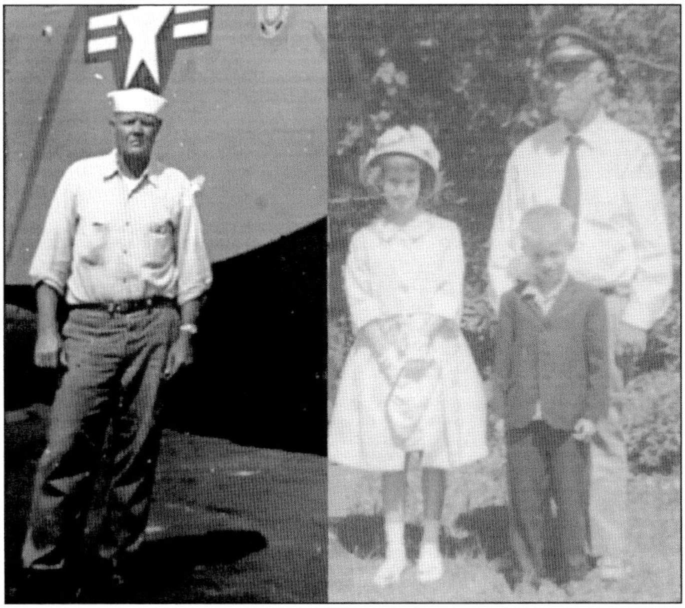

On June 7, 1939, Congress approved President Roosevelt's Reorganization Plan No. 11, which transferred the Lighthouse Service from the Department of Commerce to the Coast Guard. The plan transferred 5,200 personnel, 64 buoy tenders, 30 depots, and 17 district offices. Assistant Keeper John W. Montgomery (left) and Keeper Sullivan White (right) packed away their blue uniforms and reported for duty. Keeper White is pictured with his grandchildren, Theresa and Michael Millender. (Courtesy of Michael Millender and Leonard Montgomery.)

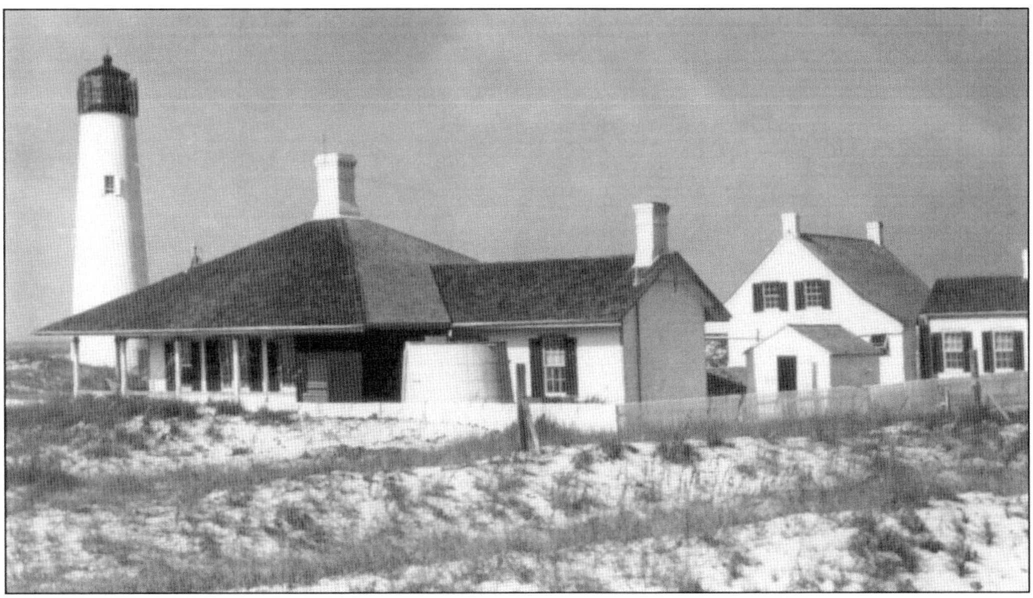

A US Coast Guard photo from about 1950 shows that Sullivan White and John Montgomery kept up the traditions of the Lighthouse Service in splendid fashion. John's son Leonard Montgomery said that every time he saw his father, he was using a paint brush, and that the keepers painted the entire establishment twice a year. Both men's families lived in the two keepers' quarters. (SGLA.)

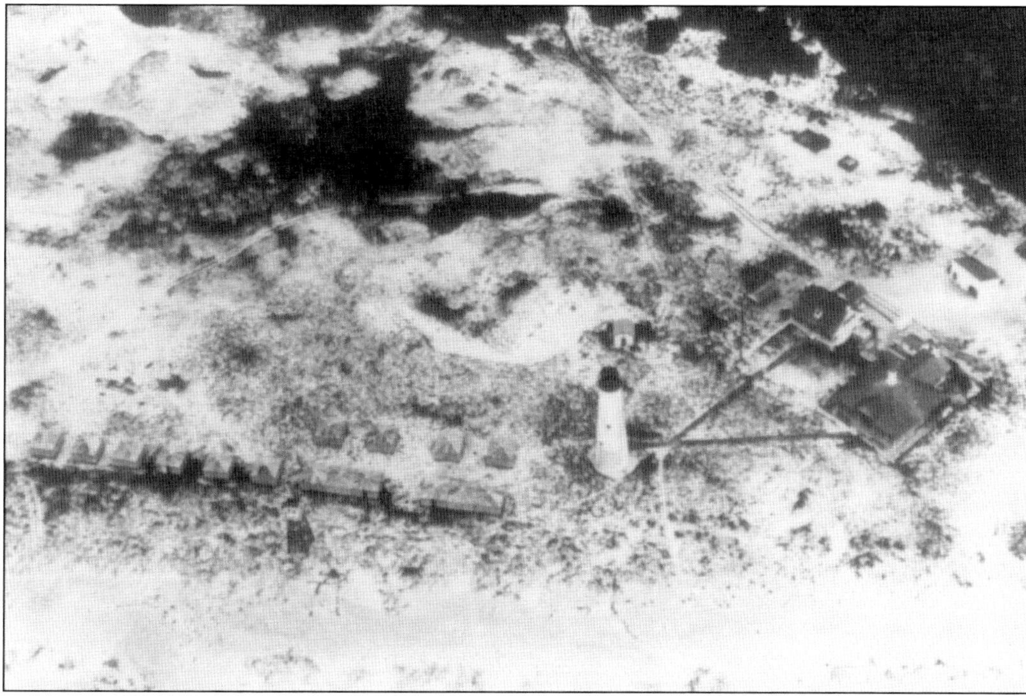

An aerial photograph taken during World War II shows US Coast Guard barracks and an observation tower that were built next to the Cape St. George Lighthouse Station to watch for enemy U-boats and aircraft. (USCG.)

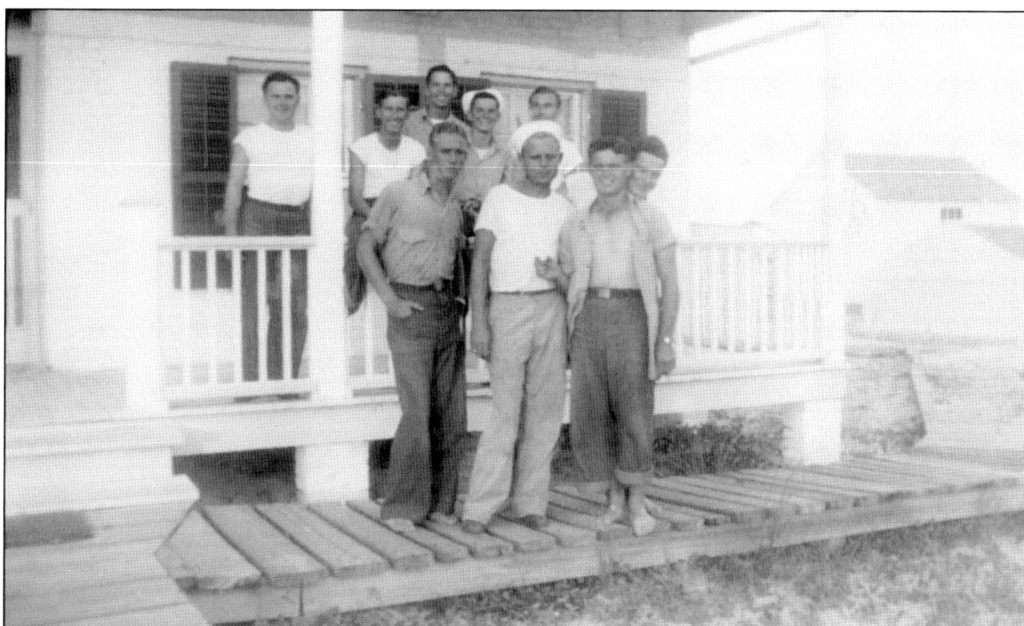

A group of US Coast Guard coast watchers poses on the porch of the lighthouse keeper's dwelling during or shortly after World War II. This period marked the end of the long era of lighthouse keepers who helped guide ship traffic along the coast, through the passes, and around the oyster bars. (SGLA.)

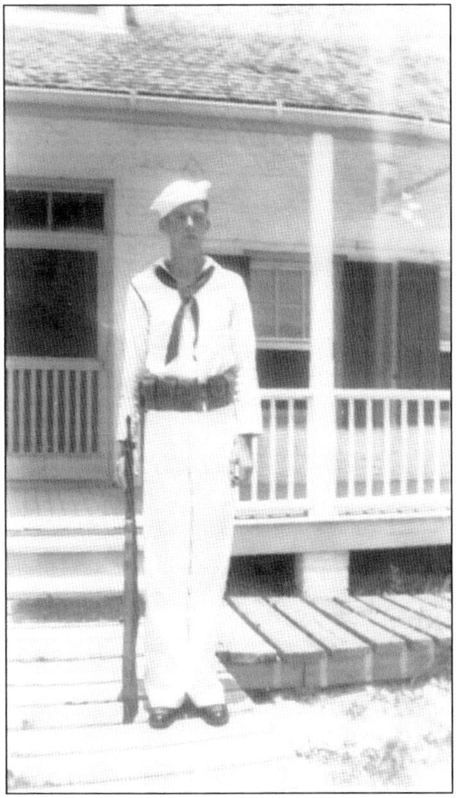

As shown by this armed serviceman, Coast Guardsmen stayed on alert to watch for U-boat activity and possible espionage along the Gulf Coast as the Germans tried to intercept oil shipments from New Orleans. (USCG.)

Just after daylight on June 29, 1942, the lighthouse keepers spotted smoke on the horizon and telephoned the Coast Guard station in Apalachicola. German U-boat *U-67* had torpedoed a British Empire-class tanker named the *Empire Mica* carrying 12,000 tons of oil. (US Naval Institute.)

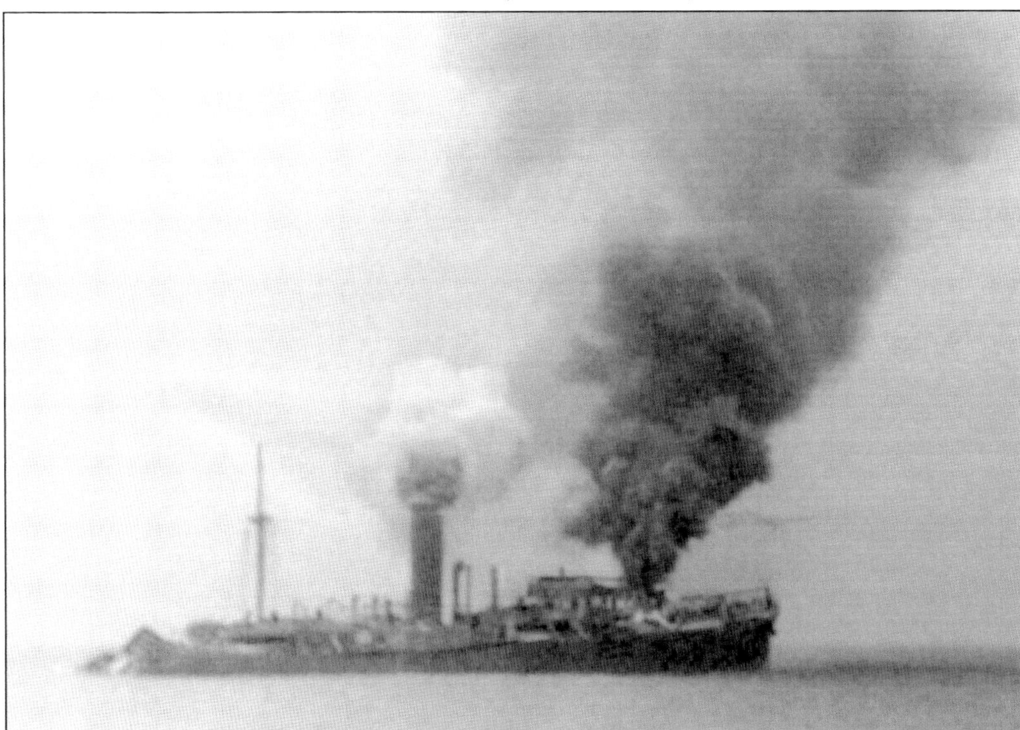

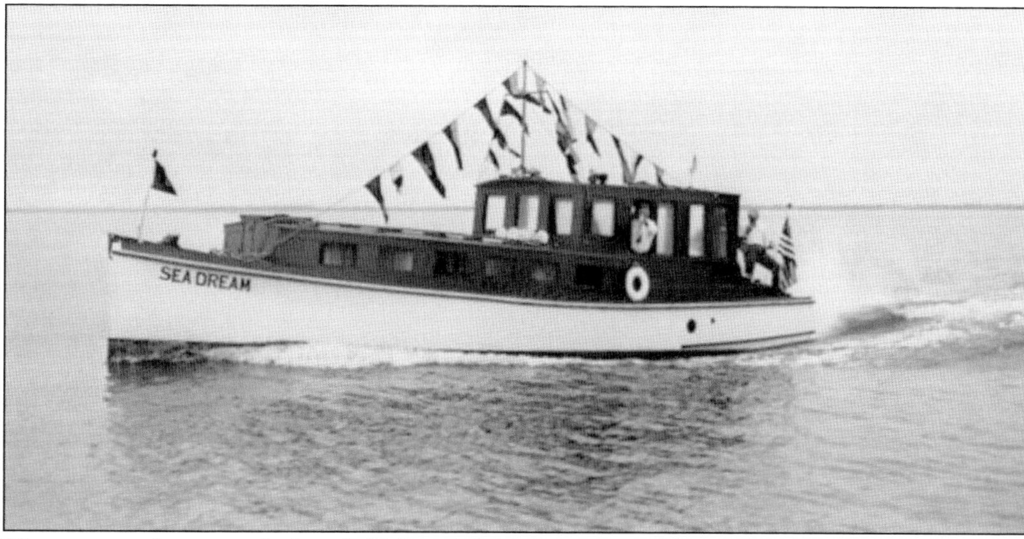

Three rescue boats, including W.F. Randolph's *Sea Dream* (shown here) sped to the burning tanker. One lifeboat with 14 survivors was found, and the men were taken to the hospital. Sadly, 33 crewmen died. The *Empire Mica* is now a diving spot and fishing reef offshore. *U-67* was sunk the next year by naval depth charges. (SAF.)

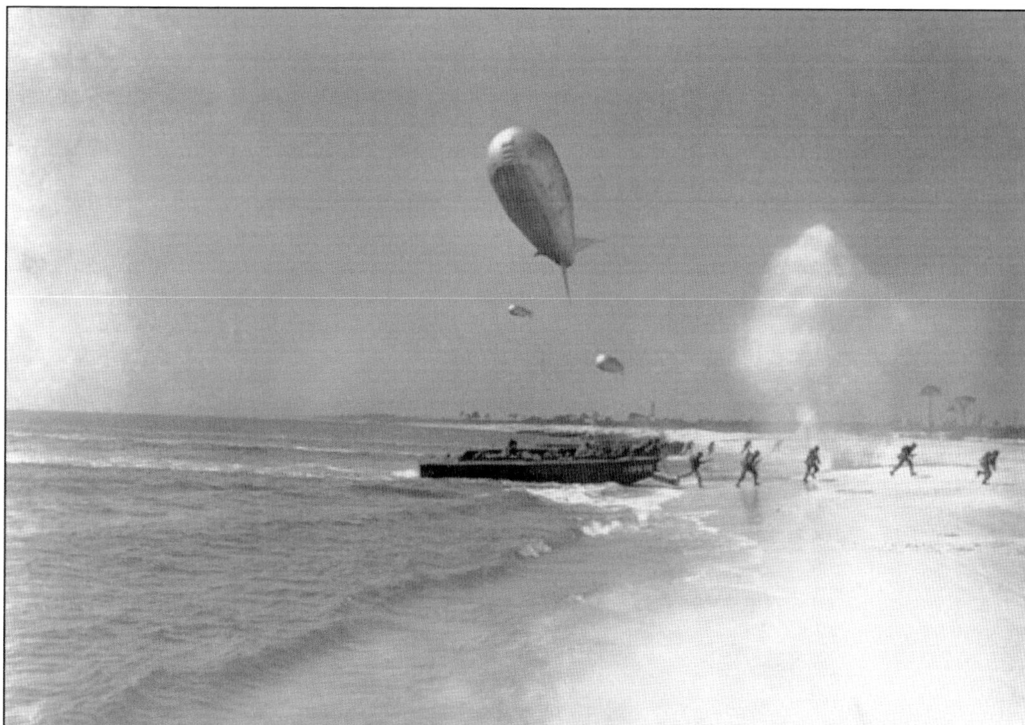

During World War II, the US Army established Camp Gordon Johnston between Carrabelle and Lanark. Barracks were built to house several thousand soldiers who were training for the invasion of Europe. Soldiers at the camp practiced landing on the beaches of St. George Island and Dog Island. In some cases, live ammunition was used, and .50 caliber ammunition casings can still be found on the islands. (SAF.)

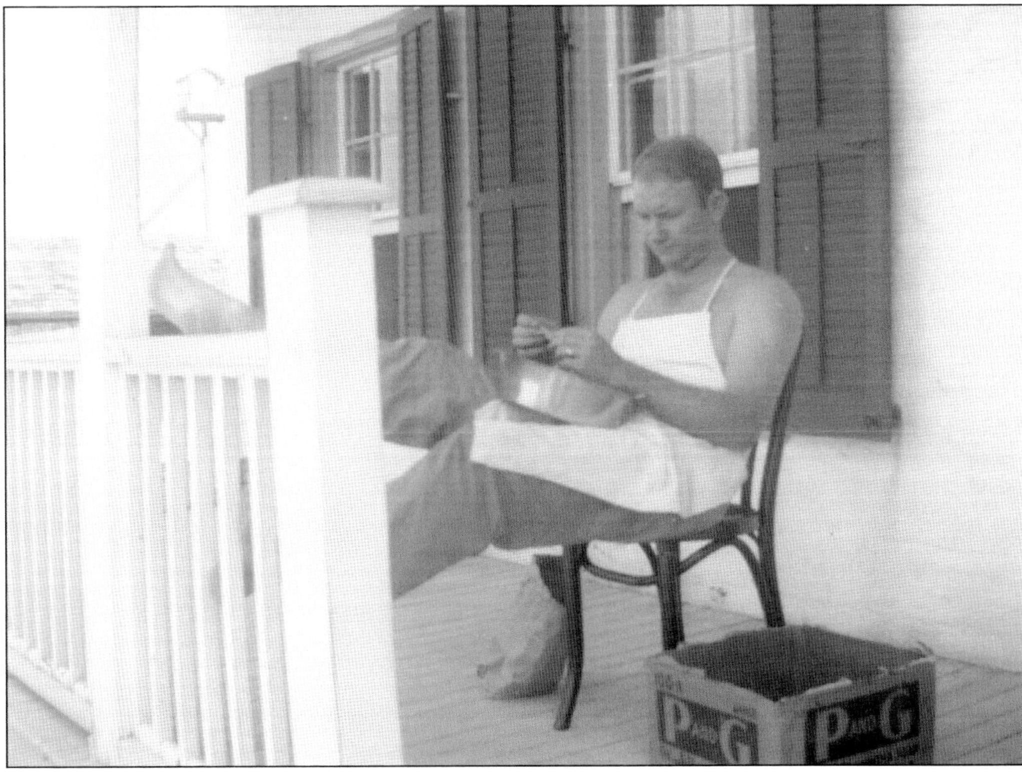

Except for the Empire Mica incident, life was quiet at Cape St. George. Here, a Coast Guardsman shells peas or beans for a meal. (SGLA.)

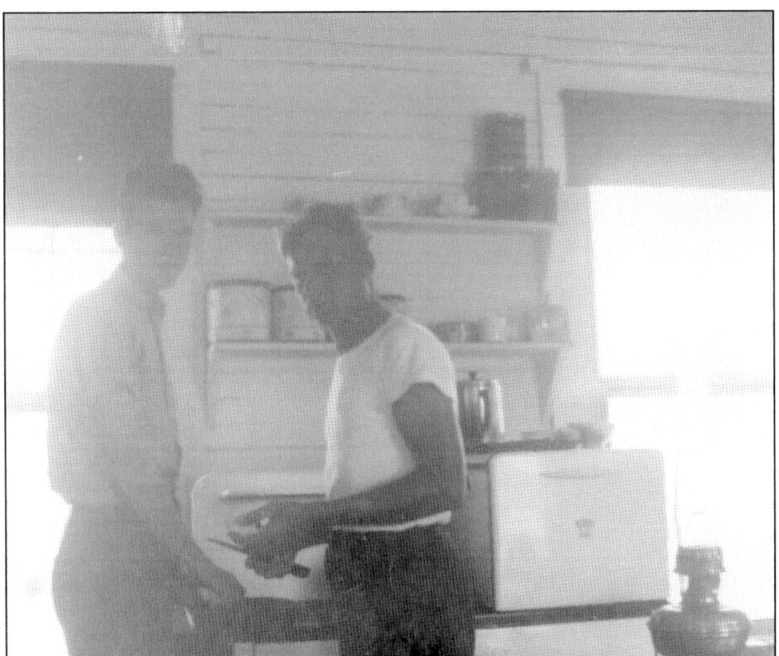

In the only interior photograph from Cape St. George, two Coast Guardsmen continue with meal preparation. Note the kerosene-powered refrigerator, coffee percolator, and Aladdin oil lamp at right. (SGLA.)

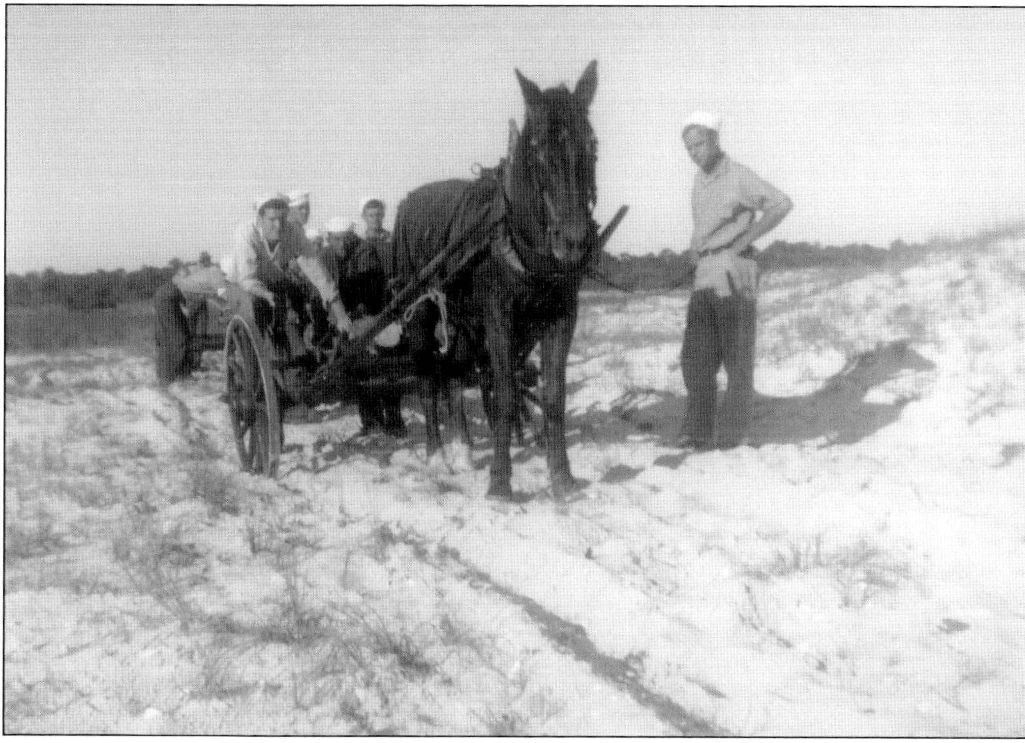

Old Neb, the lighthouse horse, stayed on long after keeper Edward Porter and his successors moved on. Here, Neb is hooked up to a wagon to pull a gang of Coast Guardsmen over the sand road to the boat dock. (SGLA.)

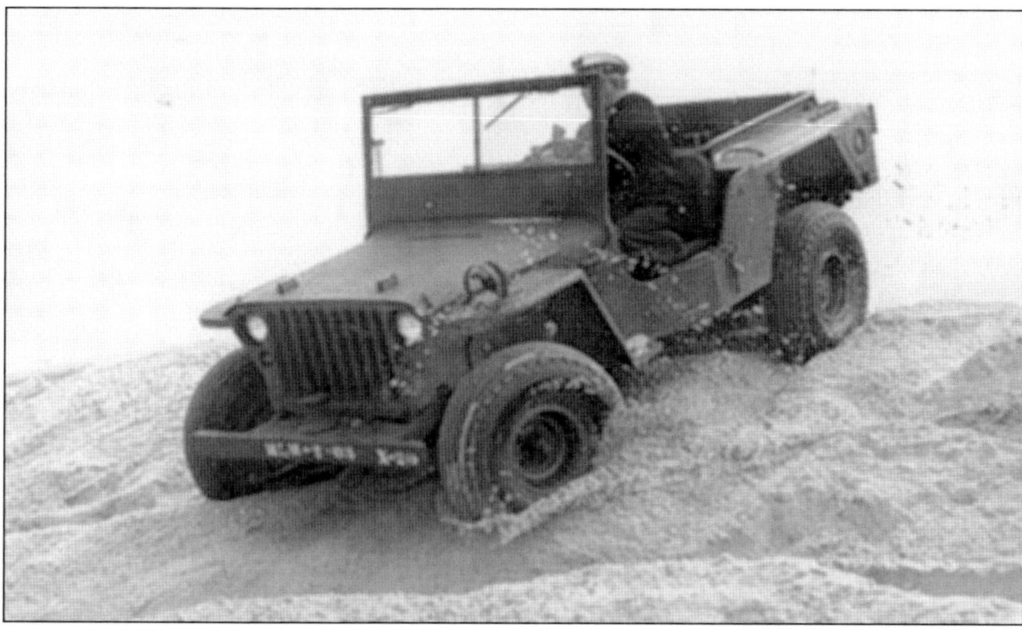

The Coast Guard sent a Jeep to replace Old Neb, but the lighthouse keepers refused to give up the horse. They secured a ration of corn and oats for him and kept him at the station until he developed severe arthritis and had to be euthanized. (USCG.)

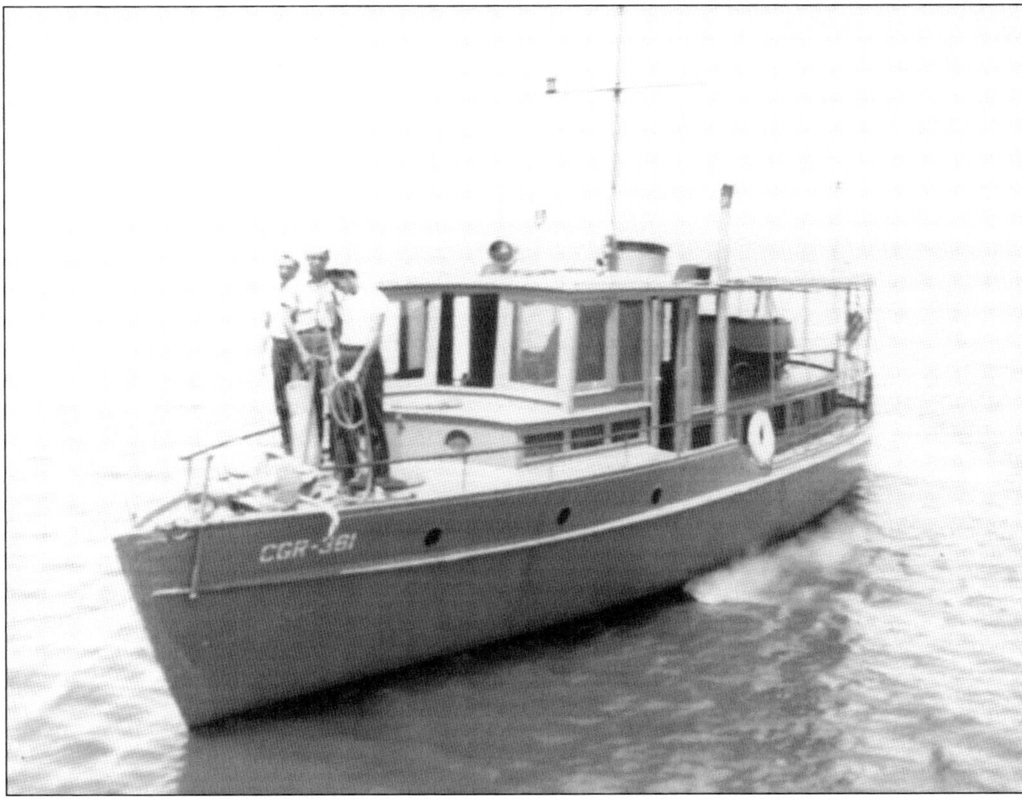

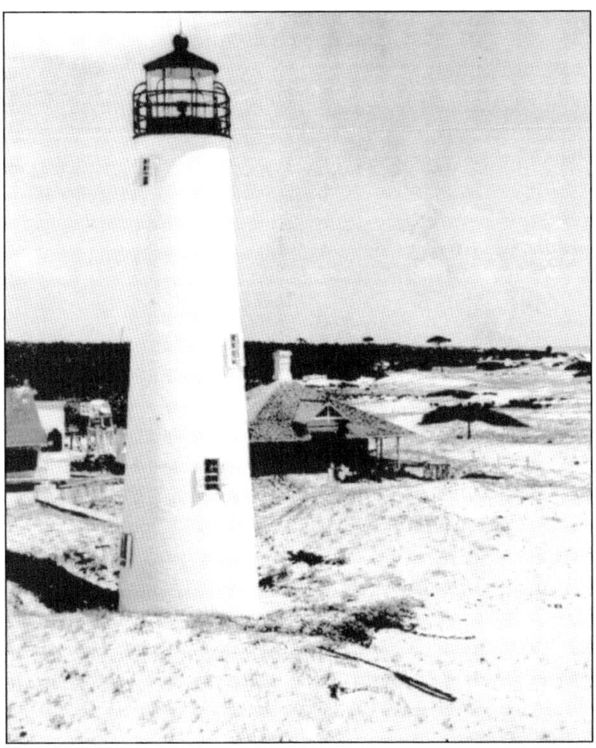

Servicemen aboard a US Coast Guard motor launch prepare to dock at the wharf on Little St. George Island. (USCG.)

In 1949, the reliable old Fresnel lens and its oil vapor lamp were removed from the Cape St. George Lighthouse, and a new, battery-powered aero beacon was installed. The beacon is visible in the lantern room in this photograph. The days of lamps with wicks fueled by whale oil or kerosene were gone, never to return. (SGLA.)

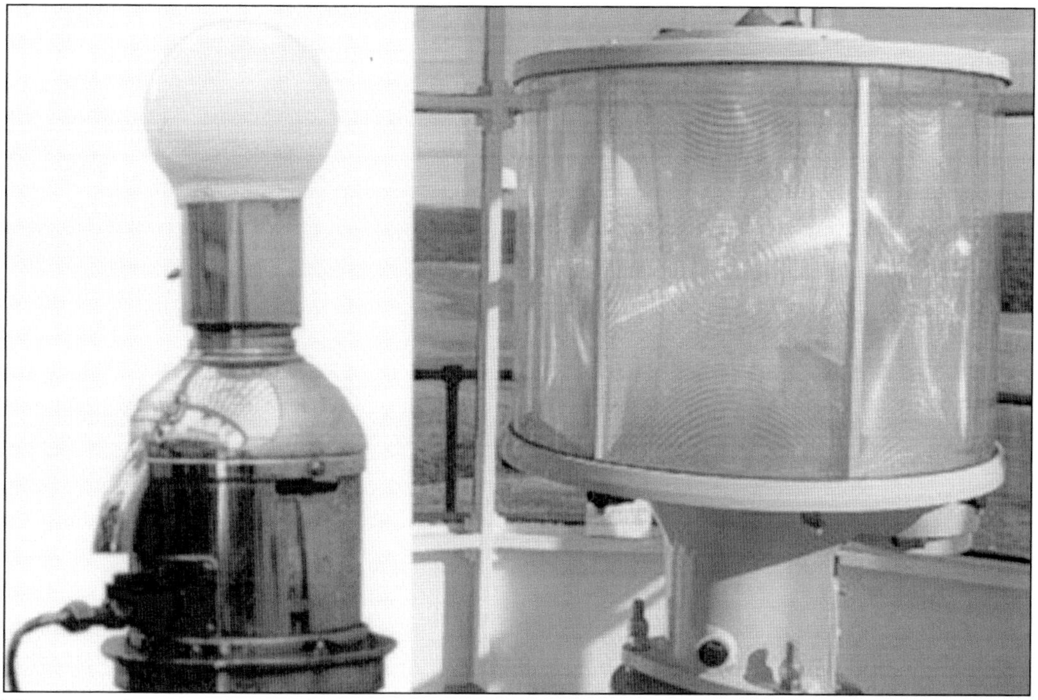

The incandescent oil vapor lamp with a mantle (left) was replaced by a new aero beacon (right) that would remain until the Coast Guard decommissioned the lighthouse in 1994. (USLHS.)

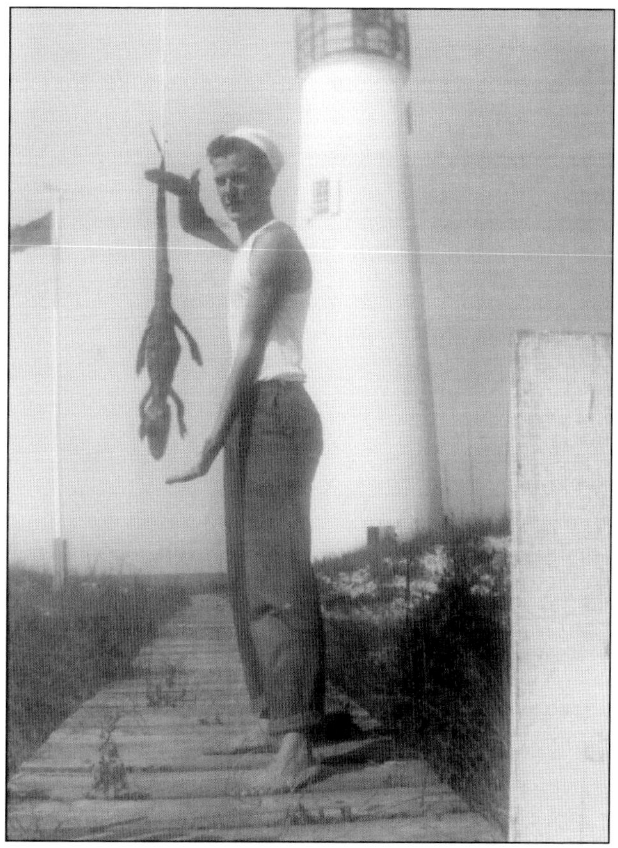

Unlike the lighthouse keepers, the Coast Guardsmen had fewer duties and were bored living on Cape St. George. Their ennui was occasionally broken when young alligators or other wildlife stopped by the lighthouse ponds and beaches. (SGLA.)

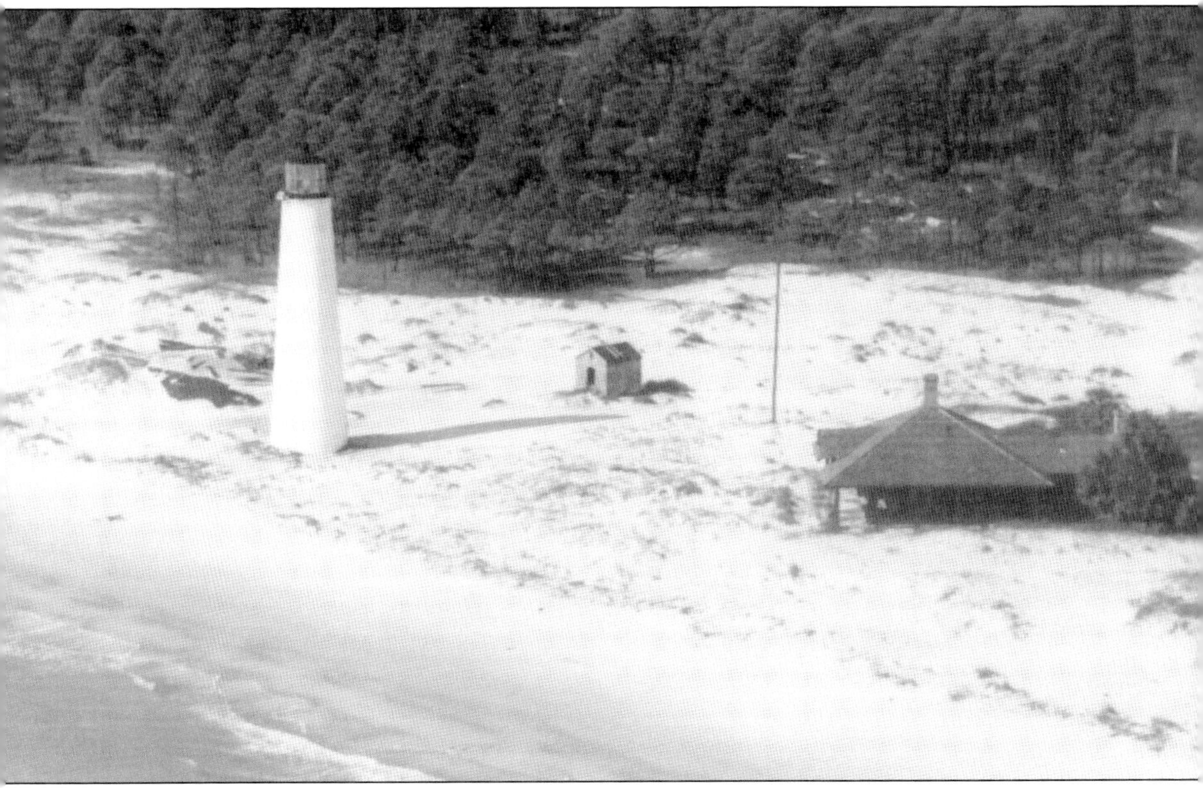

After World War II, keeper Sullivan White retired from the Coast Guard and moved to Apalachicola, and John Montgomery was sent on to other Coast Guard stations, ending his career while serving at the Carysfort Reef Lighthouse south of Miami. With no routine maintenance, the Cape St. George Light Station began to deteriorate, as shown in this aerial photograph. The weather has stripped the paint from the oil house, and the keeper's dwellings are deteriorating. The only family left on the island was Pearl Porter Marshall and her husband, Herbert, who lived in the Marshall House near the dock until Herbert died in 1976. (SGLA.)

Eight

Winds of Change

Between 1935 and 1965, major changes in transportation and navigation eliminated the need for lighthouses as aids to navigation in Apalachicola Bay. The Intracoastal Waterway was routed through the bay to the river, but was primarily used by barge traffic, commercial fishermen, and recreational boaters. Logging depleted the forests, and most sawmills closed, ending much of the large-scale shipping from the region. Longleaf forests were replanted in slash pine and loblolly. Four dams that were built on the Apalachicola and Chattahoochee Rivers between Columbus and the bay limited most river traffic to barges, and in 1954, the shipping channel called Bob Sikes Cut ended the use of West Pass for most maritime traffic. As bridges and coastal highways were completed, transportation shifted from ships and railroads to trucking and even aircraft.

By 1950, the Cape St. George Lighthouse employed an aero beacon that flashed every six seconds, but the dwellings were unoccupied. Herbert Marshall, who lived on Little St. George Island with his wife, Pearl Porter Marshall, got permission from the Coast Guard to use the floorboards from the old keeper's house in his new home near the bay, and windstorms and vandalism took their toll on the remaining structures.

Apalachicola's economy changed from lumber to seafood production, and the oyster and shrimp fisheries thrived. In the 1950s, tourism began to develop. Daily ferry service began taking visitors to St. George Island and Dog Island starting in 1955. Developers Bill Wilson and Clyde Atkinson surveyed their holdings on St. George Island and laid out plats, and state representative Bryant Patton passed legislation that allowed Franklin County to build a toll bridge. The Sikes Cut channel, thankfully, restricted the development to "big" St. George Island. Pearl Porter Marshall sold her holdings on Little St. George Island to the state, with the goal of creating an undeveloped wildlife refuge for shorebirds and sea turtles.

In 1978, the United States developed a satellite navigation system, and in 1993 launched a 24-satellite system that enabled Global Positioning to supplant LORAN as the dominant system of navigation. In 1994, the Coast Guard decommissioned the lighthouse on Cape St. George. The Coast Guard ceded the property to the State of Florida after Hurricane Opal struck in 1995 and moved the tower off its foundation. The tower was repaired and straightened but could not be moved. Storms reshaped the island, and the hurricane season of 2005 undercut the 1852 lighthouse.

Many new residents loved the old lighthouse, and, anticipating future needs, founded the St. George Lighthouse Association in 2004. Immediately after the tower toppled in 2005, they began working with the Florida Department of Environmental Protection with the goal of salvaging and rebuilding the 1852 lighthouse on St. George Island.

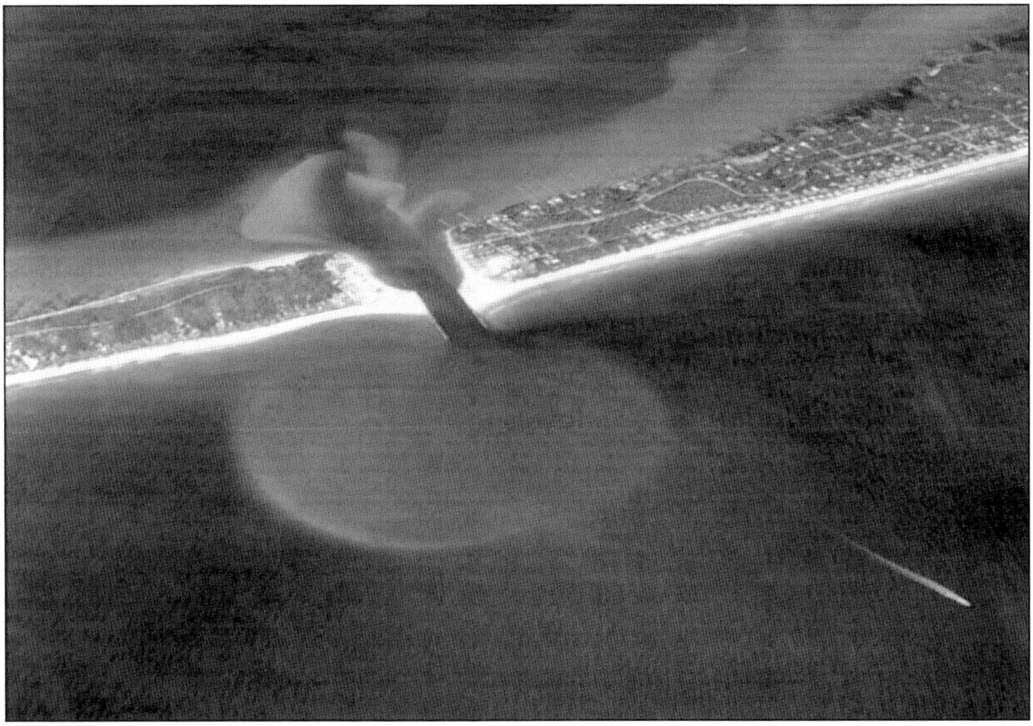

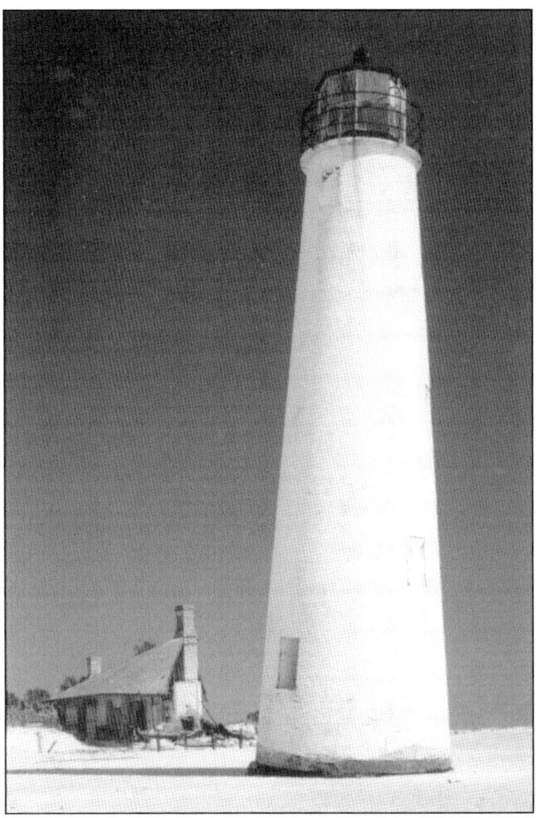

In 1954, the US Army Corps of Engineers dredged a shipping channel called Bob Sikes Cut through St. George Island. Sikes Cut permanently separated Little St. George Island from Big St. George. Development of St. George Island as a vacation destination accelerated after the Bryant Patton Bridge was completed in 1965, but Little St. George Island remained uninhabited. It is presently operated as a wildlife reserve by the Florida Department of Environmental Protection. (SGLA.)

From 1960 to 1990, the Cape St. George Lighthouse was largely unattended. The beach gradually eroded, and storm surges could easily swamp the old light station. The original keeper's dwelling was gone by 1990, and the oil house and 1878 keeper's dwelling were falling apart. (SGLA.)

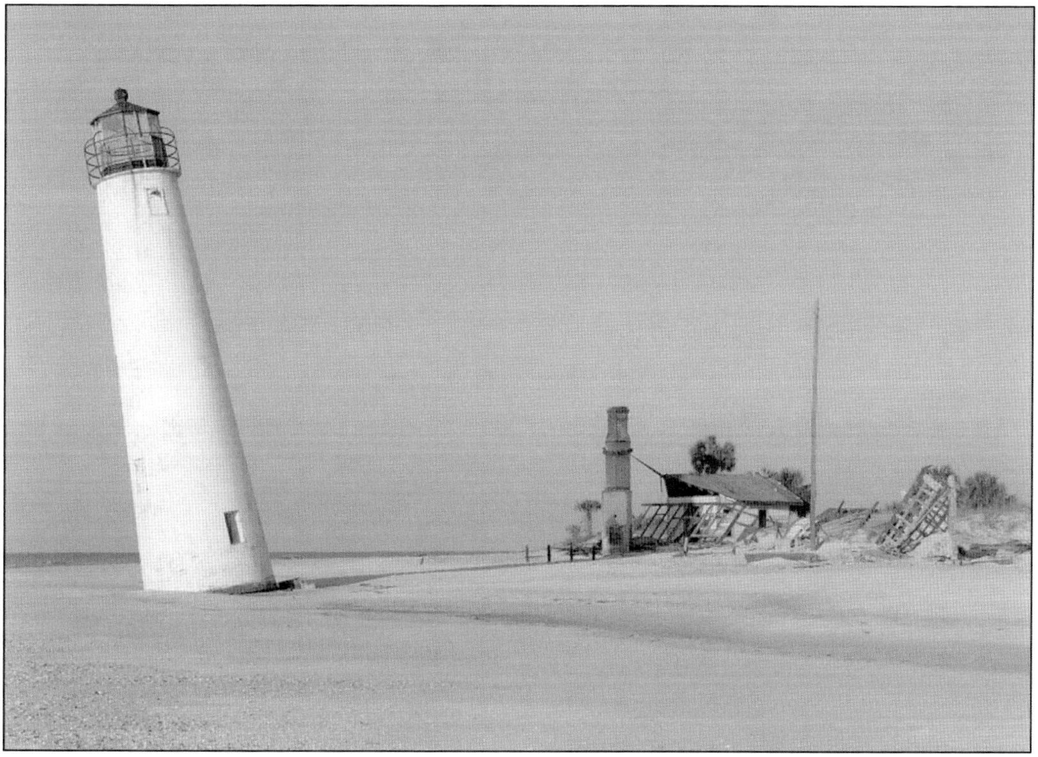

Just one year after the Coast Guard had decommissioned the lighthouse and removed the beacon, Hurricane Opal struck. The 1995 storm surge moved the lighthouse off its foundation, making it lean dramatically, and damaged all the remaining structures that had been intact in 1950. (SGLA.)

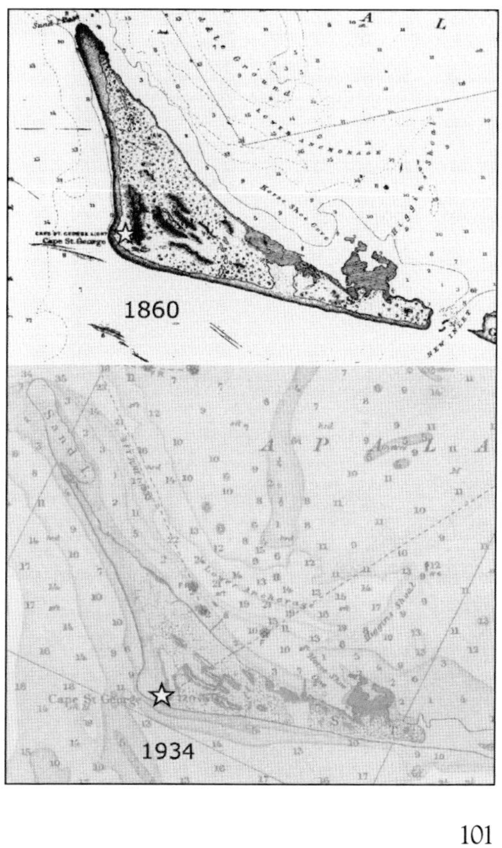

Geologists have analyzed progressive changes at Cape St. George from historical maps and aerial photographs. The position of the lighthouse relative to the "heel" where Cape St. George bends toward the northwest has changed dramatically, with progressive beach recession toward the northwest (like most of St. George Island), which removed nearly all of the original 400-yard setback seen in the 1860 map and left the lighthouse sitting at the shoreline by 1934. Also note that New Inlet and Sand Inlet closed, so Little St. George Island was part of "big" St. George Island. (JLH.)

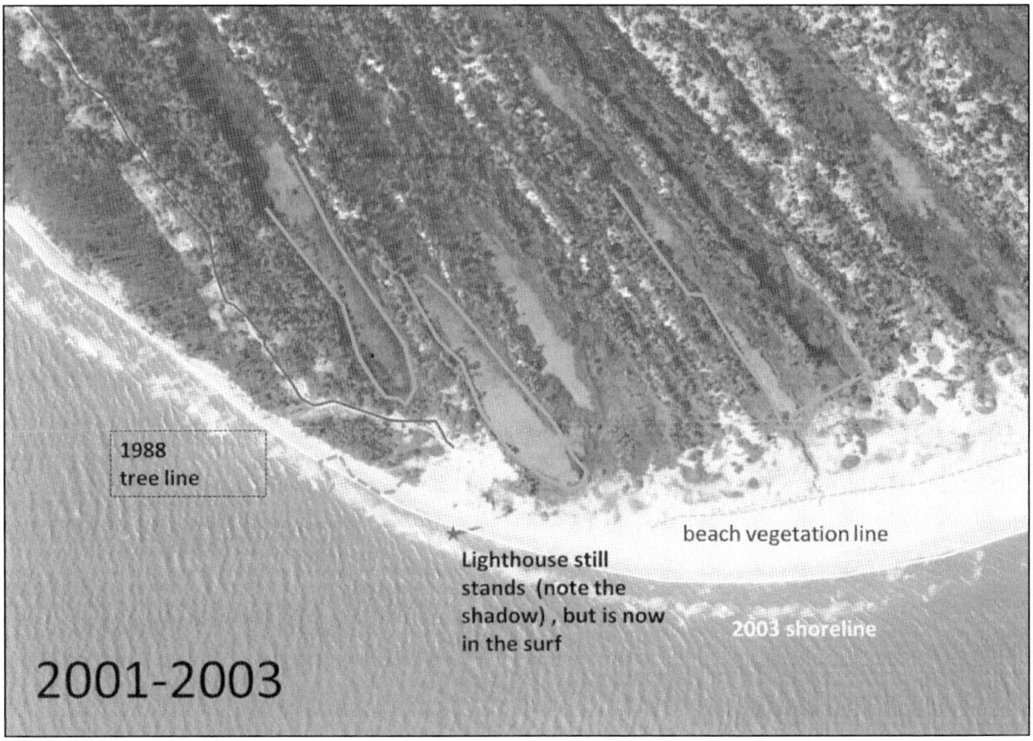

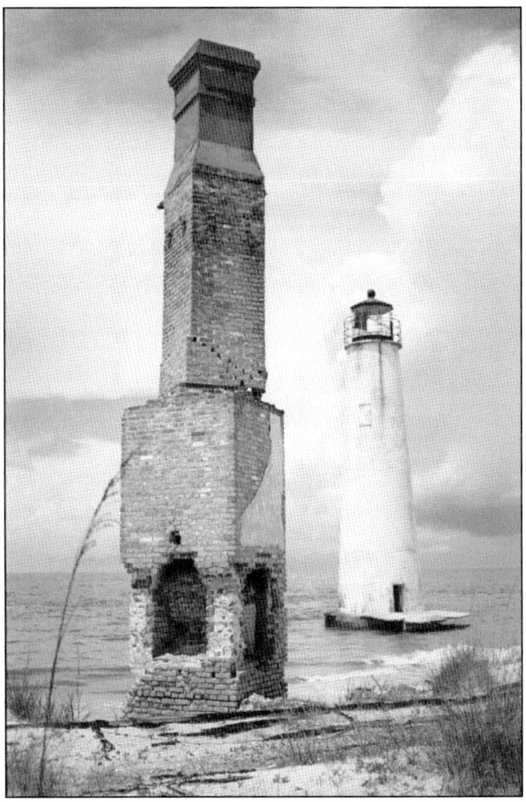

Aerial photographs show the lighthouse sitting in the surf zone by 2001. Comparison with earlier photographs indicates the migrating shoreline had encroached on the former tree line and old sand road that had served as the route to the bay for over 150 years. Despite persistent northwest beach recession that occurred for at least 100 years (which would have eventually stranded and destroyed the lighthouse), it was in fact rapid net erosion off the southwest side of the cape (a pattern reversal) starting in the 1960s that ultimately undermined the lighthouse. (Dr. Jim Mott.)

After Hurricane Opal struck, the old brick chimney was the only remnant of the 1878 keeper's dwelling. (SGLA.)

With the aero beacon and glass panes gone, only the "bird cage" and gallery remained atop the now unpainted 1852 lighthouse. Rust stains from the iron railings began seeping over the white paint. (SGLA.)

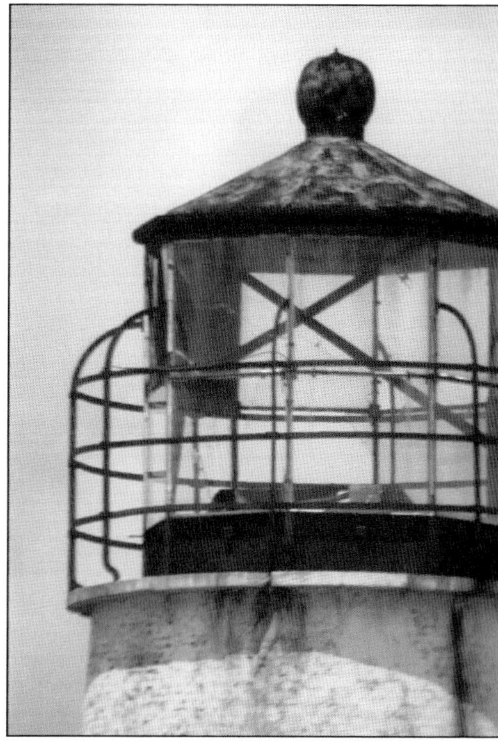

After Hurricane Opal, the Save the Light Association was founded by John Lee, editor of the *Apalachicola Times* newspaper. The organization paid Tallahassee contractor Bill Grimes to straighten the tower and protect it with a concrete collar. His crew was able to straighten the tower by digging behind it with a backhoe. Sadly, it was not possible to raise funds to move the lighthouse out of the surf zone. (SGLA.)

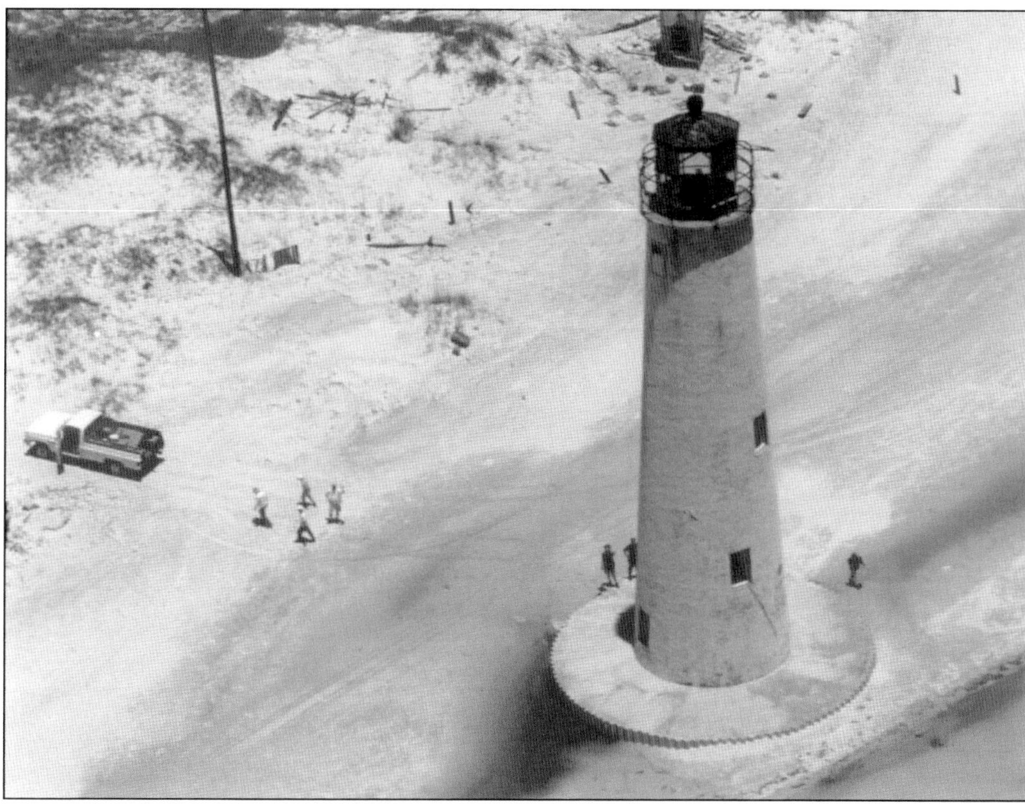

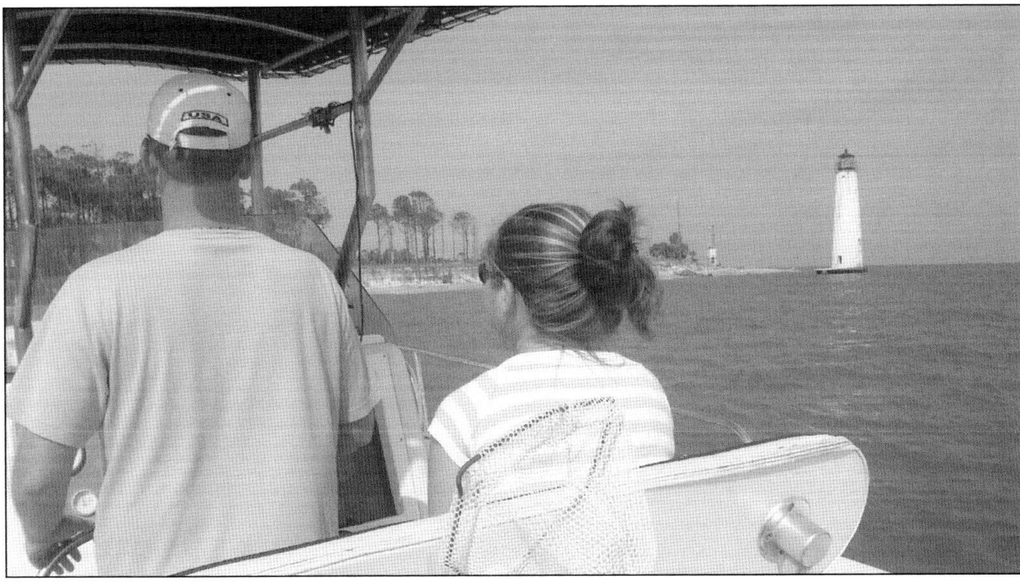

By the year 2000, the 1852 lighthouse was situated in the surf on the Little St. George Island Wildlife Refuge, which is managed by the Apalachicola National Estuarine Research Reserve as part of the Florida Department of Environmental Protection. As shown in this photograph from 2004, it was a popular destination for boaters and kayakers to picnic. (Bruce Robie.)

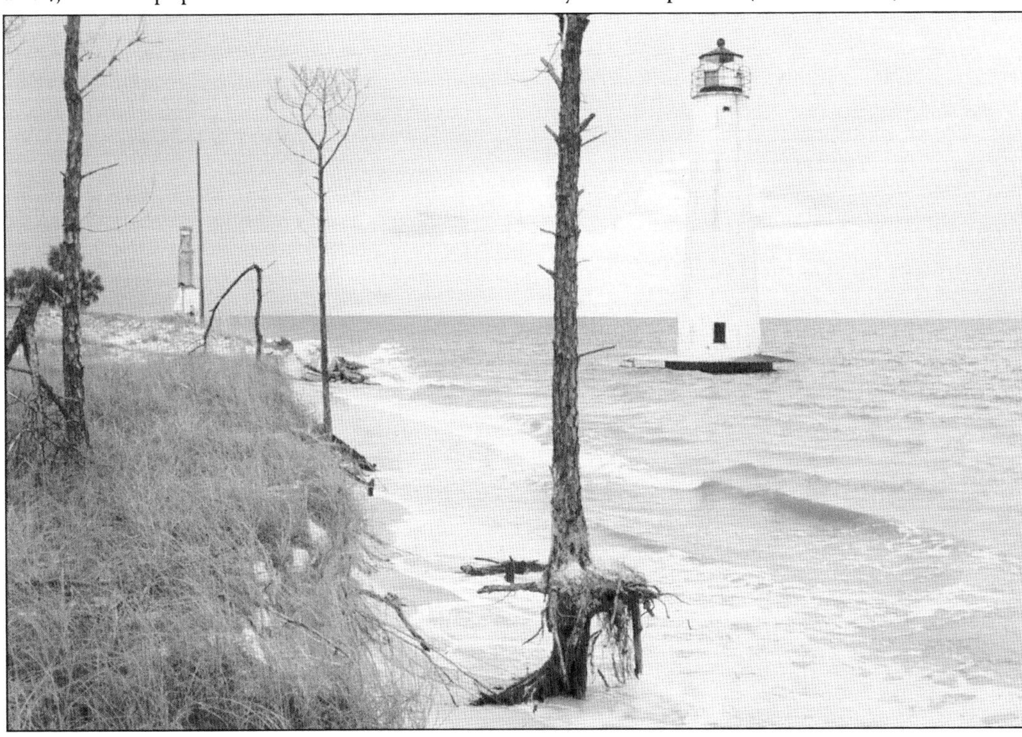

Many visitors to the 1852 lighthouse remember it being awash in the surf with pine snags that had once been live trees growing near the keeper's quarters. The concrete collar began to erode in the saltwater, and the lighthouse was in great jeopardy. The stairs had been removed to avoid accidental injury. (SGLA.)

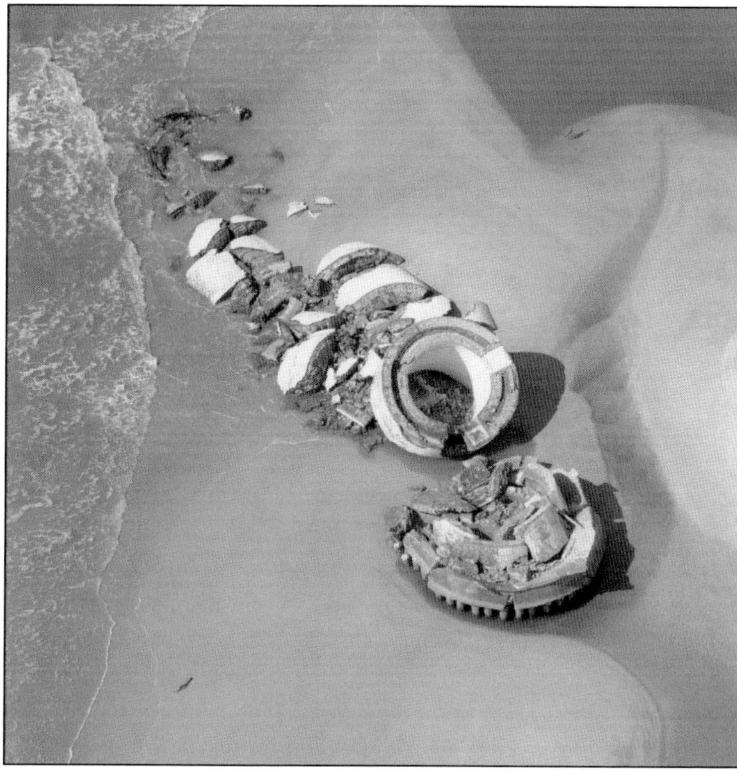

On a quiet day, George Watkins and Ricky Hathcock were working near the dock when they heard a thunderous crash. They crossed the island and found that the old tower had collapsed. The next day, aerial photographer Debbie Hooper flew over the lighthouse, now overtaken by the storm surge. In a year that had brought five hurricanes, she captioned her photograph, "One too many." (JoeBay Aerials.)

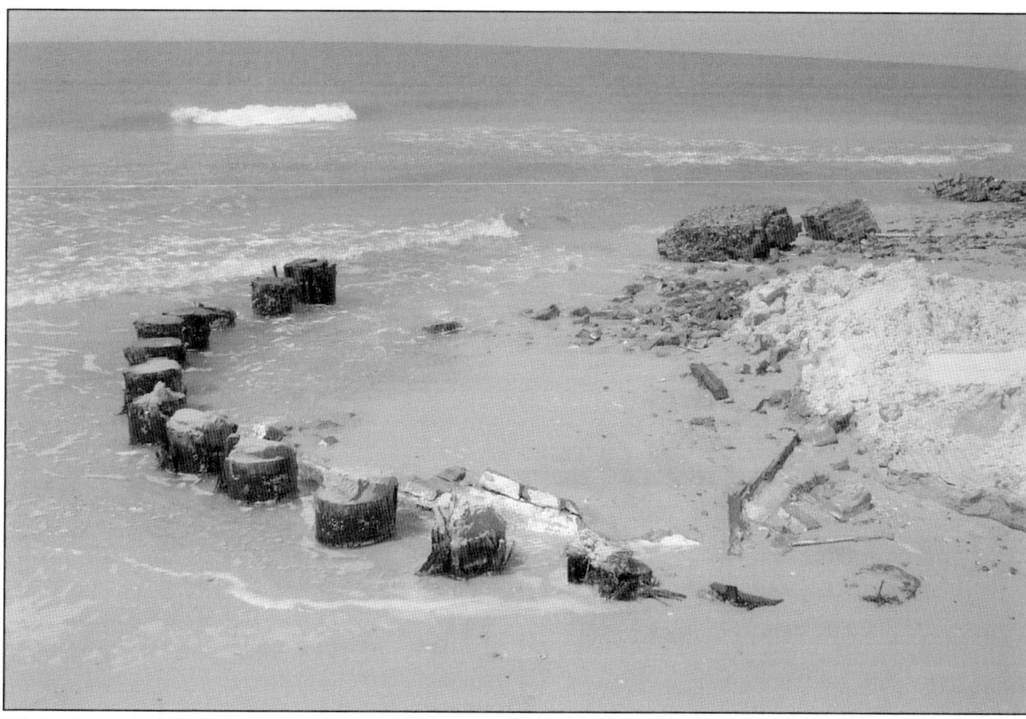

With the lighthouse lying in the surf, the pilings that had supported the concrete collar were the only remaining vestige of the 1852 lighthouse on Cape St. George. (SGLA.)

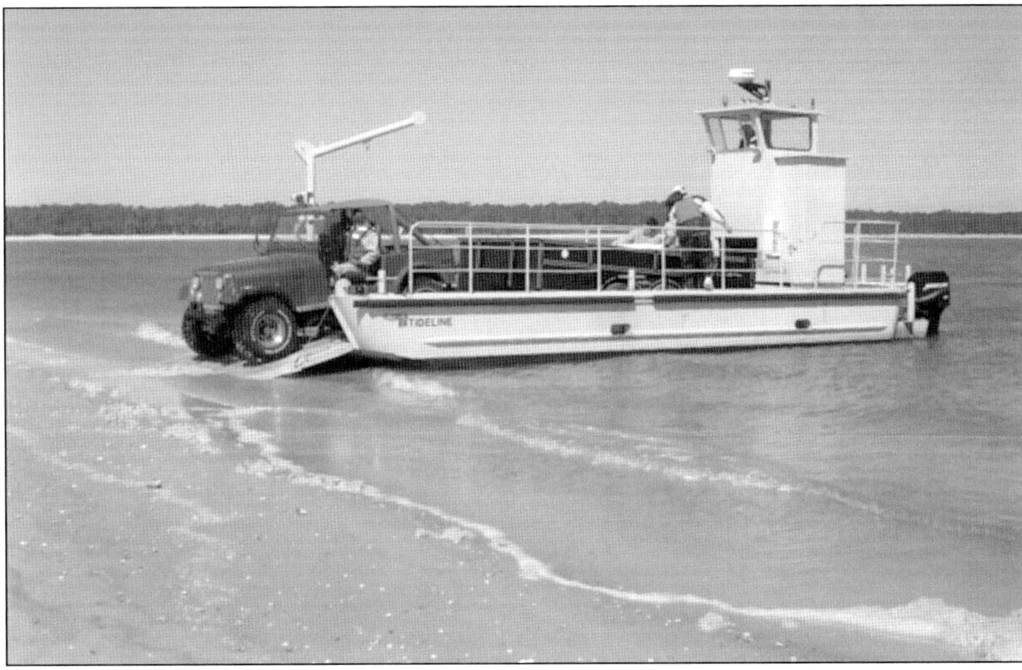

Little St. George Island was separated from the bigger island by the Sikes Cut shipping channel. The only way to salvage the 1852 lighthouse would be by barge. In 2006, members of the St. George Lighthouse Association and the Department of Environmental Protection arrived with a Jeep and dump cart to determine if it might be possible to salvage the lighthouse. (SGLA.)

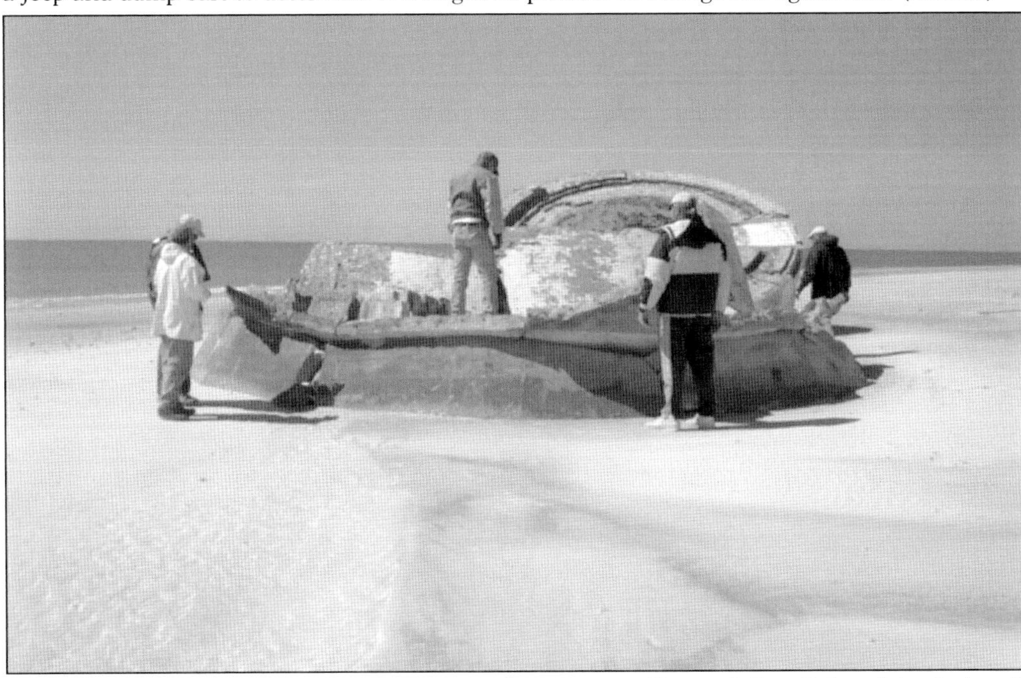

Volunteers from SGLA discuss how to manage the recovery effort with Roy Ogles of Apalachicola National Estuarine Research Reserve, which manages Little St. George Island. (Terry Kemp, SGLA.)

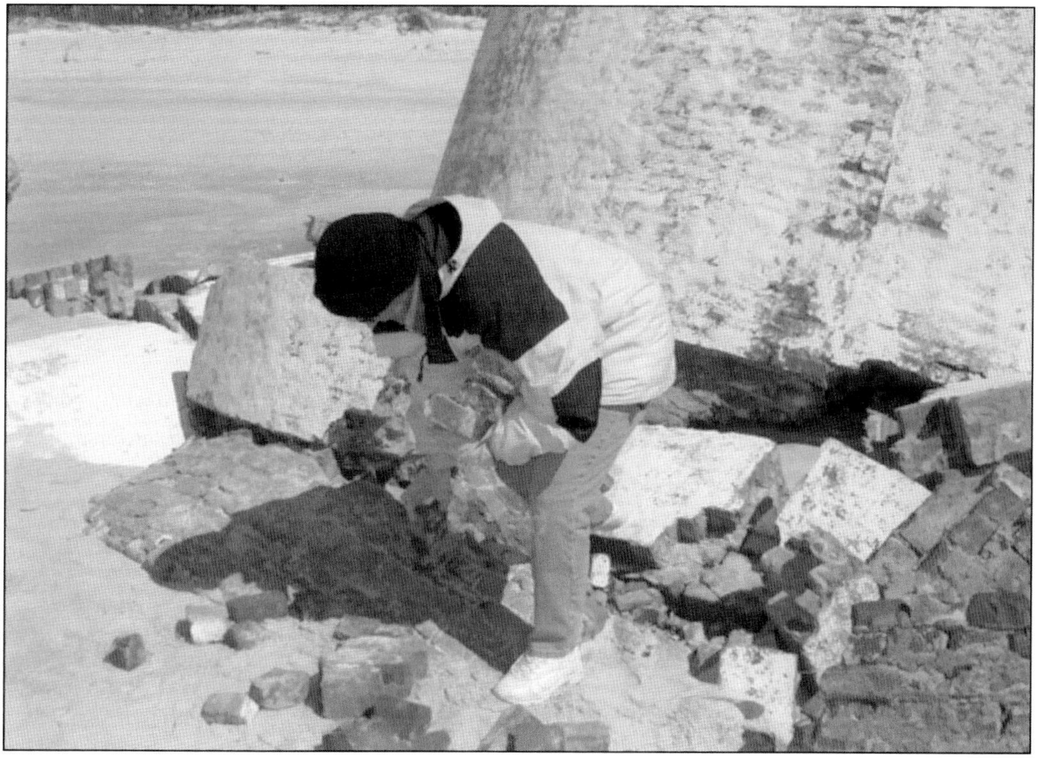

While other volunteers chisel bricks from the tower base, Sharon Poston gathers bricks to put in the dump trailer. (SGLA.)

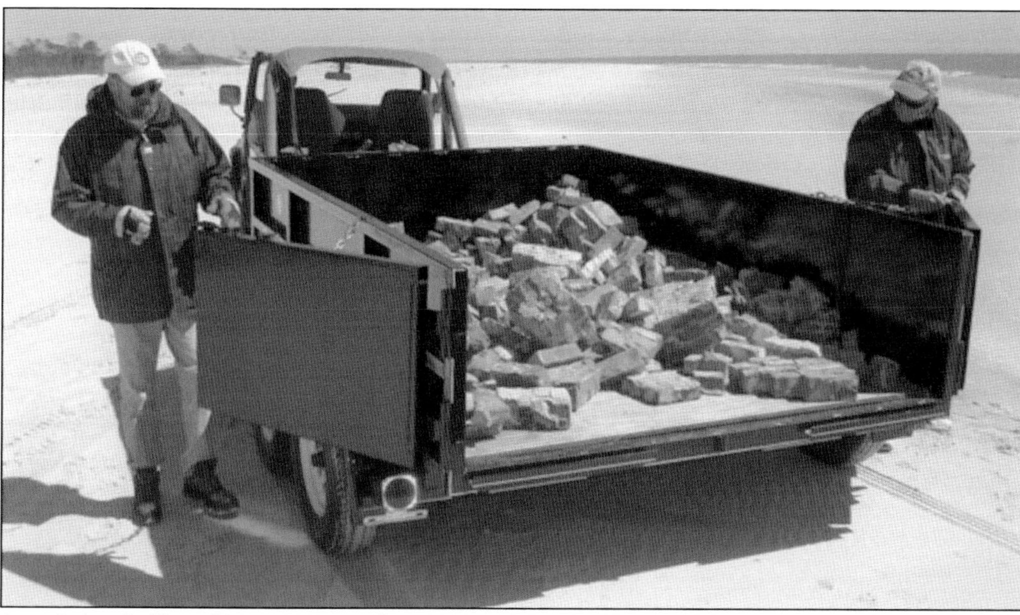

Roy Ogles (left) and Dennis Barnell examine the bricks recovered by manual labor during part of the first day. The bricks were moved away from the tideline for temporary storage. Clearly, the task of salvaging a brick lighthouse would require heavy equipment if it was to be completed in less than a year. (SGLA.)

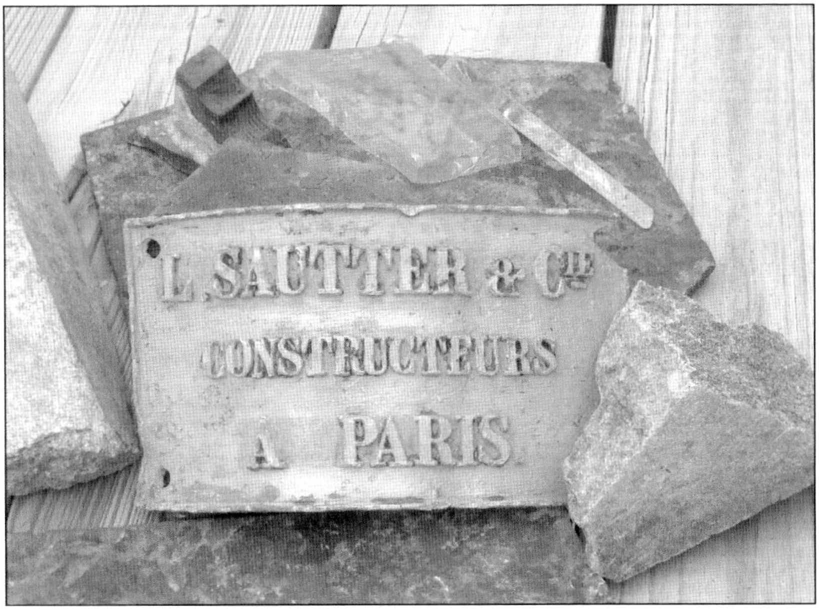

While they were searching the site, the SGLA volunteers found the original plaque that had been on the lens pedestal to identify the Sautter company in Paris that made the Fresnel lens. The lens had been transported to New Orleans by the Coast Guard in 1949 and could not be located. (SGLA.)

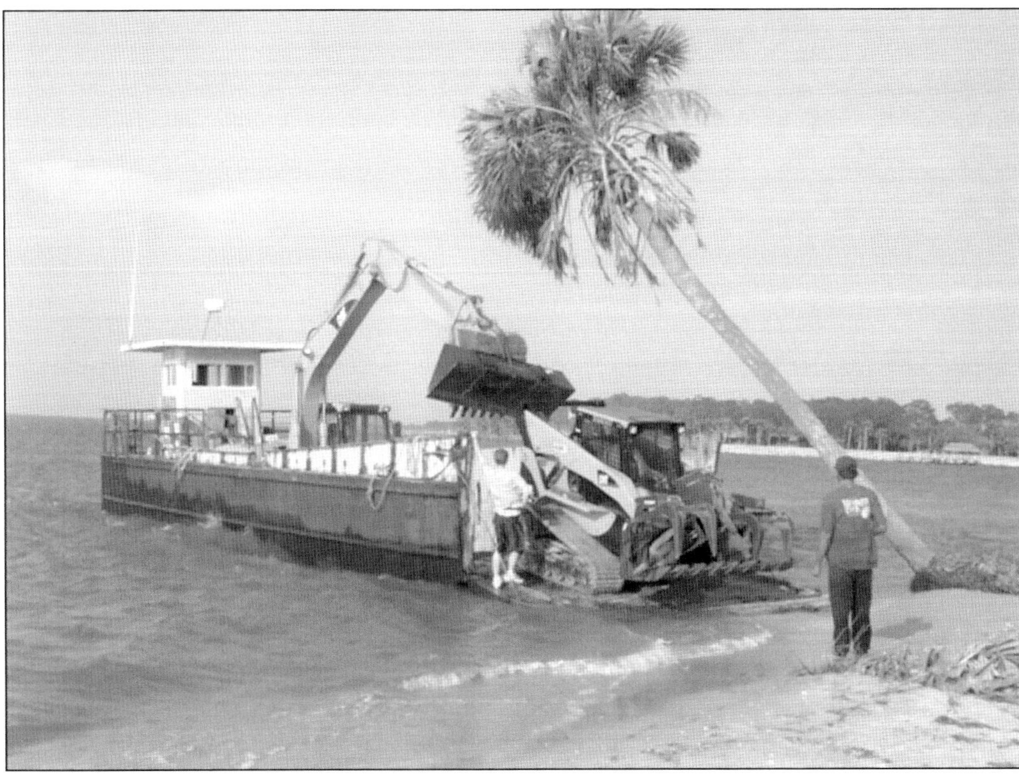

The Florida Department of Environmental Protection applied for Federal Emergency Management Agency (FEMA) funds to finance the recovery effort. In April, a grappler and excavator were brought to Cape St. George to begin dismantling the lighthouse so it could begin its journey back to St. George Island by way of Apalachicola and Eastpoint. (SGLA.)

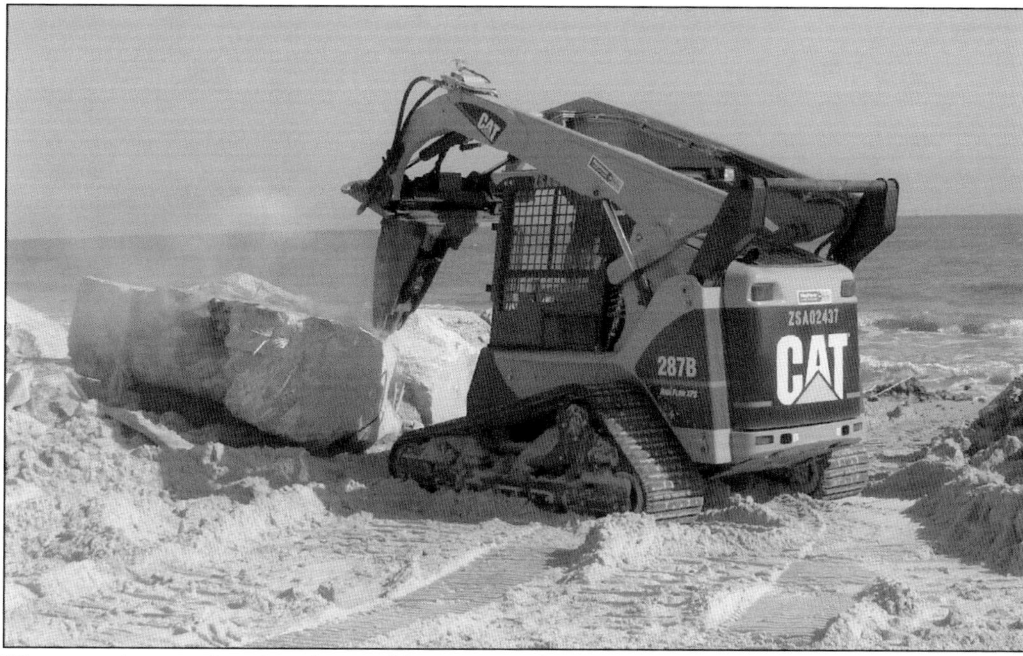

The grappler was fitted with a jackhammer to break apart the massive pieces of brick and mortar. SGLA contracted with Luberto's Sand and Gravel in Eastpoint to operate the heavy equipment. (SGLA.)

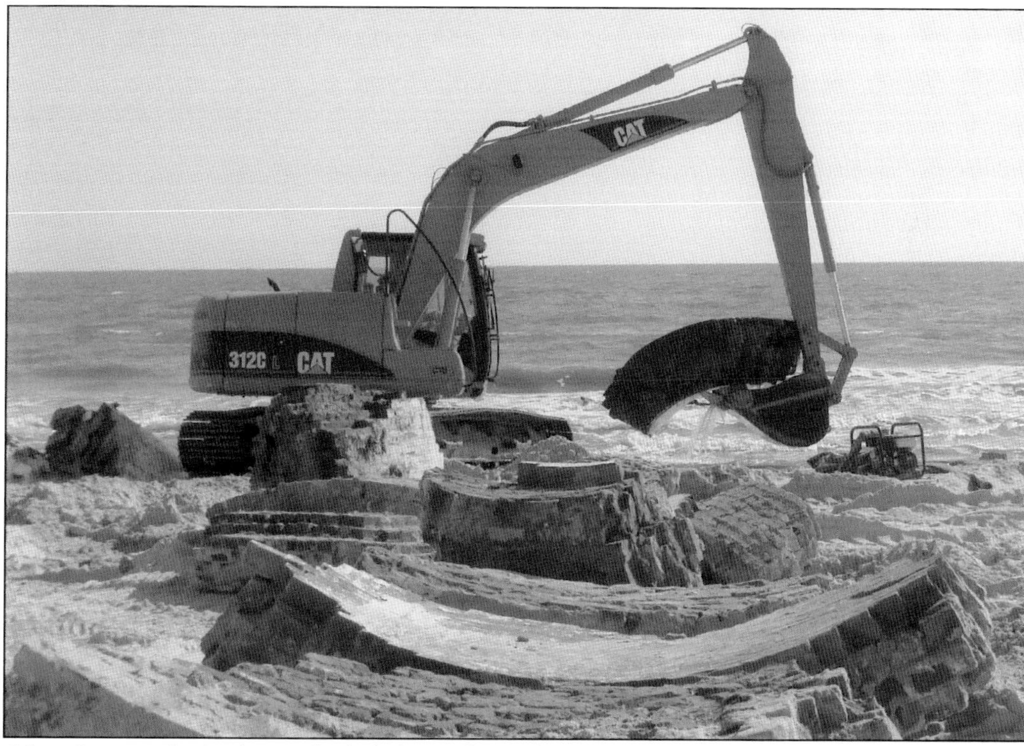

After the grappler broke up the lighthouse base, the excavator began moving the large pieces to the barge for transport to the Scipio Creek Marina in Apalachicola. (SGLA.)

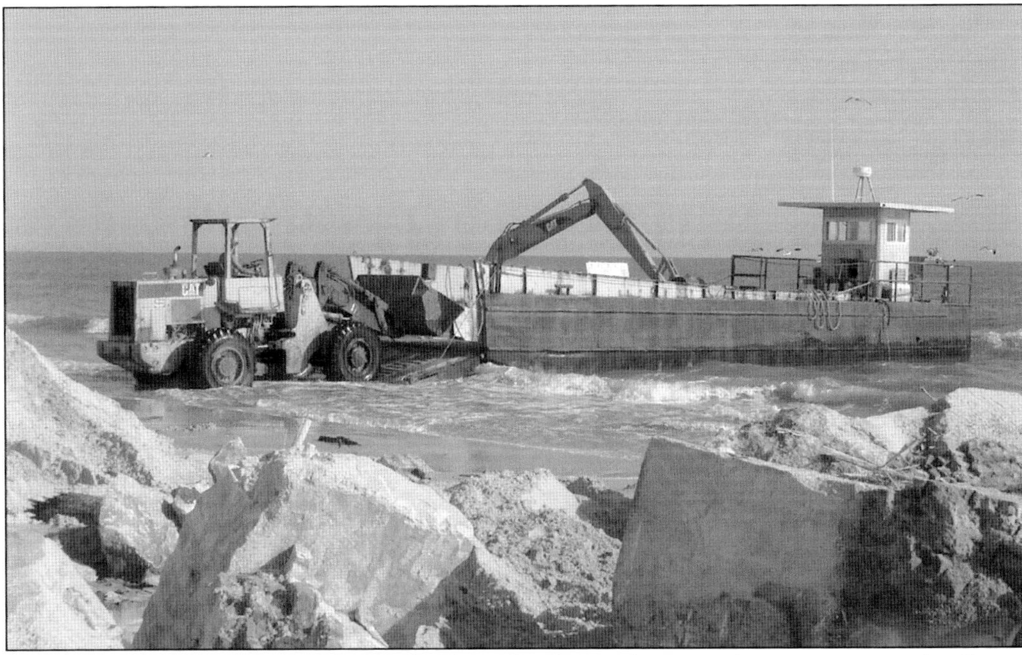

The grappler and excavator began loading the barge for one of many trips to the Scipio Creek Marina. (SGLA.)

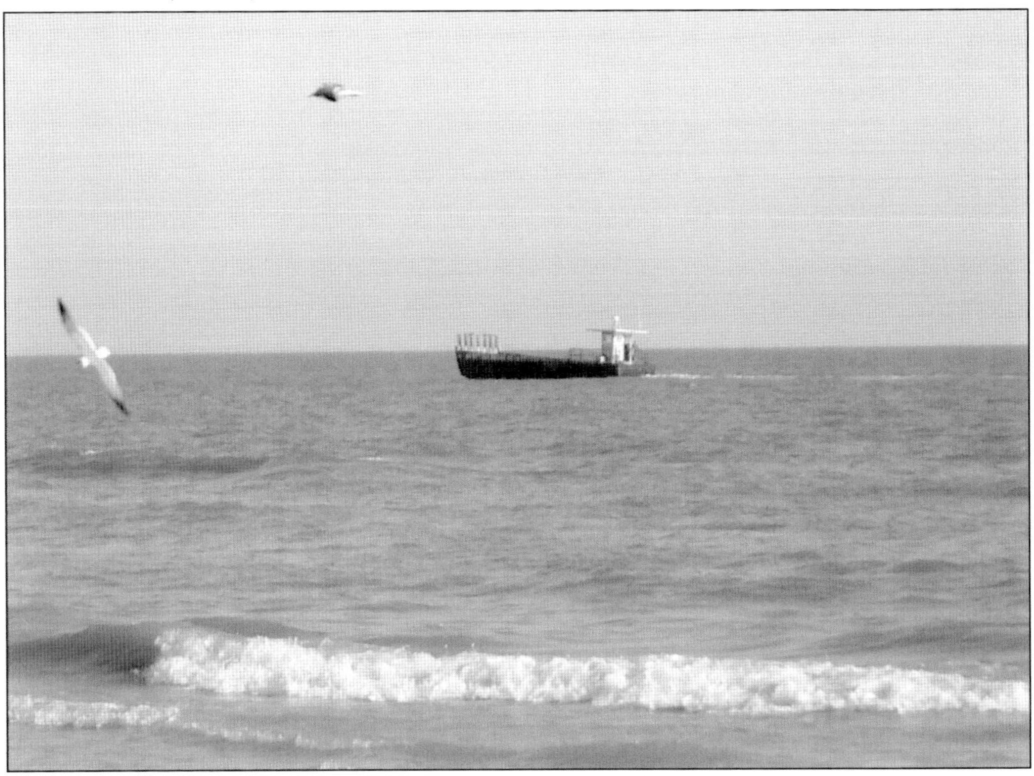

The barge heads away from Cape St. George with a load of recovered lighthouse pieces. Soon, the recovery process could begin. (Terry Kemp, SGLA.)

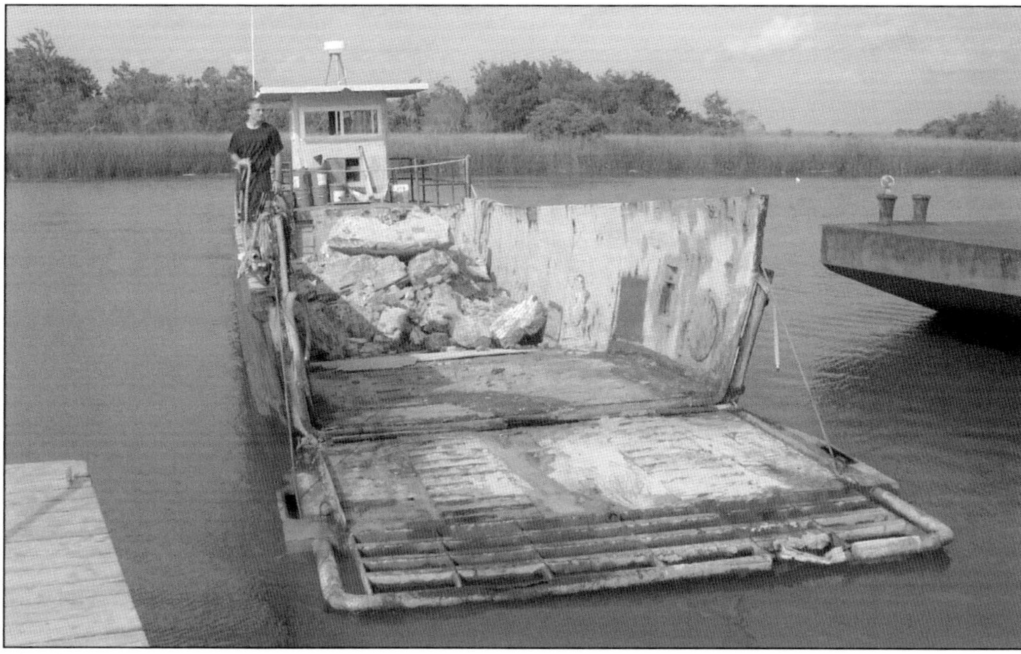

The barge pulls up to Scipio Creek, where the pieces will be transferred to a haul-off cart and taken to a lot in Eastpoint where the brick cleaning will begin. (SGLA.)

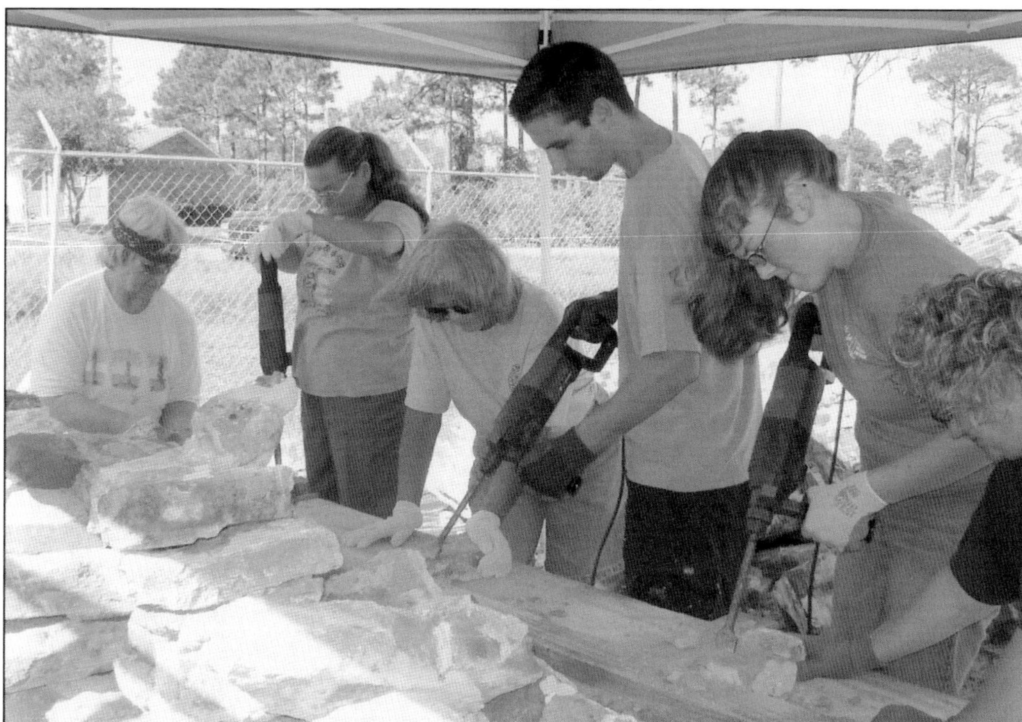

The lot behind Oyster Radio (WOYS) in Eastpoint looked chaotic and disordered under heaps of bricks, but the SGLA volunteers quickly determined how to work with 153-year-old bricks and mortar. The rescue of the Cape St. George Lighthouse had begun. (SGLA.)

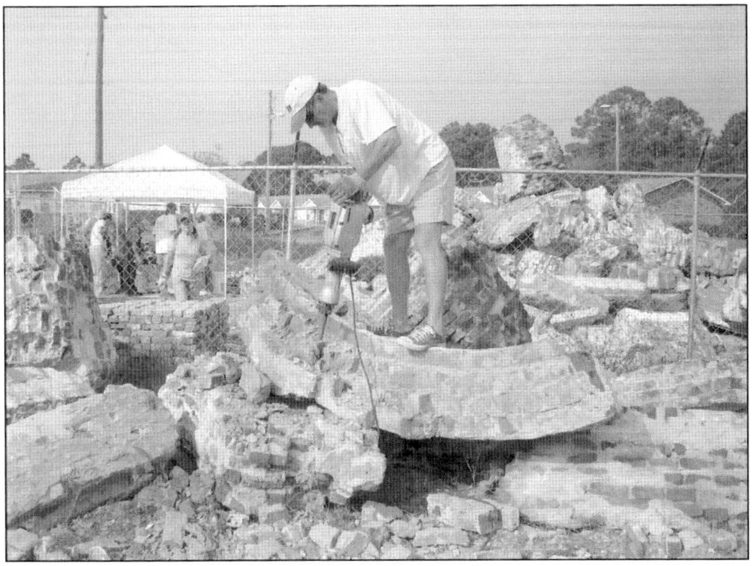

St. George Lighthouse Association volunteer Richard Saucer soon learned that an electric jackhammer was extremely useful in reducing the size of the chunks from the old lighthouse. Other volunteers worked at tables set up nearby to clean the individual bricks. (SGLA.)

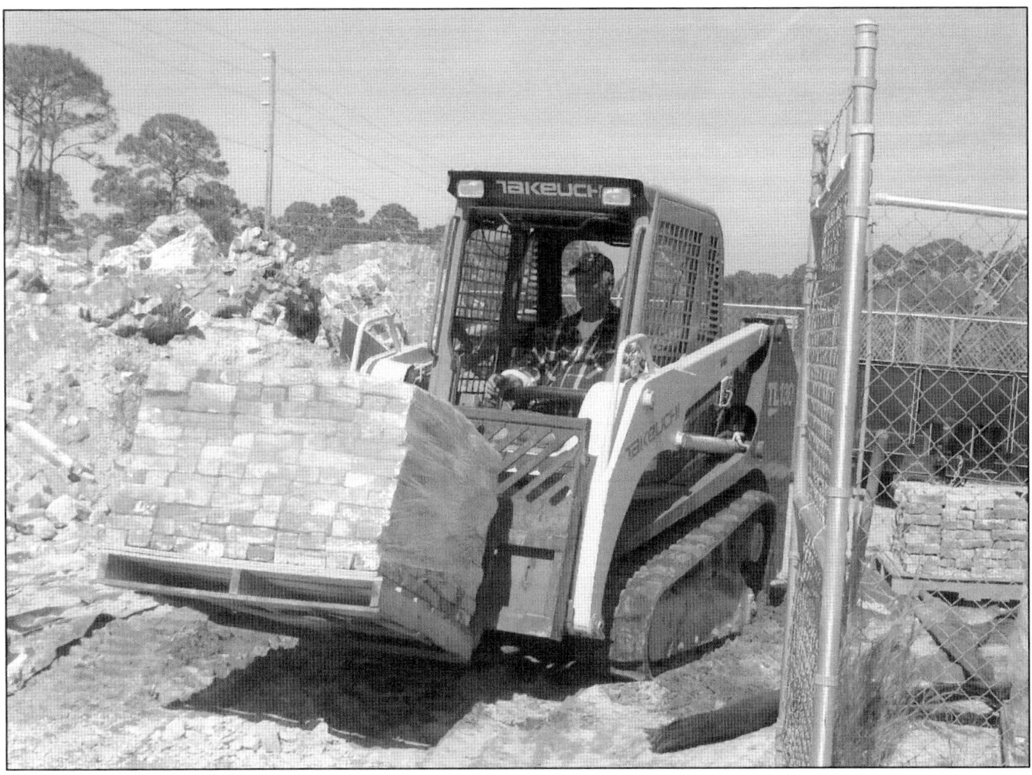

Island resident Larry Stone uses a tractor with a forklift to carry a pallet of bricks to storage, soon to be moved to the construction site in what would become Lighthouse Park on St. George Island. Over the next several months, the volunteers cleaned over 22,000 bricks, and excitement grew as the vision of rebuilding the lighthouse started to seem possible. (SGLA.)

Nine

Rebirth of the Cape St. George Lighthouse

After the 1852 lighthouse was toppled by high surf following Hurricane Wilma on October 21, 2005, members of SGLA wondered whether it should be left in place to become a future fishing reef or if it could be recovered and restored. By then, the Apalachicola National Estuarine Research Reserve, which is a part of the Florida Department of Environmental Protection, officially managed all of Little St. George Island, including the former lighthouse reservation. The two groups obtained funding from FEMA for hurricane recovery and immediately began salvaging the lighthouse.

Every part of the lighthouse that could be located was recovered and taken to a vacant lot in Eastpoint. The brick walls were broken apart and the bricks were cleaned using electric rotary hammers. The soapstone from the lantern room deck was retrieved, but a new slab needed to be obtained. The old granite threshold from the entryway was reused, as were the granite sills that once framed the windows. Twisted metal that had made up the lantern room and gallery was used as a pattern to refabricate the structure according to plans that were retrieved from the US National Archives.

Volunteers cleaned bricks for months until over 22,000 original bricks were ready. The plan was to use the original bricks for the entire inner wall of the tower, and the volunteers succeeded. Construction on the pilings and tower base began even before enough bricks were available, and by February 2008, the volunteers had finished their task.

Once the tower was finished and open for visitors, a replica of the original 1852 keeper's cottage was built to accommodate a lighthouse gift shop and a historical museum that would explain events around Apalachicola Bay from the founding of Apalachicola through the Civil War, Reconstruction, and the 20th century. Surviving members of the lighthouse keeper's families donated photographs and items that had been used at Cape St. George.

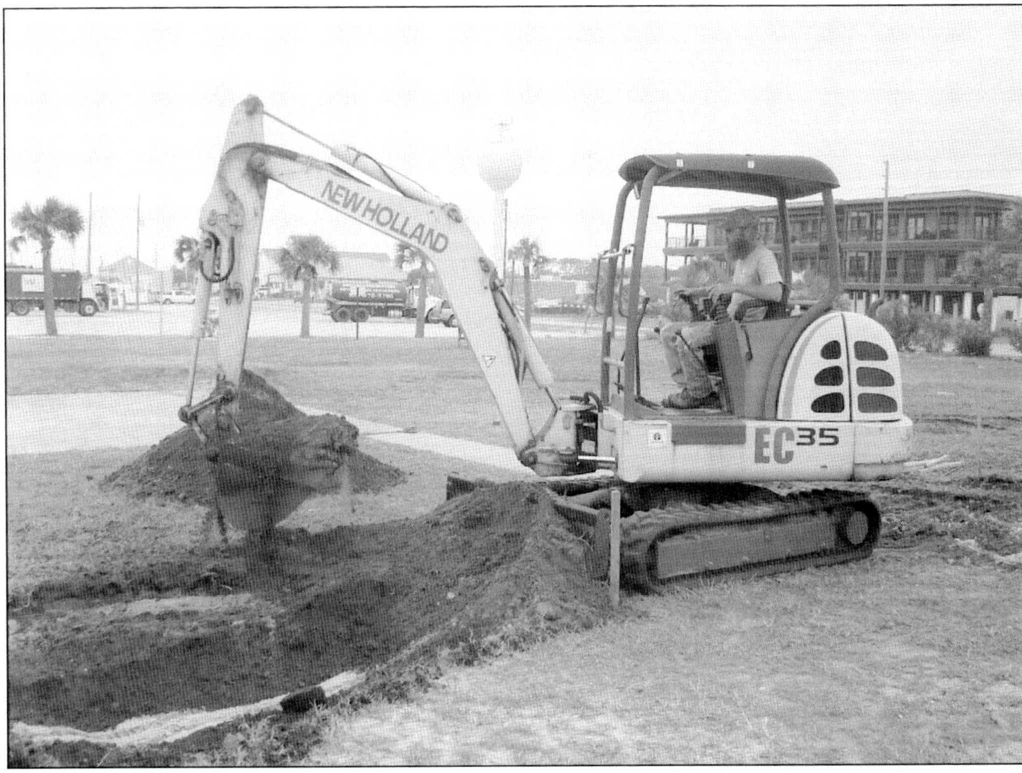

Nearly 60 volunteers worked cleaning over 22,440 historic bricks from October 21, 2006, to February 22, 2008. Actual construction began in September 2007. Ground breaking at Lighthouse Park on St. George Island began on October 22, 2007, just two years after the tower fell on October 21, 2005. Volunteers were still cleaning bricks at the Eastpoint site when the rebuilding work began. (Terry Kemp, SGLA.)

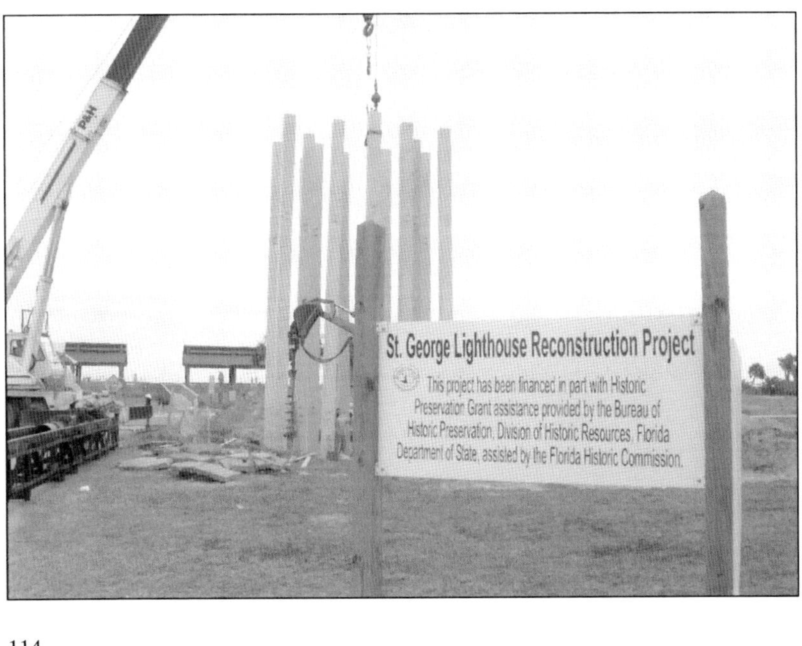

Concrete pilings were driven as much as 40 feet into limestone bedrock to provide a permanent base for the historic tower. (SGLA.)

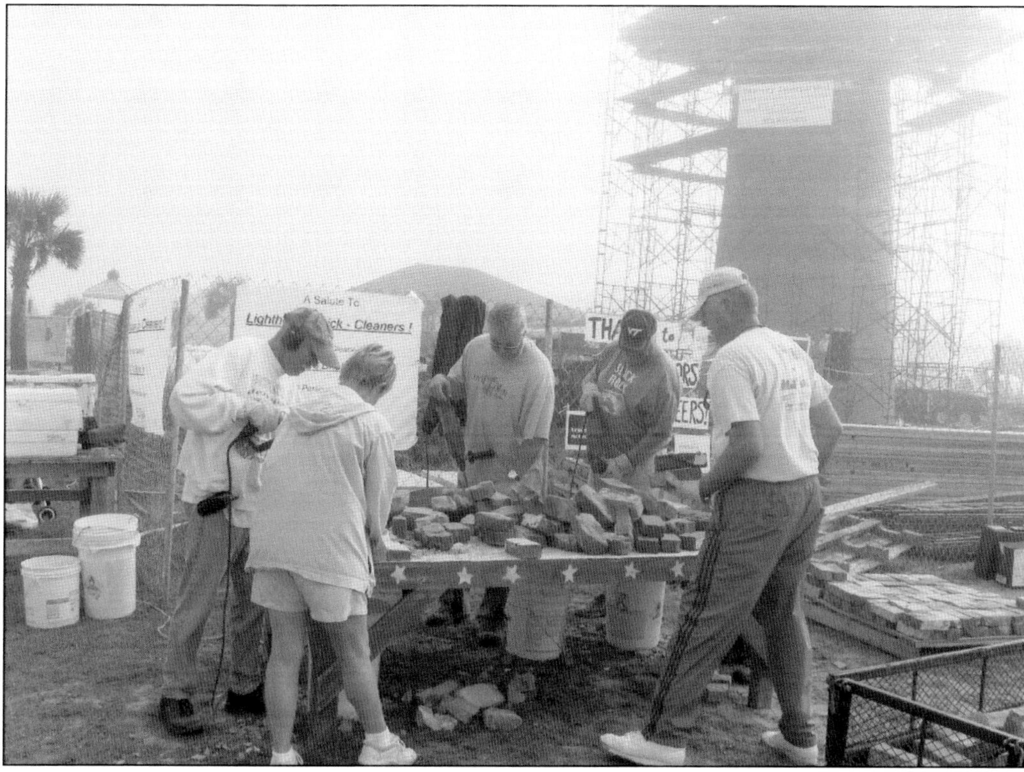

As construction began, volunteer brick-cleaners moved to the island. A formal brick-laying ceremony was held to thank the many volunteers who donated their time to the rebuilding of the Cape St. George Lighthouse. Then, following historical plans, the masons began to lay walls four feet thick at the base, tapering to two feet thick at the top of the tower. (SGLA.)

Pallets of cleaned, historic bricks were delivered to the construction site in the winter of 2007–2008, and final brick cleaning was completed in Lighthouse Park on St. George Island. By this date, masons had already begun work on the tower. (SGLA.)

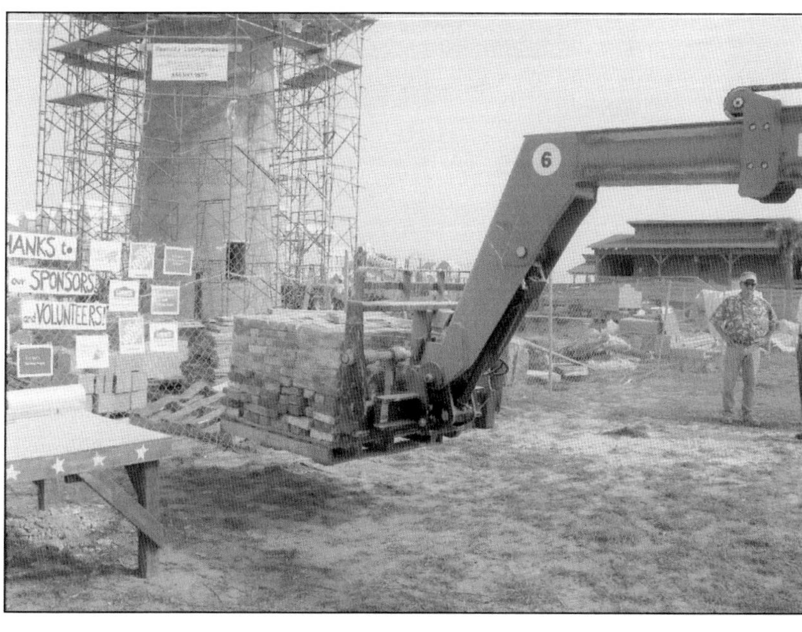

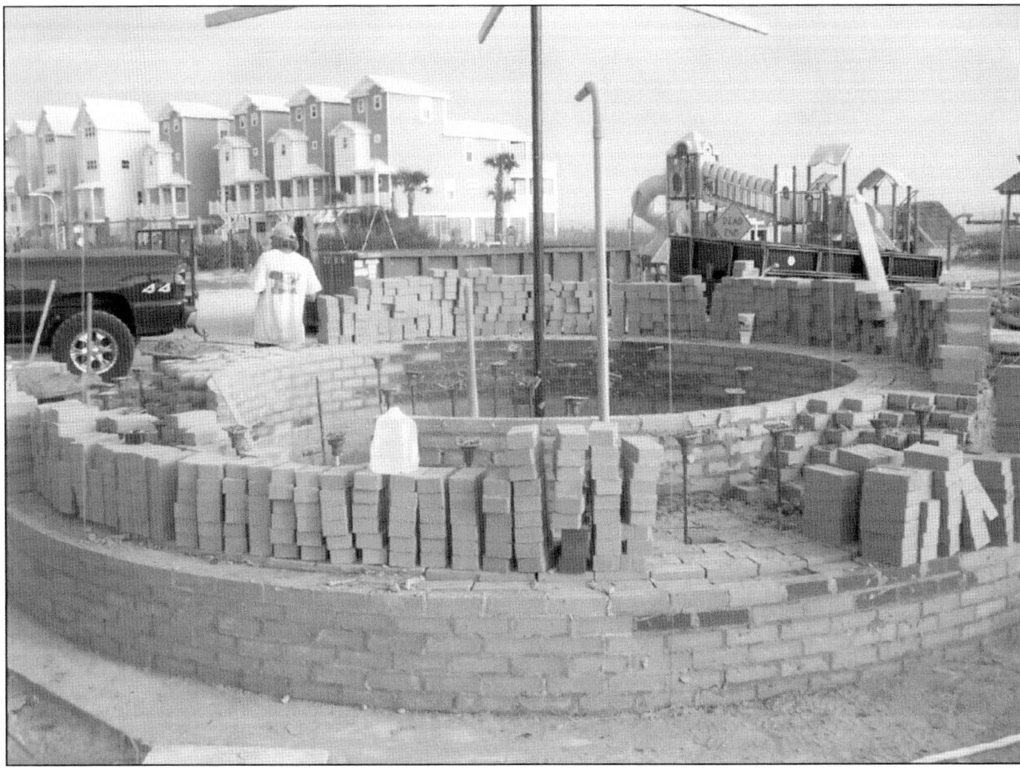

When construction began, no one had built a conical masonry lighthouse in over 70 years. To ensure that the walls followed the proper taper from the 20-foot-wide base to the 12-foot top, masons rigged up a carousel from which guide lines could be angled at the correct slant. The lines are attached to the propeller-like boards visible at the top of this photograph. (SGLA.)

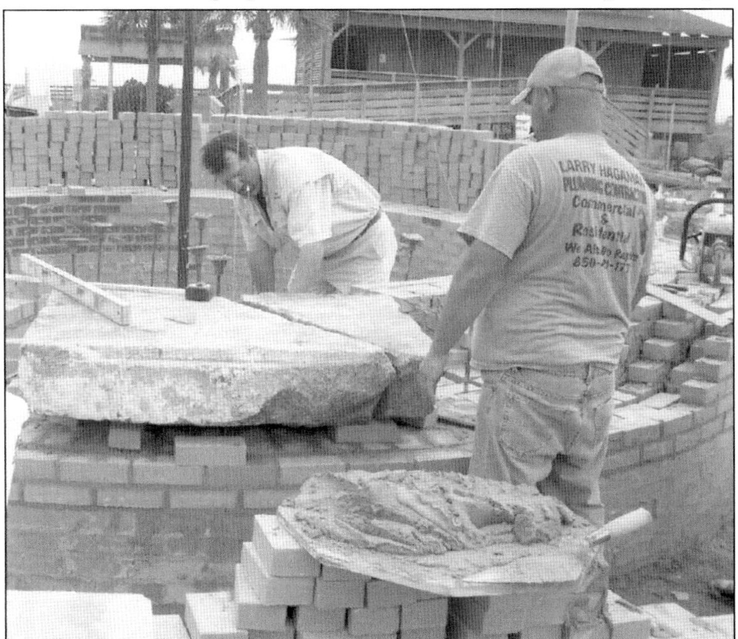

Masons carefully installed the original 1852 granite threshold in what would become the new entry door into the tower. The original granite sills and lintels from around the windows were also saved and used in the new tower. Visitors now step across the same threshold that has been used since at least 1852. (SGLA.)

The door was completely framed, and then a work platform of scaffolding was set up as the masons raised the tower walls. As the masons built the wall higher, the first of the five windows was framed up. (SGLA.)

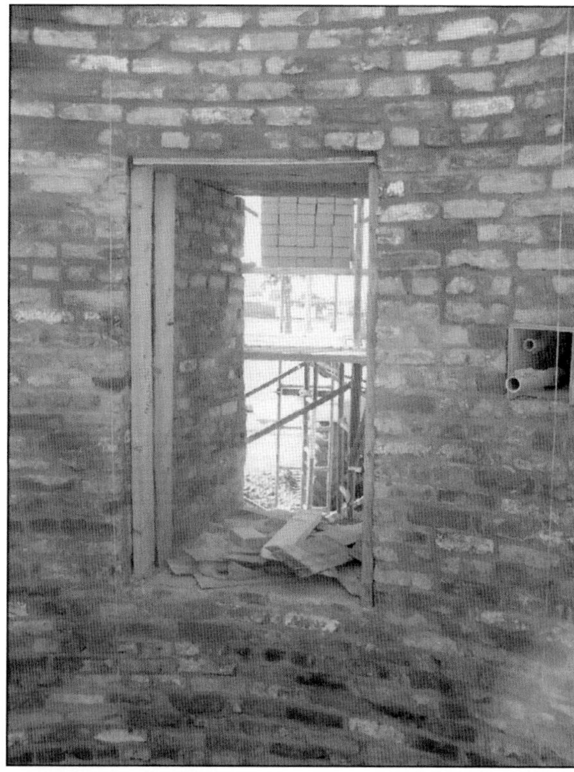

All of the interior bricks in the tower are original ones the volunteers cleaned from the 1852 Cape St. George Lighthouse. They will be left unpainted so visitors can see the historic brickwork. Much more than a replica, the tower is a historical reconstruction that uses original materials and follows original plans. (SGLA.)

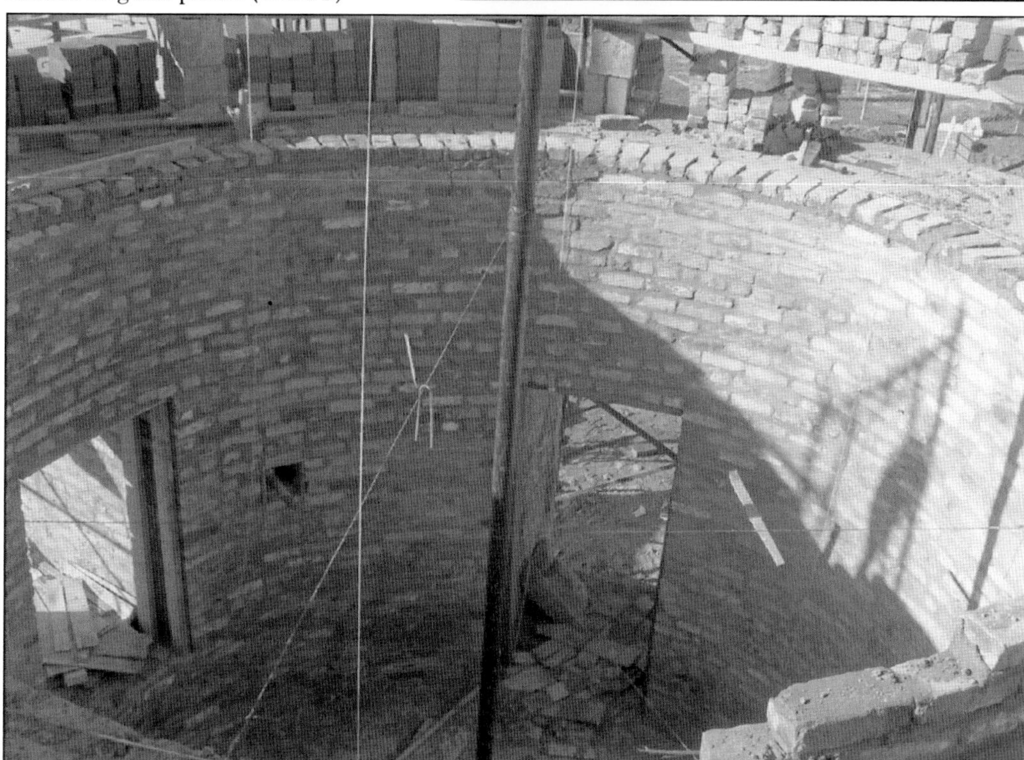

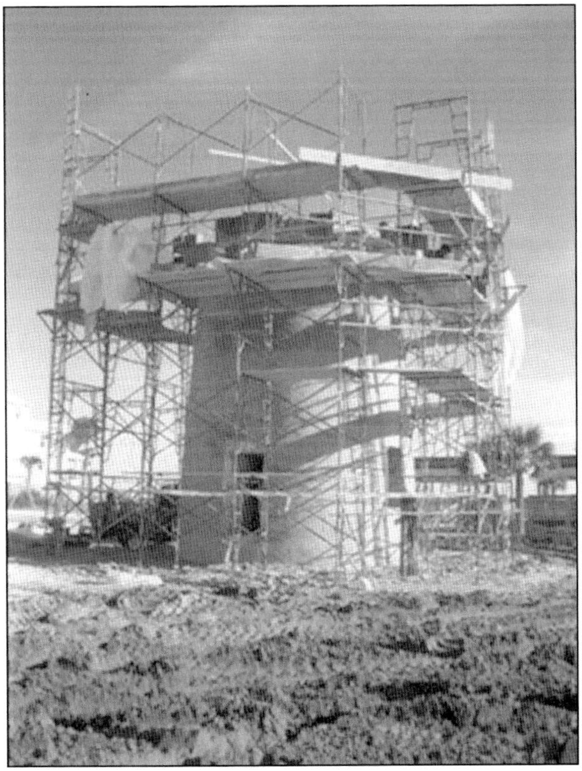

By January 28, 2008, the tower had risen to 30 feet tall. (SGLA.)

As the tower grew, a crane was brought in to lift pallets of brick to the top of the scaffolding. (SGLA.)

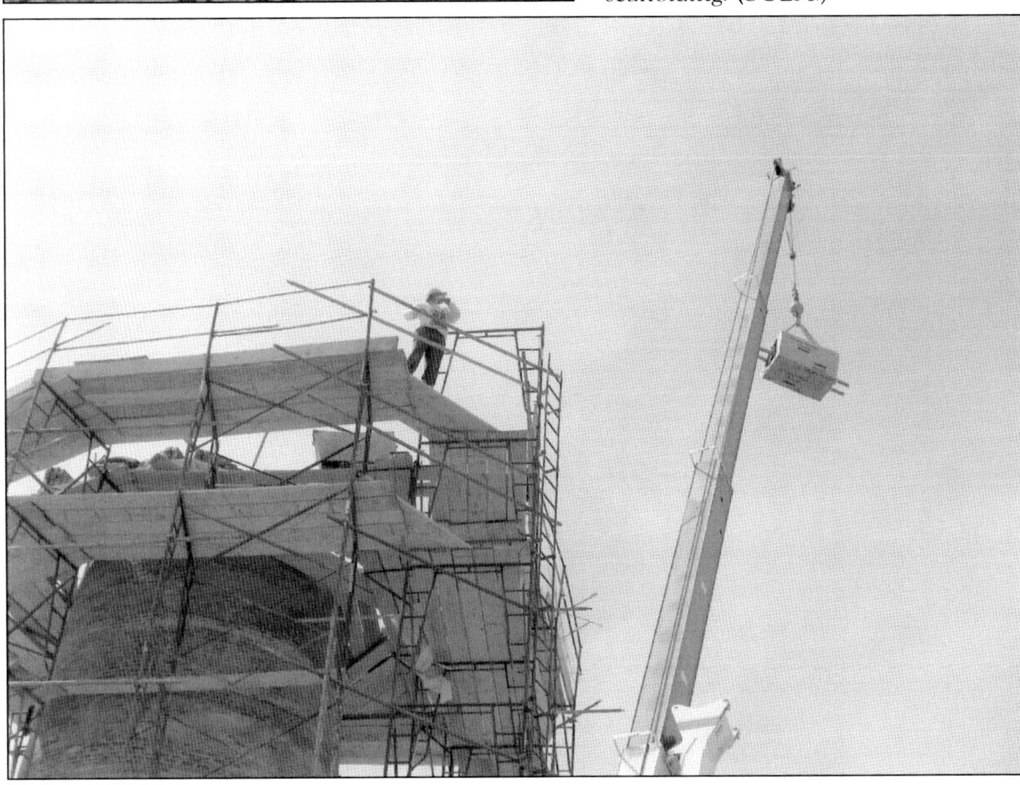

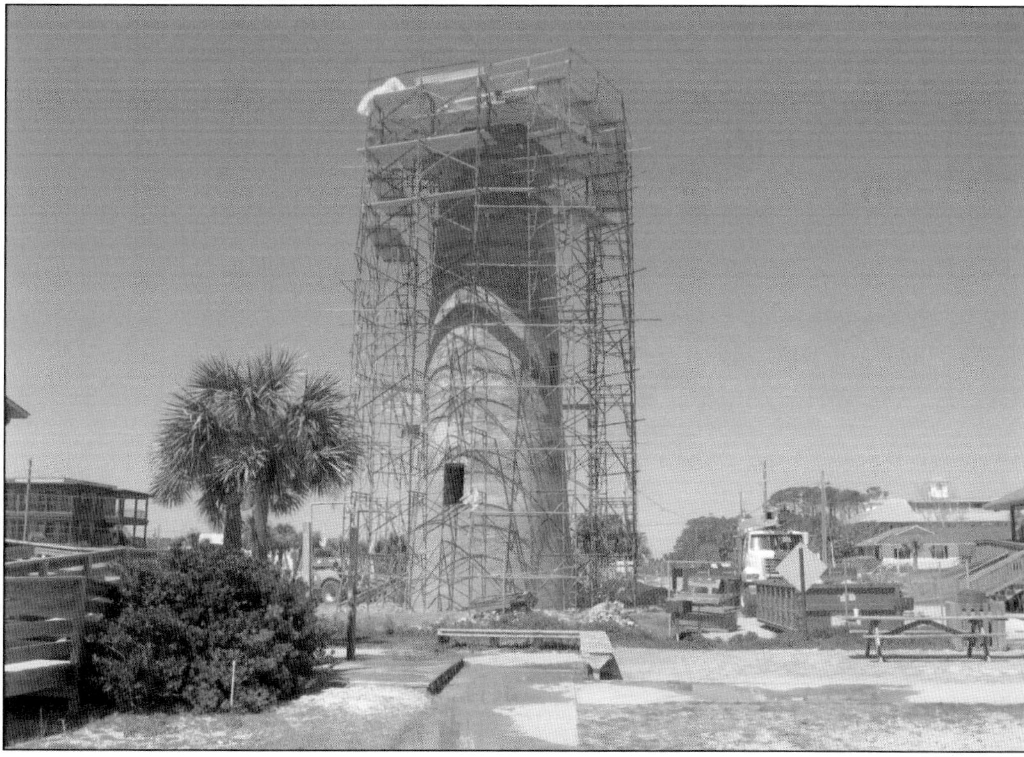

By March 13, the tower had risen to 60 feet. It was starting to show the beautiful symmetry so characteristic of lighthouses. (SGLA.)

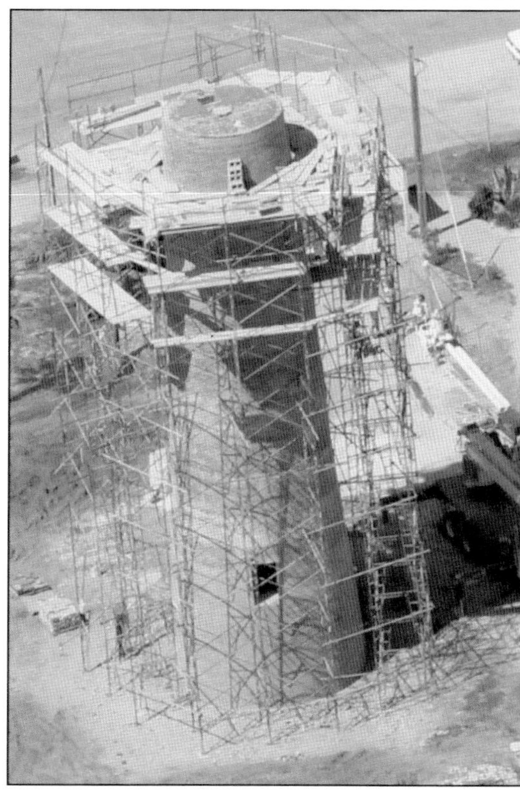

A mold was made to support the curved watch room ceiling and set in place. The dome was then bricked over to support the lantern room, with a rectangular opening that would become the access "scuttle" atop the ladder visitors use to reach the lantern room. The masonry work on the 65-foot-high tower was completed on March 22, 2008, just six months after ground breaking. It was time to begin work on the lantern room. (Debbie Hooper, JoeBay Aerials.)

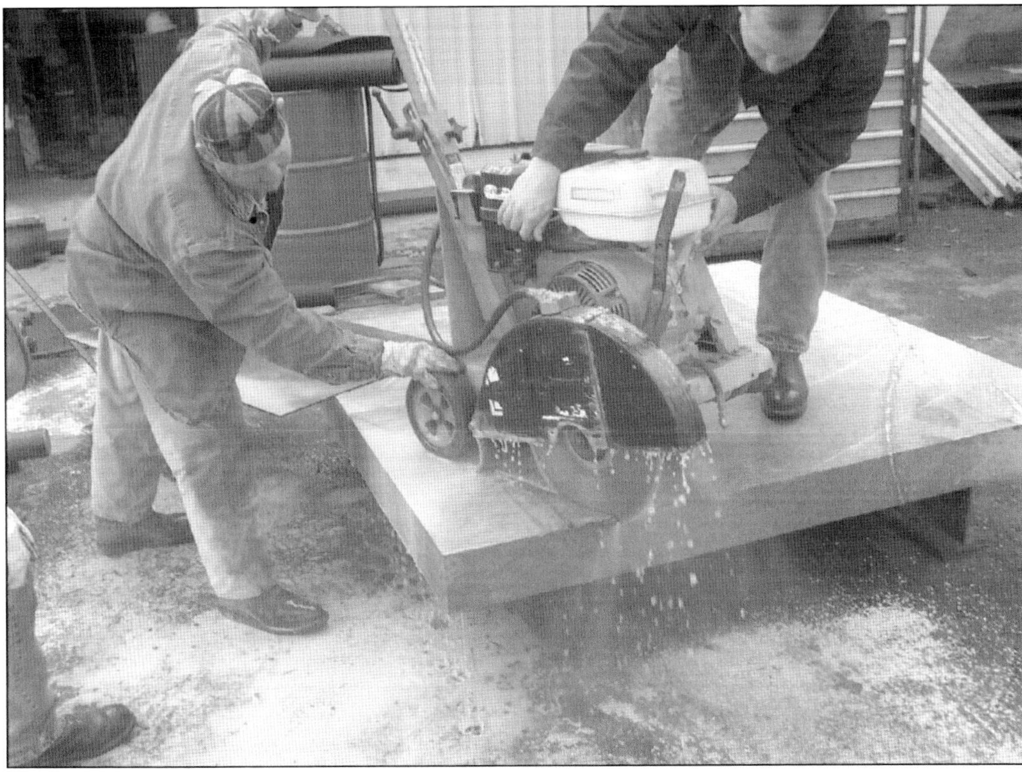

SGLA member Johnny Guy cut the soapstone for the lighthouse deck at his shop in Alabama. Many of the original soapstone pieces were recovered, but were too damaged to reuse. Once plentiful in the United States, the soapstone had to be purchased from Brazil. (SGLA.)

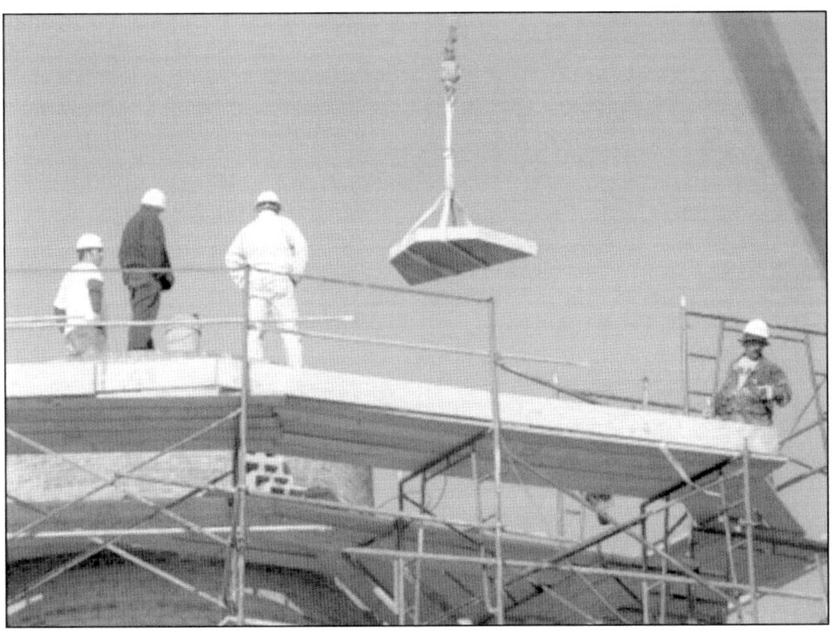

A crane raises one of the pieces of the soapstone deck to the top of the lighthouse tower in March 2008. (SGLA.)

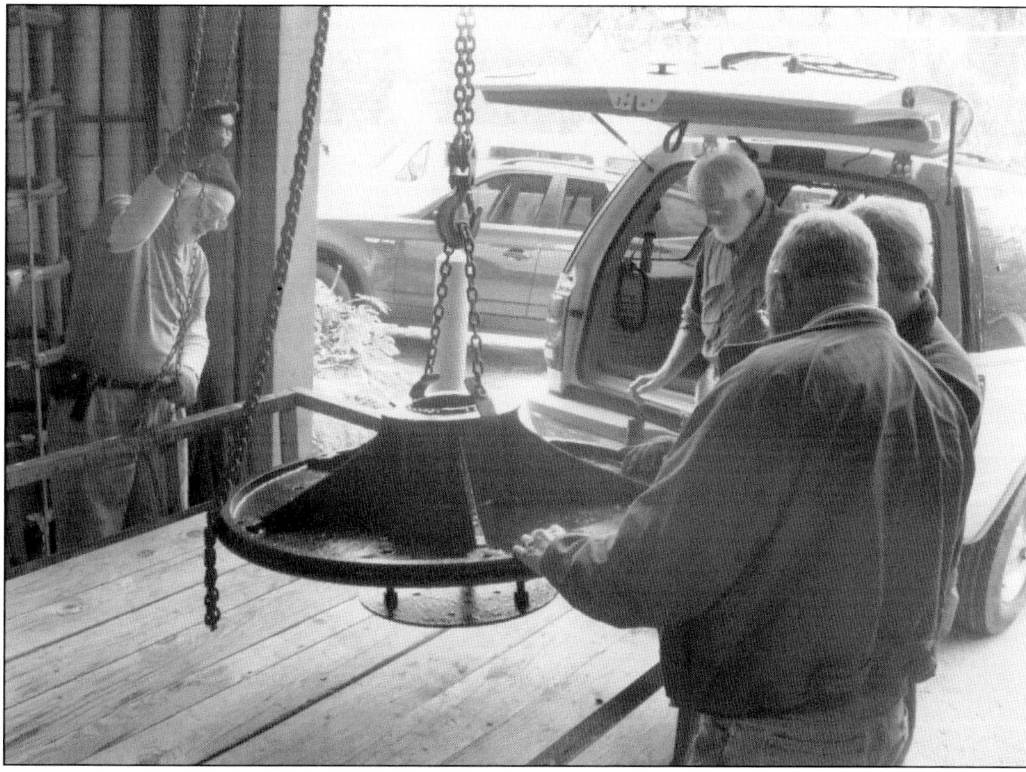

Cast-iron pieces from the lantern room were too damaged to reuse. Examples were taken to Allen Architectural Metals to refabricate identical components. The lens platform shown here was taken to a state laboratory that specializes in historical preservation. (SGLA.)

Volunteers gathered in Lighthouse Park to begin assembling the refabricated but authentic lantern room. A platform was built so the community could see the progress SGLA volunteers were making. (SGLA.)

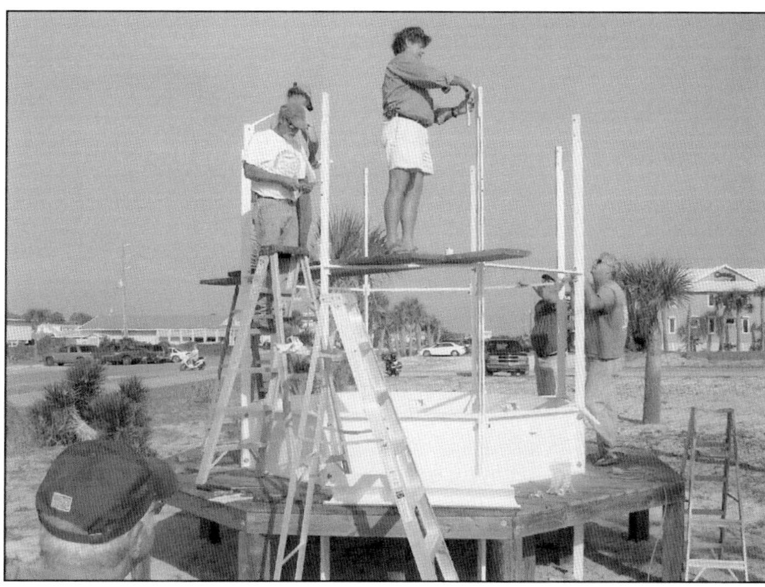

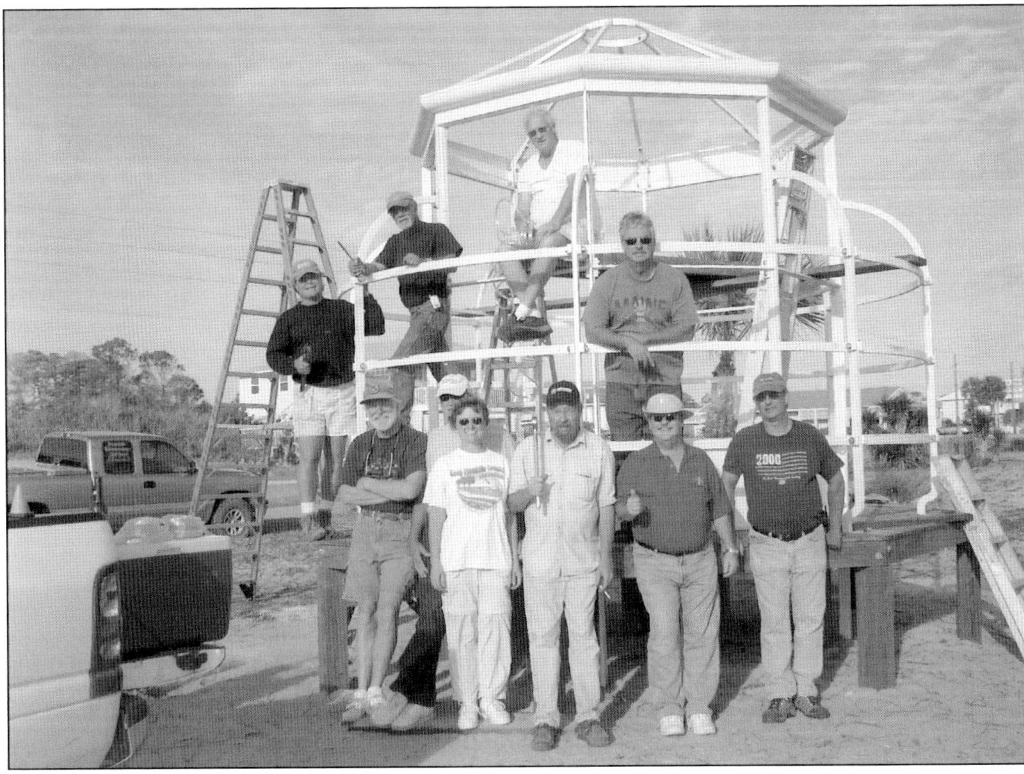

Volunteers proudly show off their completed handiwork, which would shortly be painted black. The lantern room cost $50,000 to refabricate, but labor for assembly was donated. (SGLA.)

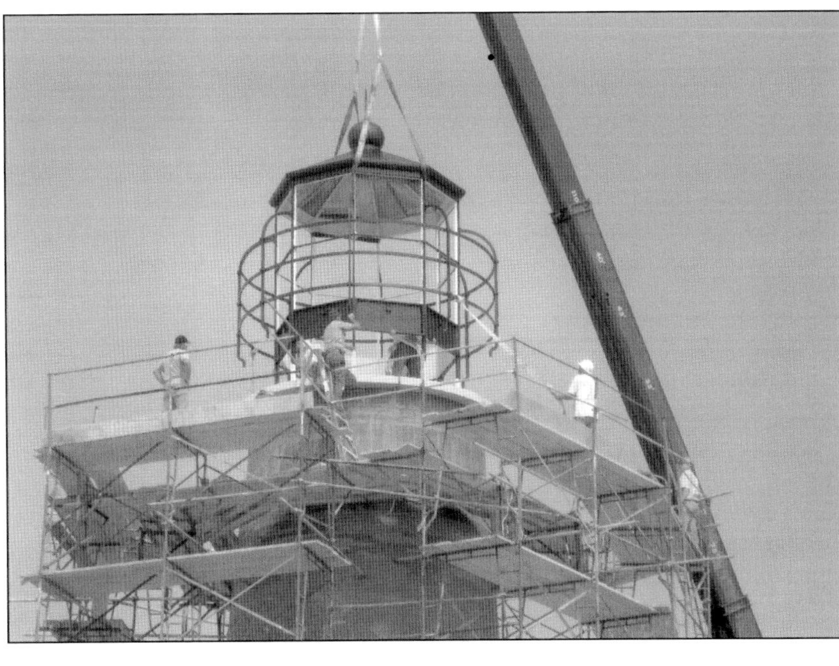

Straps were attached to the lantern room so it could be hoisted to the top of the tower after one practice lift. (SGLA.)

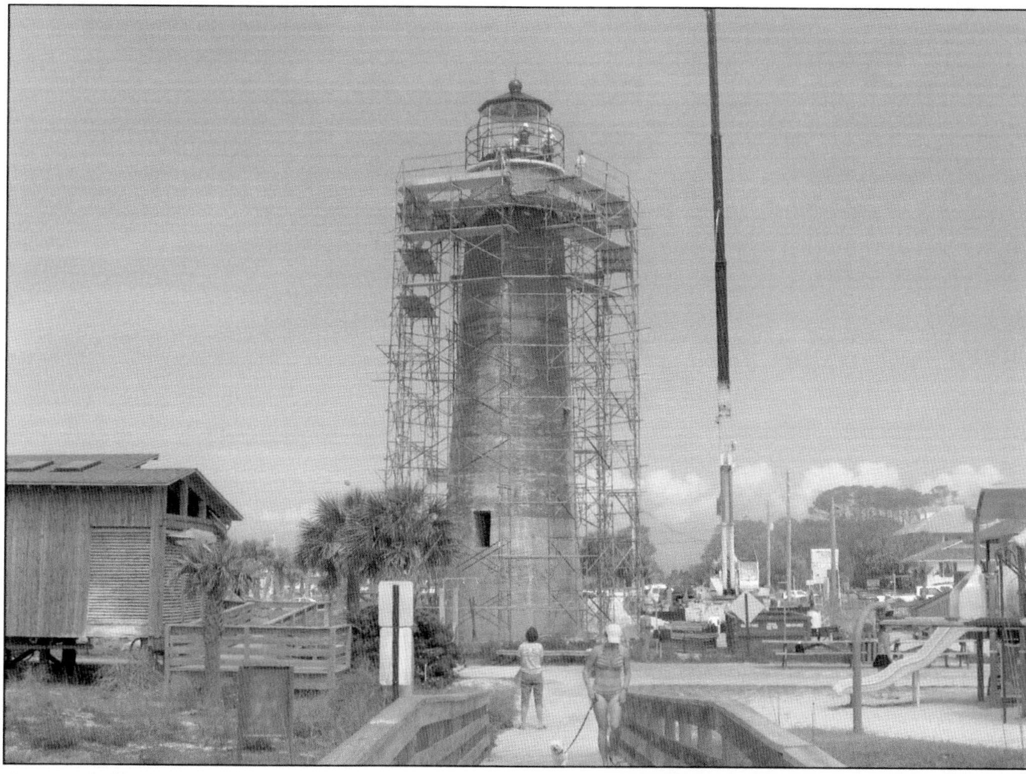

A very skilled crane operator positions the lantern room so the work crew can set the metal legs into receiving holes in the brickwork. Hardhats and steel-toed boots were required. The workmen on top of the tower cheered when the lantern room was set in place, and the crowd below echoed their cheers and celebrated the moment. (SGLA.)

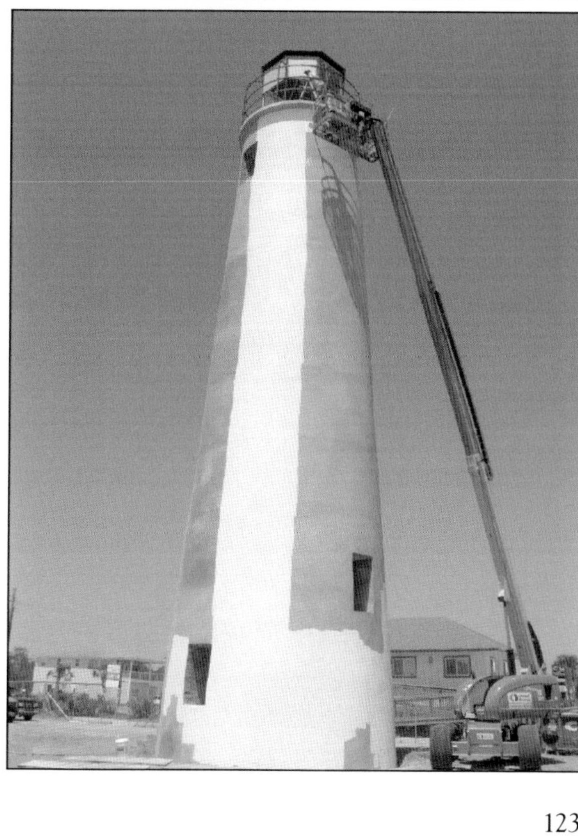

The lighthouse was stuccoed and then painted white, identical to the day mark it had shown for 153 years. (SGLA.)

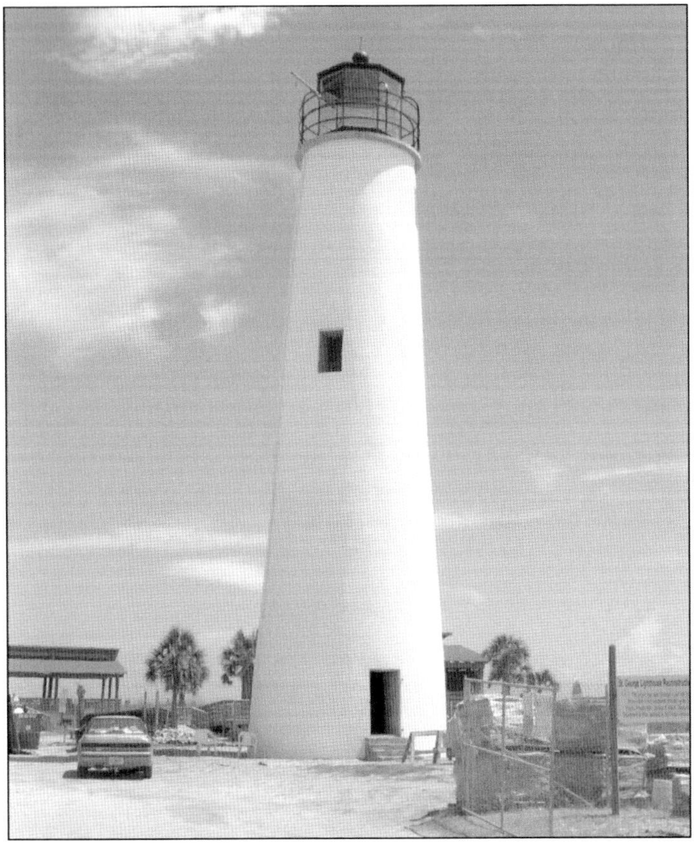

By May 13, 2008, the tower proudly displayed its white day mark, topped with a black lantern room. Now the stairway and windows needed to be installed. (SGLA.)

Each heart-pine stair tread was individually measured and cut, with one end then fitted into the brick wall. Once the staircase was completed, aluminum handrails were fabricated on site and installed. Future keepers will walk in the steps of a long line of distinguished caretakers of the Cape St. George Lighthouse. (SGLA.)

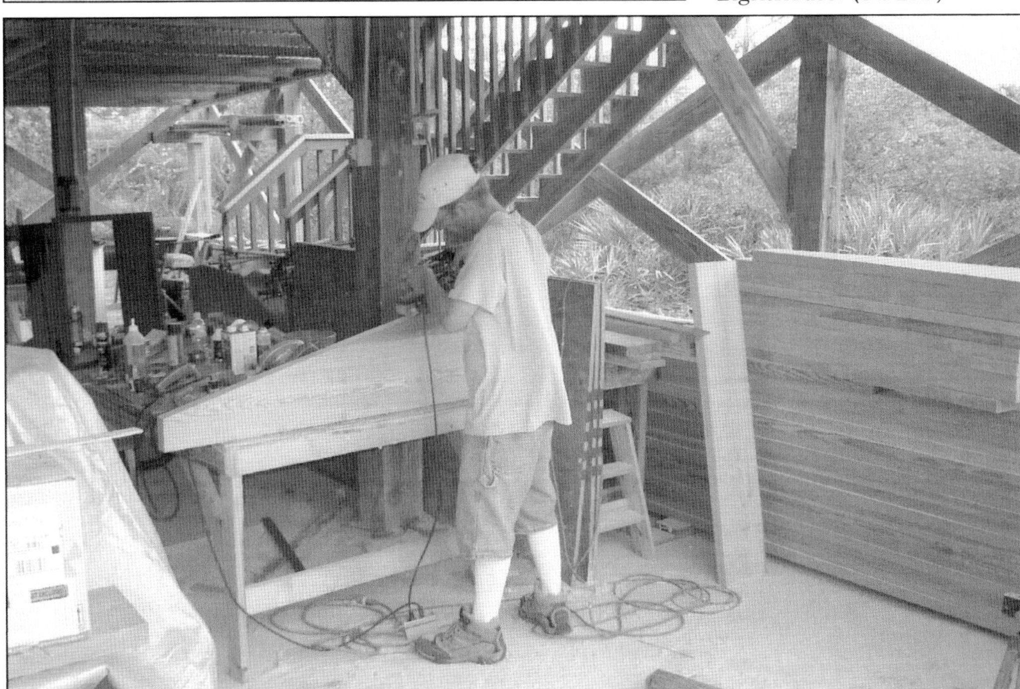

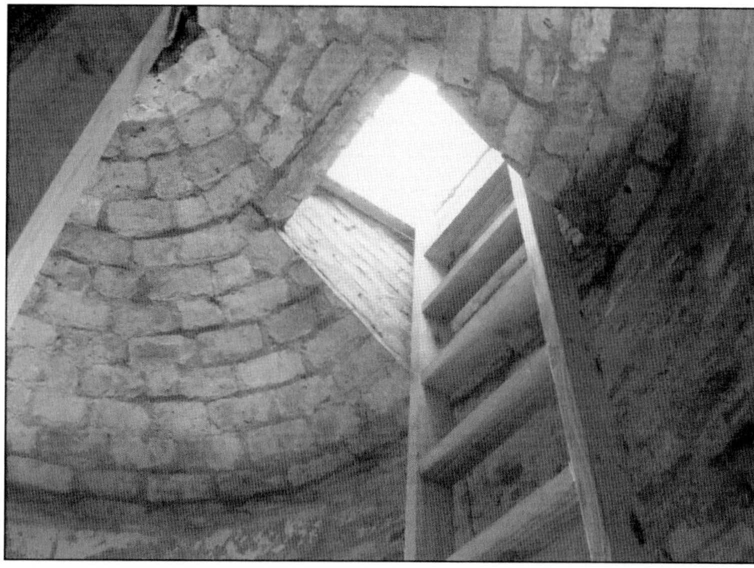

To reach the lantern room, visitors need to climb this ladder through the scuttle. A custom-made oak door was installed to duplicate the original 1852 specifications. Using a crane, shutters were installed on the windows. The shutters are held open by the long cross piece near the bottom; when the shutters are closed, a shorter piece secures them to prevent wind damage.

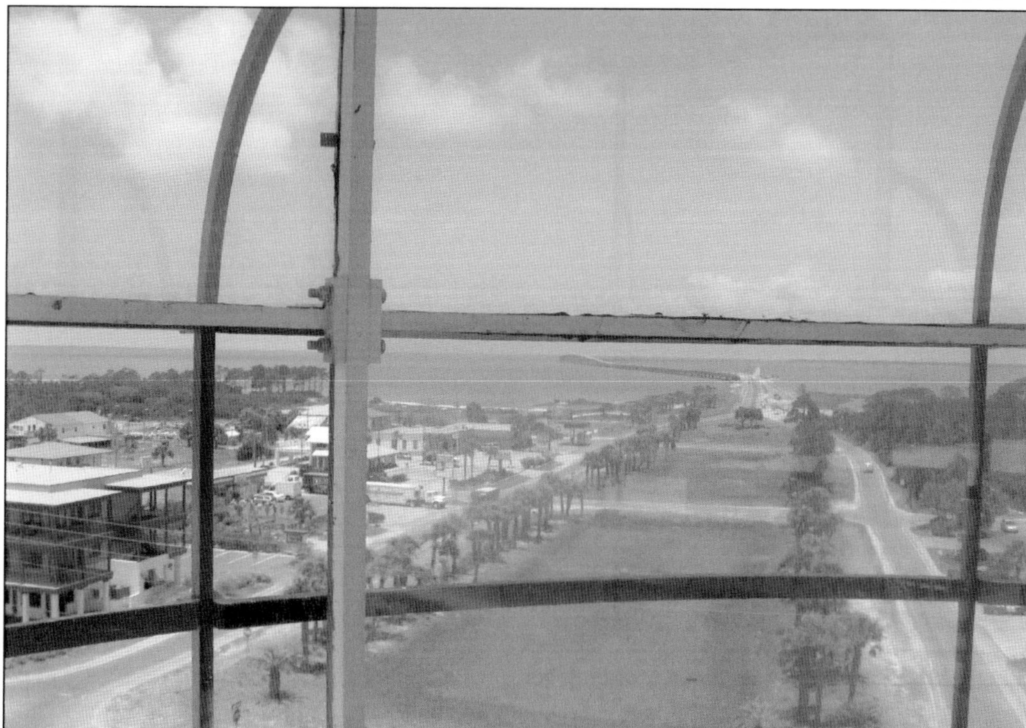

With the tower completed, the view from the lantern room shows the bridge across Apalachicola Bay on the north side and the azure waters of the Gulf of Mexico to the south. The completed lighthouse was opened to the public on December 1, 2008—a little more than a year after ground was broken and three years after a storm surge toppled the 1852 lighthouse into the Gulf. After a Vega VLB-44 LED light was installed, the Cape St. George Light was relit at midnight on Saturday, October 31, 2009, for the first time since being decommissioned by the US Coast Guard in 1994. It is now recognized as a private aid to navigation.

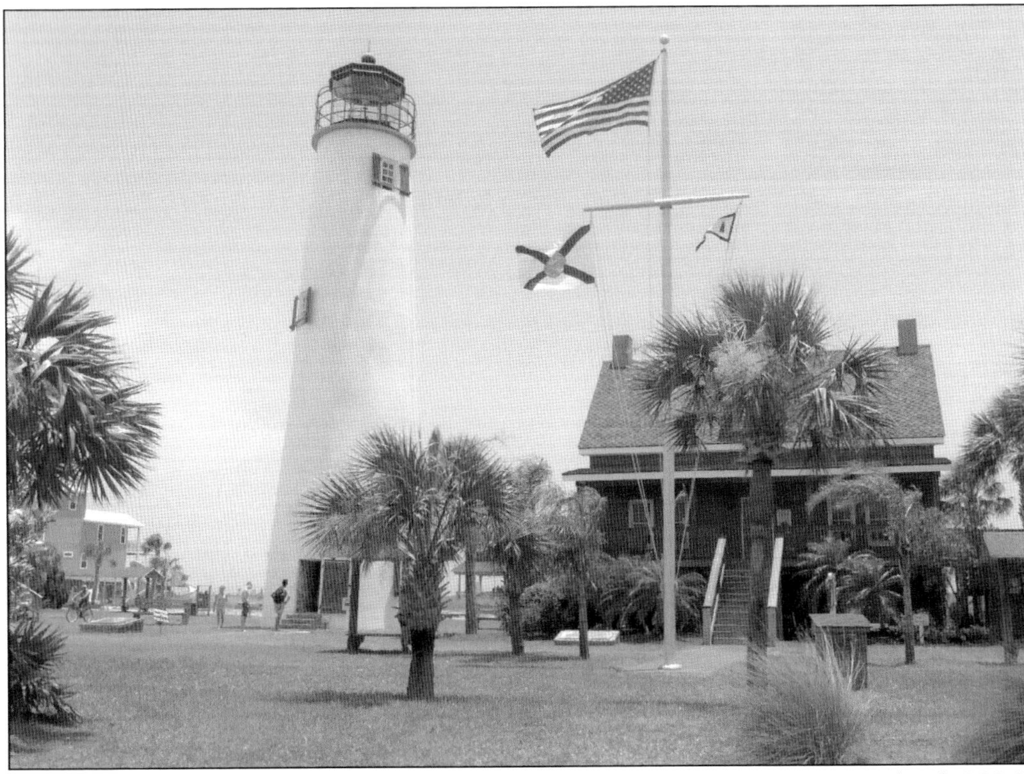

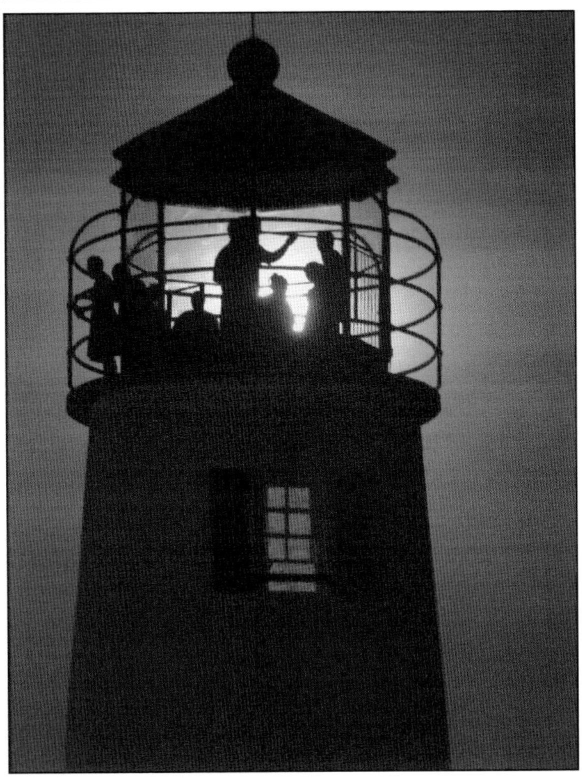

Once the tower was completed, SGLA members built a replica of the original 1852 keeper's quarters to serve as a meeting place, museum, and gift shop. To comply with modern hurricane code, the building was set on pilings that are carefully concealed behind brick pillars. Visitors can learn the history of the lighthouse in the museum and purchase tickets to climb the tower. The tickets and other gift shop sales are one source of funding to continue lighthouse operations.

When full moons arrive each month, the St. George Lighthouse Association offers special climbs so visitors can watch the moon rise over the Gulf of Mexico. (JLH.)

Bibliography

Cipra, David L. *Lighthouses, Lightships, and the Gulf of Mexico.* Alexandria, VA: Cypress Communications, 1997.

Holland, F. Ross. *Great American Lighthouses.* Washington, DC: The Preservation Press, 1989.

Hurley, Neil E. *Florida's Lighthouses in the Civil War.* Oakland Park, FL: Middle River Press, 2007.

Marshall, Pearl Porter. "Lighthouse Keeper's Daughter." *Voices of the Apalachicola.* Gainesville, FL: University Presses of Florida, 2006.

Owens, Harry P. *Apalachicola Before 1861.* Tallahassee, FL: Sentry Press, 2014.

Roberts, William. *Lighthouses and Living Along the Florida Gulf Coast.* Bloomington, IN: Author House, 2005.

Rogers, William Warren. *Outposts on the Gulf: Saint George Island and Apalachicola from Early Exploration to World War II.* Gainesville, FL: University Presses of Florida, 1992.

Swoboda, Lois. "Old Neb, the Lighthouse Horse." *Apalachicola Times,* December 5, 2012. See also Swoboda's children's stories about Old Neb from Pineapple Press, and her historical articles about Franklin County.

Taylor, Thomas W. *Florida's Territorial Lighthouses, 1821–1845: A Legacy of Concern for the Mariner.* Allandale, FL: Florida Sesquicentennial Publication, 1995.

The St. George Lighthouse Association

The St. George Lighthouse Association (SGLA), a Florida non-profit organization, was established in 2004 to conserve the Cape St. George Lighthouse, which collapsed in October 2005 after Hurricane Wilma. SGLA worked with the Florida Department of Environmental Protection to salvage the pieces of the fallen light. The lighthouse was rebuilt at the center of St. George Island and opened to the public in December 2008. The interior bricks, granite threshold, and window sills were all reclaimed from original tower of the 1852 Cape St. George Lighthouse.

In 2011, the St. George Lighthouse Association completed construction of a replica of the original Keeper's House next to the lighthouse in Lighthouse Park. The building houses the Lighthouse Museum and Gift Shop. Funds to maintain the lighthouse are raised through individual contributions, sales of tickets for climbing the lighthouse, the gift shop, and annual fund-raisers. Please visit Lighthouse Park or contact SGLA:

St. George Lighthouse Association Inc.
2B East Gulf Beach Drive
St. George Island, Florida 32328
850-927-7745
www.stgeorgelight.org